ANATOMY OF THE FOURTH GOSPEL
A Study in Literary Design

R. ALAN CULPEPPER

Foreword by

Frank Kermode

FORTRESS PRESS
PHILADELPHIA

Copyright © 1983 by Fortress Press

First paperback edition 1987
Second printing 1988

Library of Congress Cataloging in Publication Data

Culpepper, R. Alan.
   Anatomy of the Fourth Gospel.

   Bibliography: p.
   Includes indexes.
   1. Bible. N.T. John—Criticism, interpretation, etc.
I. Title. II. Series.
BS2615.2.C85   1983   226'.506   82–16302
ISBN 0-8006-2068-2

3646D88   Printed in the United States of America   1–2068

Contents

Alan Culpepper wrote much of this book in Cambridge, England, and during his stay I had the pleasure of seeing him often and reading his work in progress. At that time I was convinced of its value; but on reading it again in its final form I perceive that I had not fully grasped its significance.

For a Christian minister there must always be a difference between the word of the secular text and the Word of the gospel. He or she will therefore want to avoid the dilemma in which Shakespeare's Richard II found himself, of setting "the Word itself / Against the word." Culpepper has acquired techniques of narrative analysis which originate in secular scholarship. For example, when he treats of time relations in narrative he uses methods brought to a high state of refinement by Gérard Genette, who honed them on Proust. But he does so in full knowledge of the proper relationship between word and Word. The sharp severance between gospel narrative and objective history has, over more than two centuries, caused deep disturbances in biblical scholarship and divisions among the faithful. Culpepper rejects unreflecting literalism on the one part and easy skepticism on the other; he maintains that the only way to heal these divisions is to achieve a proper understanding of the gospel as story, and of the relation of story to truth. Can a story be true if it is not "history"? This is a question, according to Culpepper, on which "the future role of the gospel in the life of the church will depend. . . . When art and history, fiction and truth, are again reconciled we will again be able to read the gospel as the author's original audience read it." Of course we will bring to it our own conditioning, the new shapes of our minds as they have been formed by the pressure of so long a tradition.

It may be, as Culpepper conjectures, that it is our lengthening experience with secular narrative—with the rich and various history of the novel—that has made possible this kind of return to John and the other evangelists. In a book of which Culpepper has taken due note, Hans Frei acutely remarked that at the crisis of historical narrative the Germans developed Higher Criticism, which painfully called into question the veracity of the gospel narratives, and the English invented the novel. If that is so, there seems to be a certain propriety in attempts to apply to the study of the gospel lessons learned in the study of the novel.

Culpepper is not the first to make such an attempt, but it seems fair to say that no one else has shown such eclectic thoroughness in the use of modern narratological techniques. He owes a good deal to Seymour Chatman, and through him to Roman Jakobson and others; but he adapts his model to his own proper purposes, and takes what he needs from others, such as the Russian narratologist Boris Uspensky and the Israeli Meir Sternberg, to name only two. Terms which may be new to readers whose orientation is primarily to biblical scholarship—"implied author," "implied reader," "narratee," and so forth—are lucidly explained. Readers who already have an acquaintance with these terms, and with the works of such theorists as Wayne Booth, Wolfgang Iser, Genette, and Chatman, should be grateful for the clarity with which Culpepper presents the material of modern biblical scholarship, with which they are equally unlikely to be familiar. This book strongly upholds the position, long since enunciated but still widely ignored or disputed, that there can be no sharp distinction between sacred and profane hermeneutics.

In claiming that position, Culpepper is required to be at once tenacious, bold, and modest. He has maintained this posture admirably, so that neither proponents of the sacred nor proponents of the profane may legitimately take offense, for neither could claim to have been neglected or treated with disrespect. And, to end more positively, I think that anybody who reads this book will be rewarded by a deeper understanding of John, and of narrative generally.

Frank Kermode

It may be the experience of all authors to find that their books interest them as much as this one has interested me, but I doubt it. Writing it has been a fascinating and joyful experience: fascinating because of the new directions which are being opened for students of the gospels by current literary studies, and joyful in large measure because of the help and encouragement I received from so many sources. The writing of any book is usually a shared adventure; such has certainly been the case with this one.

Without the time and income provided by The Southern Baptist Theological Seminary's sabbatical leave program I would never have been able to do the research which has cultivated my interest in literary criticism of the gospels. Southern also provided a special grant from a donor and the equipment and assistance needed for the preparation of the manuscript. The Association of Theological Schools and the Education Commission of the Southern Baptist Convention provided a research grant and financial assistance which made it possible for me to spend the academic year of 1980–81 in Cambridge, England. There, through the hospitality of Professor Ronald E. Clements, Fitzwilliam College, and the Divinity School, I was able to use the fine resources of the University Library and work in an environment which has stimulated academic pursuits for centuries. The opportunity to study in that setting and participate in the Cambridge New Testament Seminar is one for which I am deeply grateful. Professor Frank Kermode graciously encouraged me to pursue this project, recommended sources I had not yet discovered, and read the first draft of each chapter. His guidance made it possible for me to work into the field of current literary theory, poetics, and narratology, a field in which I am still a novice. My mentor, Professor D. Moody Smith, has again shown the personal warmth and wisdom his friends and students admire as he read the manuscript and made numerous well-founded suggestions. David Rhoads, my friend and fellow pilgrim in literary criticism of the gospels, worked through the manuscript with meticulous care, making critical comments and suggestions which have been of tremendous value in helping me to make the book both more precise and more readable. Every writer should have such friends!

The first draft of Chapter 2 was presented to the Johannine Seminar of the Society for New Testament Studies in August 1980, and an abridgement of the final draft of this chapter was printed in the SBL 1982 *Seminar Papers* for the Literary Aspects of the Gospels and Acts Group. Parts of Chapters 7 and 8 were presented to the Arts, Literature, and Religion Section of the American Academy of Religion and the Biblical Section of the Theological Education Association of Mid-America in the fall of 1981. The discussion and responses of colleagues at each of these meetings helped me shape the material in these chapters. My graduate seminar in the fall of 1981 perceptively distinguished what made sense from what did not, and from Paul D. Duke in particular I have learned a great deal about John's use of irony. As typists, Peggy Shaw and Terri Mathews demonstrated both professional skill and a patience and tolerance worthy of saints. From the beginning, Fortress Press has provided the level of support and technical assistance which has helped them earn a place of distinction as publishers in the field of biblical research. Professor Robert W. Funk graciously suggested publishing this volume, and he and Char Matejovsky at Polebridge Press have produced it accurately and efficiently. Through it all, my family has patiently endured my obsession with this manuscript with love and understanding, celebrated the passing of milestones toward its completion, and reminded me that there is much more to life than the consumption and production of books.

Without all these important people this book could not have been written, but for the imperfections and weaknesses that remain I am entirely responsible. Every book—and certainly this one—is a confession of ignorance and an invitation to criticism. My hope, however, is that readers will find the book as interesting and stimulating as I have, and find that as a result of it they are able to read the Gospel of John more perceptively and perhaps even to reach some new insights about what the gospel is and what we do when we read it.

R. Alan Culpepper

Writing a preface for another printing of one's book is much like writing a postscript: it gives the author a chance to reflect on the book at some distance from it.

Anatomy of the Fourth Gospel (1983) was written at a significant juncture in the discovery of the importance of current narrative theory and literary criticism for biblical studies. At the time I was engaged in this writing, my friend David Rhoads and his colleague Donald Michie were writing *Mark as Story* (1982). Together we explored some of the same questions: What is involved in the shift from a historical-critical analysis to a narrative-critical analysis of a gospel? Given the diverse schools of thought in the field of narratology, how can students of the Bible begin to enter into interdisciplinary research? Can a model for such study be developed—one that would introduce key concepts, survey narrative theory on specific topics, and then explore its significance for the study of a gospel?

Especially important for this project was the question: Is John sufficiently coherent as narrative to sustain such a study? Whereas earlier Johannine studies often emphasized the discontinuities in John and postulated the use of sources drawn from different settings, I believe *Anatomy of the Fourth Gospel* demonstrated that the Fourth Gospel develops narration, themes, characterization, ironies, and symbolism with a great deal of internal consistency.

Hindsight, assisted by perceptive reviews of the book,[1] reveals a number of points at which research can now build on, sharpen, or correct the work I have done. Since the model used in this book depends heavily on the work of Roman Jakobson, more direct interaction with Jakobson is in order. The model might also be revised to call interpreters to be more sensitive to the Gospel of John as interpretation of other narratives, and hence to its relationships to other texts and other interpretations of Jesus. A part of the meaning of this gospel is its distinctiveness from other narratives and other narrative interpretations of Jesus.

---

[1] Among the reviews from which I have learned the most, and for which I am most grateful, are the following: Donald A. Carson, *Trinity Journal* 4 (1983): 122–26; William G. Doty, *Interpretation* 39 (1985): 78–80; Richard B. Hays, *TSF Bulletin* 7/5 (1984): 20–21; Xavier Léon-Dufour, *Recherches de Science Religieuse* 73/2 (1985): 249–53; D. Moody Smith, in *John*, Proclamation Commentaries, 2d ed. rev. and enl. (Philadelphia: Fortress Press, 1986), 94–104.

Jeffrey Staley used sections of *Anatomy of the Fourth Gospel,* especially those dealing with the narrator and narration, as a springboard for his fine dissertation *The Print's First Kiss: A Rhetorical Investigation of the Implied Reader in the Fourth Gospel.*[2] His thesis follows the lead of my work by "paying close attention to the different levels of narrative and to the temporal reading process." On the other hand, Staley argues that the narrator is not consistently reliable but is at times self-contradictory and engages in a strategy of reader entrapment or reader victimization. The role of reader entrapment in the Gospel of John will have to be assessed carefully. Clearly the narrator withholds essential information from the reader until it can have a dramatic impact, and in the course of the reading experience the reader finds expectations created and then dashed. But the reader is still given privileged information—from the prologue on—which is not significantly undermined by the twists and turns in the story that are so important in Staley's reading of the Gospel of John. At points his definitions of the implied author, narrator, narratee, and implied reader differ from those I have used. The result is not always clarifying. For example, Staley argues that "the narrator of the Fourth Gospel must be male" because of the masculine references in 19:35 (*ho heōrakōs*) and 21:24 (*houtos estin ho mathētēs*). In both of these instances, however, the narrator is referring to a character in the story. Staley proceeds to identify the Beloved Disciple as the narrator, but he has just indicated that the narrator can be "omnipresent." Some distinction between the narrator and the character in the story must therefore be maintained. In contrast, I have argued that at the end of the Fourth Gospel the narrative voice identifies the implied author as the Beloved Disciple (pp. 44–49). Staley's term, "fictive author," is appropriate, but the fact remains that by this point the reader is ready to accept that the narrative has been constructed by one who has both the insight and the reliability that the narrative attributes to the Beloved Disciple. I hope that further dialogue over the artistry and rhetorical effects of the Fourth Gospel will follow. A full response to Staley's provocative and significant work will have to wait for another context.

The chapter on narrative time (chap. 3) uses terminology defined by Gérard Genette to explore the relationship between story time and narrative time. Interesting insights into the handling of time in this gospel emerge. One might extend my treatment of time by exploring the significance of the distinction between Jesus' time (especially his "hour") and the time of the Jewish festivals in John.

My analysis of the plot of the gospel (chap. 4) as conflict between belief and unbelief in response to the revealer, developed in a series of episodes,

---

[2] Society of Biblical Literature Dissertation Series (Atlanta: Scholars Press, forthcoming).

still seems to me to be basically correct.[3] The relationship between these episodes and the four "ministry tours" proposed by Jeffrey Staley also merits further reflection.[4] Study of the rhetorical effects of an episodic plot can now take advantage of Janice Capel Anderson's use of "redundancy" in her study of the Gospel of Matthew.[5] Norman R. Petersen's analysis of types of gospels based on their handling of revelation and concealment also offers a promising avenue for extending the study of the Fourth Gospel's plot.[6]

The study of characters (chap. 5) is important because it is the first treatment I know of that looks at all the main characters in the gospel and asks questions about the means and effects of characterization. In earlier treatments of the characters scholars looked for actual groups at the time of the composition of the gospel which might have been evoked by the characters. In chapter 5, by contrast, I described the role of the characters in shaping the range of responses readers may make to this gospel. In keeping with the guiding concern of the volume, attention is focused on literary rather than historical matters, and a comprehensive design is proposed.

The narrator's use of implicit commentary is one of the most engaging aspects of the Fourth Gospel, which is nothing if not subtle. Statements often communicate more than their first, apparent meaning. The three topics treated in chapter 6 are interrelated in John: misunderstanding, irony, and symbolism. The first two in particular play important roles in teaching the reader how to read this gospel. Whereas I concentrated primarily on a set of identifiable misunderstandings in John, more might be said about the role of misunderstanding throughout this gospel—and in the experience of reading it. Don A. Carson's article points the way here, but his interest is primarily historical rather than literary.[7] Two fine volumes, by Paul D. Duke and Gail R. O'Day,[8] now offer complementary treatments of the literary devices, social functions, and theological significance of John's ironies. I welcome similar volumes devoted to symbolism in John, ones which might test the relevance of E. K. Brown's discussion of "expanding symbols" for this gospel and treat the "signs" as symbolic actions.

---

[3] The episodes in John 1–12 are now treated in more detail in "The Gospel of John and the Jews," *Review and Expositor* 84 (1987): 276–79.

[4] "The Structure of John's Prologue: Its Implications for the Gospel's Narrative Structure," *Catholic Biblical Quarterly* 48 (1986): 249–64.

[5] "Double and Triple Stories, the Implied Reader, and Redundancy in Matthew," *Semeia* 31 (1985): 71–89.

[6] "Myth and Characterization in Mark and John," A Working Paper for the Society of Biblical Literature Literary Aspects of the Gospels Group, 1985.

[7] "Understanding Misunderstandings in the Fourth Gospel," *Tyndale Bulletin* 33 (1982): 59–91.

[8] Paul D. Duke, *Irony in the Fourth Gospel* (Atlanta: John Knox Press, 1985); and Gail R. O'Day, *Revelation in the Fourth Gospel: Narrative Mode and Theological Claim* (Philadelphia: Fortress Press, 1986).

The chapter on the implied reader (chap. 7) should be regarded as a beginning, but only as a beginning. It offers a significant advance over earlier efforts to identify the audience of the Fourth Gospel, but more remains to be done. What is the relationship between characterization, the issues and tensions in the story, and the definition of the implied reader? How does this gospel evoke and interact with this reader as it unfolds chapter by chapter? These are questions that still await our attention.

Other, more general issues call for further discussion also. The function of the large blocks of discourse material in the Fourth Gospel must be studied carefully. In this respect, John seems to be a compromise between a narrative gospel (like Mark) and a sayings gospel (like Q, Thomas, and some of the gnostic materials). The just-completed dissertation by Linda McKinnish Bridges contains a rewarding analysis of the function of selected aphorisms in John.[9] A subgroup of the Jesus Seminar is currently working toward the production of a list of the aphorisms in John that have a high probability of being pre-Johannine, and therefore possibly authentic logia of Jesus. Such work is tentative at best but offers the prospect of significant dialogue between narrative criticism of John and more traditional historical-critical issues (especially the life setting of the gospel).

Finally, of course, the delicate relationship between history and art as these are related in this gospel is still unresolved, sensed but not yet clarified. But then, it is characteristic of John to convey much that the reader senses but cannot define.

In keeping with the original aim for this volume, my hope is that it will now guide many others, students all, in reading this gospel more perceptively and delighting in its subtlety, truth, and mystery.

June 1987   R. Alan Culpepper

---

[9] "Aphorisms in the Gospel of John: A Transmissional, Literary, and Sociological Analysis of Selected Sayings" (Ph.D. diss., Southern Baptist Theological Seminary, 1987).

Chapter One

INTRODUCTION

This world is very fair to see.
The artist will not let it be.
He fiddles with the works of God
And makes them look uncommon odd.

Sir Walter Raleigh

The historian who succeeds in marrying science and art
with the fewest sacrifices on either side is no doubt the
one with whom Clio, Muse of history, is best pleased.
But, like its younger relative the novel, historical narrative is an unstable compound, always threatening to
give way too much to one or the other of the opposed
fictional and empirical pressures which continually
beset it.

Robert Scholes and Robert Kellogg
The Nature of Narrative

Perusal of Robert Kysar's *The Fourth Evangelist and His Gospel* reveals the extent to which recent criticism of the Gospel of John has been dominated by historical, sociological, and theological concerns. In the majority of studies the gospel has been used as a source for evidence of the process by which it was composed, the theology of the evangelist, or the character and circumstances of the Johannine community. Relying on the standard critical methods, Johannine scholars have generally approached the text looking for tensions, inconsistencies, or "aporias" which suggest that separate strains or layers of material are present in the text. The next step is usually to place the "layers" in some sequence by noting the way they are embedded in the gospel and the probable direction of theological development. On the basis of this stratification, the history of the material, the process by which the gospel was composed, and developments within the Johannine community can all be studied. The gospel is seen as preserving evidence of various stages of its origin and various, at times sharply different, theological emphases. The model of research is that of a "tell" in which archaeologists can unearth strata which derive from different historical periods. This model depends on dissection and differentiation of elements within the gospel. Consequently, little attention has been given to the integrity of the whole, the way its component parts interrelate, its effects upon the reader, or the way it achieves its effects.

Using the images proposed by Murray Krieger,[1] it is clear that John has been used as a "window" through which the critic can catch "glimpses" of the history of the Johannine community. The meaning of the gospel derives from the way it was related to that history.[2] The meaning of the text, therefore, is assumed to lie on the other side of the window. The task of the reader, then, is to become sensitive to the two historical levels lurking in the gospel, the historical level (the ministry of Jesus) and the contemporary level (the situation of the Johannine community). By observing how the latter is reflected in an ostensible

---

[1] *A Window to Criticism,* pp. 3–4. See also Norman R. Petersen, *Literary Criticism for New Testament Critics,* p. 19.

[2] See also the protest of Hans W. Frei, *The Eclipse of Biblical Narrative,* e.g., pp. 135, 280–81.

account of the former, the reader is able to grasp the gospel's message for its first-century readers. Insofar as parallels and similarities can be drawn between the first- and twentieth-century contexts, the gospel may continue to speak to twentieth-century readers. This approach to the gospel has been immensely fruitful and exciting, but it ties the gospel's meaning to historical considerations which are forbidding for all but New Testament specialists, neglects the essential unity of "the most literary of the gospels," and overlooks the importance of the relationship between text and reader.

In contrast to the approach to a text as a "window," Krieger offers the metaphor of the text as a "mirror." This model assumes that the meaning of the text lies on this side of it, between mirror and observer, text and reader. Meaning is produced in the experience of reading the text as a whole and making the mental moves the text calls for its reader to make, quite apart from questions concerning its sources and origin. As one reads the gospel, the voice of the narrator introduces the narrative world of the text, its characters, values, norms, conflicts, and the events which constitute the plot of the story. The narrator conveys the author's perspective to the reader and sends signals which establish expectations, distance and intimacy, and powerfully affect the reader's sense of identification and involvement. The narrator's claims and the norms of the story woo, beckon, and challenge the reader to believe that the story, its narrative world, and its central character reveal something profoundly true about the "real" world in which the reader lives. As Robert Scholes and Robert Kellogg observed,

> Meaning, in a work of narrative art, is a function of the relationship between two worlds: the fictional world created by the author and the "real" world, the apprehendable universe. When we say we "understand" a narrative, we mean that we have found a satisfactory relationship or set of relationships between these two worlds.[3]

The implicit purpose of the gospel narrative is to alter irrevocably the reader's perception of the real world. The narrative world of the gospel is therefore neither a window on the ministry of Jesus nor a window on the history of the Johannine community. Primarily at least, it is the literary creation of the evangelist, which is crafted with the purpose of leading readers to "see" the world as the evangelist sees it so that in reading the gospel they will be forced to test their perceptions and beliefs about the "real" world against the evangelist's perspective on the world they have

---

[3] *The Nature of Narrative*, p. 82; cf. pp. 84, 98. Cf. William A. Beardslee, *Literary Criticism of the New Testament*, p. 13.

encountered in the gospel.[4] The gospel claims that its world is, or at least reflects something that is, more "real" than the world the reader has encountered previously. The text is therefore a mirror in which readers can "see" the world in which they live. Its meaning is produced in the experience of reading the gospel and lies on this side of the text, between the reader and the text.[5]

According to this model, dissection and stratification have no place in the study of the gospel and may distort and confuse one's view of the text. Every element of the gospel contributes to the production of its meaning,[6] and the experience of reading the text is more important than understanding the process of its composition. While the approach of literary criticism is clearly distinct from that of historical-critical scholarship, there needs to be dialogue between the two so that each may be informed by the other. This book is an attempt to make some initial tracings of what the gospel looks like through the lens of "secular" literary criticism. As an interdisciplinary study, the work is an effort to contribute to that dialogue by studying the narrative elements of the Fourth Gospel while interacting occasionally with current Johannine research. It is intended not as a challenge to historical criticism or the results of previous research but as an alternative by means of which new data may be collected and readers may be helped to read the gospel more perceptively by *looking at* certain features of the gospel. This process is to be distinguished from reading the gospel *looking for* particular kinds of historical evidence.

Our aim is to contribute to understanding the gospel as a narrative text, what it is, and how it works. The emphasis will be upon analysis and interpretation rather than upon the construction of hypotheses or critique of methods. The gospel as it stands rather than its sources, historical background, or themes is the subject of this study. "Text" here means simply the words or signifiers of the story as recorded in the 26th edition of the Nestle-Aland *Novum Testamentum Graece*. The phrase, "what it is," signals discussion of both the character of this particular narrative and gospel genre more generally.[7] By understanding more clearly the nature and functions of a gospel, avenues may be opened for a more precise definition of the genre. By "how it works" I intend questions regarding how the

---

[4] Cf. Raymond E. Brown, *The Community of the Beloved Disciple*, p. 17.

[5] Cf. Wolfgang Iser, *The Act of Reading*, p. 18; Giles Gunn, *The Interpretation of Otherness*, p. 120.

[6] Cf. Marinus de Jonge, *Jesus: Stranger from Heaven and Son of God*, p. 198: "In the present approach both supposedly redactional and supposedly traditional elements are treated as integral parts of a new literary entity, which has to be studied on its own, because it functioned as a whole among people who did *not* take its prehistory into account."

[7] Cf. Susan Sontag, *Against Interpretation and Other Essays*, p. 14.

narrative components of the gospel interact with each other and involve
and affect the reader. Ultimately we may be in a better position to understand what the gospel requires of its readers, how it directs the production
of its meaning, and what happens when someone reads it.

The theoretical model employed here is derived from Seymour
Chatman[8] and owes a great deal to the communicational model of Roman
Jakobson. Insofar as it differs from Chatman's the modifications are my
own.

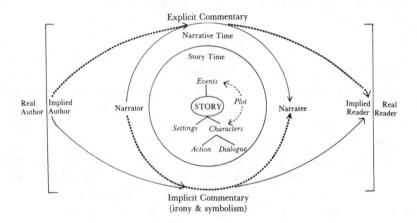

This diagram shows how a story is transmitted from the author to the
reader. The choice of a communicational model is dictated both by its
currency in contemporary literary criticism and its suitability for understanding afresh what the gospel is and how it achieves its effects. Each
element in the diagram is defined further at appropriate points below, but
a provisional definition of its key elements will indicate the concerns of the
chapters which follow and justify their place in a work of this sort. Every
story presupposes a teller, the story, and an audience. Chapter 2 is devoted
to discussion of the teller, the narrator. Chapters 3 through 6 are devoted
to various components of the story, its time, its plot, its characters, and the
implicit commentary which makes it so intriguing. Chapter 7 analyzes the
audience, or reader, it assumes. Between author and reader is the text,
enclosed above in brackets. Literary critics distinguish between the real
author and reader and their counterparts within the text. As the real
author writes, he or she makes decisions about the narrative, constructs
the story, and tells it through the narrator in such a way that the narrative
projects an image of the author, but the image may not conform to the
identity of the real author at all. The "implied author" is defined by the

---

[8] *Story and Discourse*, p. 267.

sum of the choices reflected in the writing of the narrative, choices of the use of settings, irony, characterization, the handling of time, suspense, distance, and all the problematics and potential of narrative writing which must be dealt with in one way or another. The choices determine the reader's response to the narrative and the mental image the reader will have of the author. In John it is difficult to say what the relationship between the real author and the implied author is, but there is no real difference between the point of view of the narrator, i.e., the voice which tells the story, and the perspective of the implied author which is projected by the text. The narrator, point of view, and the relationship of the narrator to the implied author are treated in detail in Chapter 2.

The story itself consists of characters, events, and their settings. The plot is worked out primarily through the conflict of forces and characters, and the plot too has tremendous power to affect the reader. In the Gospel of John, the story depends upon both events which preceded the ministry of Jesus and events which follow it. The gospel insists that the story itself cannot be understood apart from these events. Moreover, not all of the ministry is included in the story. There are gaps in it, and the reader is told about some events before others so that the sequence in which it is told will have the desired effect upon the reader. All of these matters are treated in Chapter 3, "Narrative Time," and Chapter 4, "Plot."

One of the most interesting elements of any story is the cast of characters which populate it. Characters are defined and shaped for the reader by what they do (action) and what they say (dialogue) as well as what is said about them by the narrator or by other characters. The reader may also be led to react to each of the characters in a particular way and to identify with facets of their characterization. Much of the power of the Fourth Gospel comes from its vivid characterizations and their effects upon the reader.

The reader's response is further shaped by both the narrator's overt commentary and by the more subtle implicit commentary which permeates the narrative. By such means as the recurring misunderstandings, sharp, witty irony, and profound, moving symbolism the gospel moves the reader to soul-searching insights and compelling invitations to faith. The lines in the diagram indicate that overt commentary is primarily communication between the narrator and the narratee (the one to whom the narrator tells the story), while irony and symbolism are means by which the implied author communicates tacitly with the implied reader.

The implied reader is defined by the text as the one who performs all the mental moves required to enter into the narrative world and respond to it as the implied author intends. Although there are various definitions of the implied reader, as Chapter 7 will make clear, a narrative inevitably projects a picture of the reader for which it was intended. When an explanation is offered, for example, the intended reader would not have understood that point without it. On the other hand, when characters, places, customs, and terms are not explained, the interpreter can assume that the intended reader was capable of understanding them without any explanation from the narrator. By systematically collecting and analyzing such data one can construct a portrait of the gospel's implied reader. In John the implied reader is scarcely distinguishable from the narratee, just as the implied author can hardly be separated from the narrator.

Even this cursory survey of the elements of the diagram should suggest its potential for contributing to the study of the Fourth Gospel. By understanding the crafting and function in John of each of the diagram's elements, one will discover fresh insights and an enhanced appreciation for the way the gospel shapes the reader's production of its message.

The venture is certain to evoke a chorus of objections from different quarters. Three can be anticipated at the outset: (1) it is not legitimate to apply methods developed for the study of modern literature to ancient writings; (2) methods developed for the study of fiction are inappropriate for the study of scripture; and (3) literary criticism ignores the gains of historical criticism and the nature of the gospels as historical accounts.

In response to the first, one would certainly want to recognize the differences between ancient and modern literary art. Biblical and literary critics have both observed, however, that the gospels are unlike anything else which has survived of first-century literature.[9] On the other hand, they are not direct precursors of novels and modern fictional literature either. Still, C. S. Lewis' objection, in spite of the false dichotomy he poses, is interesting because of its implicit admission that there are significant similarities between the gospels and modern narrative literature:

> Of this text [the Gospel of John] there are only two possible views. Either this is reportage—though it may no doubt contain errors—pretty close up to the facts; nearly as close as Boswell. Or else, some unknown writer in the second century, without known predecessors or successors, suddenly anticipated the whole technique of modern, novelistic, realistic narrative.[10]

John is, at points at least, "novelistic, realistic narrative." In the gospel narratives, individual units of the Jesus tradition, whether oral or written,

---

[9] Erich Auerbach, *Mimesis*, pp. 40–49; Amos N. Wilder, *Early Christian Rhetoric*, p. 36; Beardslee, *Literary Criticism of the New Testament*, pp. 3–5. Charles H. Talbert, *What is a Gospel*, however, has demonstrated similarities between the gospels and ancient cultic biographies.

[10] "Modern Theology and Biblical Criticism," p. 155.

became parts of a larger entity in which they perform functions they did not have previously; they build characterization and have a place in the development of themes and the plot. The narration becomes part of the voice of the narrator throughout. Literary criticism can help us to understand how the units of tradition cohere and function together within the gospel, and it can do so more successfully than form and redaction criticism have.

George A. Kennedy has observed that great art always goes "beyond anything which can be analyzed in the critical systems of their own times." John is almost certainly a work which "bursts the limits of rhetoric as known" previously.[11] It is not surprising that the evangelists, and John in particular, went beyond the level of narrative art in their time. In writing realistic narrative the evangelists could not avoid using and dealing with all of the components of narrative literature. They may not have been aware of their handling of characters, the narrator, or the implied reader, but they could not write a narrative without dealing with them in one way or another. When, in the ensuing chapters, we use concepts and examine narrative components which were unknown to ancient writers, we are still dealing with features of the text that are actually there and which had to be handled by the evangelist, whether unconsciously, instinctively, or deliberately. Distortion can be minimized by taking into account the state of literary art in the first century and by not expecting to find such modern devices as an unreliable narrator, distance between the narrator and the implied author, or between the narratee and the implied reader. Literary criticism, however, is basically an inductive method in that one works from observations on the text being studied. Features of the narrative can be observed and analyzed using modern concepts without presuming that they were understood by the ancient writer. It would be preferable if we could utilize literary categories which are peculiarly suitable for the study of the gospels rather than those which have been developed from the study of other literary genres,[12] but perhaps some progress toward that ability can be made by a study such as the present one.

The second objection which can be lodged against this approach to the Fourth Gospel is that perspectives and methods drawn from the study of fiction are inappropriate for the study of scripture and therefore will inevitably distort the interpretation and prejudice the interpreter toward treating the gospel as fiction.

The danger of distortion must be faced constantly when techniques developed for the study of one genre are applied to another, but in prin-

---

[11] *Classical Rhetoric*, p. 6.
[12] Cf. E. D. Hirsch, Jr., *Validity in Interpretation*, pp. 116, 120.

ciple the question of whether there can be a separate set of hermeneutical principles for the study of scripture should have been settled as long ago as Schleiermacher. As Boeckh, Schleiermacher's disciple, put it:

> Since the principles under which understanding must occur and the functions of understanding are everywhere the same, there can be no specific differences in hermeneutic theory corresponding to different objects of interpretation. The distinction between *hermeneutica sacra* and *profana* is therefore thoroughly untenable.[13]

Scripture must be studied with the same methods that are applied to the study of "secular" literature.

While critics of the gospels have ardently defended this principle, in practice they have developed their own peculiar methods for the study of the gospels and have not, until recently, sought to learn how secular critics study narrative literature. This curious development may be clearly seen from the way biblical scholars have understood the task of literary criticism. Klaus Koch, for example, wrote that the literary critic

> approaches the text with, so to say, a dissecting knife in his hand, looks out particularly for breaks in continuity, or missing links in the train of thought, and also for disturbing duplications and factual inconsistencies, and for variations in the use of language which will have originated in another set of circumstances or at a period of different religious concepts. The literary-critical method leads to a determination of sources.[14]

In the section of his massive commentary on the Gospel of John entitled "Literary Criticism of the Gospel of St. John," Rudolf Schnackenburg is likewise concerned primarily with those data which indicate a complex composition history involving sources, the evangelist, displacements and rearrangements (which he generally rejects), and redaction.[15] There is no discussion of the textual features with which we shall be concerned.

It is interesting that not only have biblical scholars been slow to appropriate the perspectives used by literary critics, but literary critics themselves have rarely treated the gospels as narratives which have a place in the history of western literature. Auerbach is the great exception, and others have followed his lead. Scholes and Kellogg, however, survey the emerging genres of narrative literature in the ancient world without dis-

---

[13] *Encyclopädie*, cited by Hirsch, *Validity in Interpretation*, pp. 112–13.

[14] Klaus Koch, *The Growth of the Biblical Tradition*, p. 69. Cf. Northrop Frye, *Anatomy of Criticism*, p. 315; and Leland Ryken, "Literary Criticism of the Bible," pp. 24–40.

[15] *The Gospel According to St. John*, vol. 1, pp. 44–58.

cussing the gospels. At best there are references to Old Testament narratives in such discussions. Recently, however, both biblical and literary scholars have begun to cross the traditional barriers which have kept the former from using the latter's methods and the latter from studying the former's literature.[16] The result promises to be a gain for both. Readers of the gospels have much to gain from a clearer understanding of the relationship between sacred and secular literature, what the experience of reading the gospels involves, and how these texts call for the reader to interact with them.

The third objection which may be raised is that literary criticism ignores the gains of historical criticism and the historical nature of the gospel itself. The revolution in shifting from a historical to a literary model for gospel studies has indeed led some advocates of the new methods to view with animosity any hint of contamination of the new lump with the leaven of the old. Questions of historicity need not enter the discussion because the literary critic is concerned with the gospel and its meaning rather than with Jesus or the Johannine community. Appeals to general historical considerations regarding the age of the story, the culture it assumes, and the meaning of the words with which it is told are, of course, necessary if one is to understand the dynamics of the narrative, but using historical data as aids to interpretation is quite different from using the gospel story for historical reconstruction. On the other hand, our effort to set aside interest in the Johannine community or the historical Jesus should not be interpreted as a denial of any historical core or matrix of the gospel. Once the effort has been made to understand the narrative character of the gospels, some rapprochement with the traditional, historical issues will be necessary. Questions about how the story is told inevitably raise interest in why it is told and why it is told as it is.

Objections may still be raised. This is a tentative step in a new direction. It will be enough, however, if one gains a clearer view of how the Fourth Gospel tells its story. My hope is that the present effort will be judged on the basis of its capacity to expose new considerations, explain features of the gospel, and stimulate greater appreciation for its literary design.[17]

---

[16] Especially noteworthy is Frank Kermode, *The Genesis of Secrecy,* which takes the Gospel of Mark as its central text, and Northrop Frye, *The Great Code.*

[17] Cf. Wolfgang Iser, *The Implied Reader,* p. 290: "Perhaps this is the prime usefulness of literary criticism—it helps to make conscious those aspects of the text which would otherwise remain concealed in the subconscious: it satisfies (or helps to satisfy) our desire to talk about what we have read."

Chapter Two

NARRATOR AND POINT OF VIEW

The whole intricate question of method, in the craft of fiction, I take to be governed by the question of the point of view—the question of the relation in which the narrator stands to the story.

Percy Lubbock
The Craft of Fiction

. . . novelists' ethical beliefs, opinions, and prejudices are expressed as the formal signals which control our response to the characters, acts, and thoughts represented in their novels.

The more precise our knowledge of how a writer has accomplished the artistic end of his work, the more accurate will be the inferences we make about his ethical beliefs, notions, prejudices.

Sheldon Sacks
Fiction and the Shape of Belief

Stories must be in the past, and the more in the past they are, one might say, the better it is for them, in their capacity as stories, and for the narrator, the whispering wizard of the imperfect tense.

Thomas Mann
Der Zauberberg

Our doctrine is, that the author and the reader should move along together in full confidence with each other. Let the personages of the drama undergo ever so complete a comedy of errors among themselves, but let the spectator never mistake the Syracusan for the Ephesian; otherwise he is one of the dupes, and the part of a dupe is never dignified.

Anthony Trollope
Barchester Towers

The specter of a "whispering wizard," a narrator, inhabiting the Fourth Gospel and wooing us to his side may understandably be unsettling. How is the narrator related to the evangelist? What does he do, and what do we know about him? Since these are the questions in search of answers in this chapter, our present task is to "name the wizard."

DEFINITIONS

Three elements of the diagram in the Chapter 1 can now be defined further: the real author, the implied author, and the narrator.

The real author. The real author of the gospel needs little definition, although he has been the object of an enormous amount of scholarship.[1] The concern here is not to continue the discussion of the identity of the gospel's author or authors, but to understand the gospel itself more clearly. In the following pages, therefore, references to the "author" do not exclude the possibility, indeed the probability, that the gospel is the product of several writers. Moreover, while a clearer understanding of how the author accomplished "the artistic end of his work" may enable one to make more accurate inferences about "his ethical beliefs, notions, and prejudices," understanding the interests and theology of the real author is not our primary concern.[2]

The implied author. The implied author is always distinct from the real author and is always evoked by a narrative. The Gospel of John, therefore, has an implied author simply by virtue of its being a narrative. Wayne Booth, who coined the term, defined the implied author as follows: "The 'implied author' chooses, consciously or unconsciously, what we read; we infer him as an ideal, literary, created version of the real man; he

---

[1] See R. Alan Culpepper, *The Johannine School*, pp. 1–60, and the standard critical commentaries.
[2] Sheldon Sacks, *Fiction and the Shape of Belief*, pp. 231, 251.

is the sum of his own choices."[3] Unlike the narrator, the implied author has no voice and never communicates directly with the reader. The implied author is the sum of the choices made by the real author in writing the narrative, but the implied author is neither the real author (who wrote) nor the narrator (who tells). The implied author must be inferred from the narrative. The whole work conveys to the reader an impression of the implied author, not the real flesh and blood author, but the literary artist or creative intellect at work in the narrative. This impression may be more or less accurate as a picture of the real author depending on how he or she has crafted the work. Various works by the same author will therefore present different images of their implied authors, and a single work touched by several writing hands presents a single implied author. As Seymour Chatman suggests

> There is always an implied author, though there might not be a single real author in the ordinary sense: the narrative may have been composed by committee (Hollywood films), by a disparate group of people over a long period of time (many folk ballads), or by random-number generation by a computer, or whatever.[4]

Or, we might add, by an evangelist, who used material derived from an authoritative source, and at least one redactor who later edited the evangelist's gospel, as is commonly supposed by Johannine scholars.

The narrator. The voice that tells the story and speaks to the reader is a rhetorical device. Narrators may be dramatized as a character in the story, or left undramatized. They may serve as the implied author's voice or the voice of a character whose perspective differs from the implied author's. The narrator may also be more or less present and audible in the narrative. The more overt the address to the reader, the stronger is our sense of the narrator's presence.[5] In John, the narrator is undramatized and serves as the voice of the implied author. Since the narrator shares the author's point of view, the two are not usually distinguished. Booth's warning is therefore appropriate: "One of the most frequent reading faults comes from a naive identification of such [undramatized] narrators with the authors who create them. But in fact there is always a distinction, even though the author himself may not have been aware of it as he wrote."[6] The narrator guides the reader through the narrative, introduces the

---

[3] *The Rhetoric of Fiction*, pp. 74–75, cf. pp. 71–73, 151.
[4] *Story and Discourse*, p. 149.
[5] *Story and Discourse*, pp. 216–28.
[6] "Distance and Point of View," p. 65; cf. Meir Sternberg, *Expositional Modes and Temporal Ordering in Fiction*, p. 256: ". . . the omniscient narrator is as much a

reader to the world of the narrative and the characters which populate it, and provides the proper perspective from which to view the action.[7] In John, the narrator is the one who speaks in the prologue, tells the story, introduces the dialogue, provides explanations, translates terms, and tells us what various characters knew or did not know. In short, the narrator tells us what to think. Because he, or she, makes comments to the reader which interrupt the flow of the narrative, the narrator is *intrusive*. We have a clear sense of his presence and relate to him as a person.[8] The Johannine narrator is not identified as male or female; we will refer to the narrator with masculine pronouns, however, for the sake of convenience and simplicity. The narrator is *self-conscious* in the sense that he is aware that he is speaking to a reader or audience.[9] As the narrator tells the story, and because of the way he tells it, we soon accept him as a reliable guide to the meaning of Jesus' life and death.

Important as this literary device is, there is scarcely any literature on the narrator in John.[10] The explanatory comments were collected and analyzed by M. C. Tenney over twenty years ago. Commenting that "to the best knowledge of this writer there is no separate treatment of this phenomenon to be found in the vast literature on the Fourth Gospel," Tenney located fifty-nine "footnotes" or explanatory comments interjected into the narrative.[11] Tenney's list is helpful, but the distinction between

---

creation of the author's as are dramatized narrators that are obviously distant from him."

[7] Norman R. Petersen, "When is the End not the End," p. 156.

[8] M. H. Abrams, *A Glossary of Literary Terms*, p. 134: "Within this mode [omniscient] the *intrusive narrator* is one who not only reports but freely comments on his characters, evaluating their actions and motives and expressing his views about human life in general; ordinarily, all the omniscient narrator's reports and judgments are to be taken as authoritative." Booth, *The Rhetoric of Fiction*, p. 273: ". . . we react to all narrators as persons."

[9] Sternberg, *Expositional Modes*, p. 254.

[10] See, however: David W. Wead, *The Literary Devices in John's Gospel*, pp. 1–11. The most sophisticated analysis to date, which came to my attention after this chapter was written, is in Wilhelm Wuellner's unpublished SNTS seminar paper, "Narrative Criticism and the Lazarus Story."

[11] "The Footnotes of John's Gospel," p. 350. Tenney's list of 59 comments includes: 1:14, 16, 38, 41, 42; 2:9, 11, 22, 24–25; 3:16–21, 31–36; 4:2, 9, 25, 54; 6:6, 23, 59, 64, 71; 7:2, 5, 39, 50; 8:20, 27; 9:7, 14; 10:6, 22–23; 11:2, 18, 30, 51; 12:6, 16, 37–43; 13:11, 23, 28; 18:10, 14, 40; 19:13, 14, 17, 31, 35, 36, 42; 20:9, 16, 30–31; 21:7, 8, 14, 19, 23, 24–25. He divides the comments by subject matter into ten groups: (1) translation, (2) time or place, (3) custom, (4) allusion to author, (5) memory of disciples, (6) explanatory, (7) enumeration and summary, (8) identification of person, (9) knowledge of Jesus, and (10) theological discussion. Chatman, *Story and Discourse*, p. 228, observes that commentary may be either implicit (ironic) or explicit, and that the latter "includes interpretation, judgment, generalization, and 'self-conscious' narration. . . . 'Interpretation' (in this special sense) is open explanation of the gist, relevance, or significance of a story element.

narration and commentary is a precarious one. Commentary can be suggested or implied in the course of the narration, and even "intrusive" commentary is not always clearly distinguishable. John J. O'Rourke expanded Tenney's list of 59 to 109 "asides" (including 3:16–21, 31–36), although he marks 18 of these as "doubtful."[12] Even if we confine ourselves to intrusive commentary as Tenney and O'Rourke do, other verses could be added to the list. In the first few chapters the following verses (which do not appear in either of their lists) could be proposed: 1:39 "for it was about the tenth hour," 4:4 "he had to pass through Samaria," and 4:8 "for his disciples had gone away into the city to buy food." However much one might want to expand or reduce the list, the role of the narrator, "the whispering wizard of the imperfect tense," cannot be defined adequately solely on the basis of intrusive comments. Nevertheless, Tenney helpfully observes that intrusive comments occur throughout the gospel except between 13:31 and 17:26, that there is no relation between their distribution and the structure of the gospel, and that they are not interpolations but an essential part of the text.

Since the Johannine narrator has emerged as a significant rhetorical device, we shall want to know as much as possible about him. "Naming the whispering wizard" will mean defining the location and function of his comments, his point of view, and his relationships to the characters and the author. The rest of the chapter is organized around these three topics.

Expositional Mode

Narrators vary with respect to how much they know, how much they tell, and when they tell the reader what must be known in order to understand the narrative world and its characters. Meir Sternberg calls this necessary, introductory or orienting information "exposition."[13] Sternberg observes that the exposition given by the narrator may either be concentrated in one place or distributed throughout a narrative. It may be preliminary (i.e., given before the beginning of the story itself) or delayed until it will have its desired effect at a later point in the narrative. It may either be

---

'Judgment' expresses moral or other value opinions. 'Generalization' makes reference outward from the fictional to the real world, either to 'universal truths' or to actual historical facts. 'Self-conscious' narration is a term recently coined to describe comments on the discourse [i.e., narrative] rather than the story, whether serious or facetious." All four kinds appear in John (e.g., 4:8; 19:35; 21:23, 24), though some comments fit more than one of these categories.

[12] "Asides in the Gospel of John," pp. 210–19.

[13] *Expositional Modes*, p. 1.

given to the reader in chronological order or in some other order so that the reader must work out the chronological sequence. Exposition which is chronological, preliminary, and concentrated is "the basic norm of straightforward communication."[14] This "expositional mode" allows the reader's first impressions to be confirmed as the story progresses. Sternberg subsequently analyzes deviations from this expositional mode which have the effect of qualifying, modifying, or demolishing the reader's first impressions of a character or situation in the narrative world. In summary, he shows that an author's handling of the expositional material has a powerful effect upon the reader.

John's strategy conforms closely to the norm of chronological, preliminary, concentrated exposition. The narrator gives the reader a concentrated, more or less chronologically arranged, block of exposition in the prologue, which proves to be reliable as the work progresses. Comments by the narrator are also distributed throughout the narrative and generally serve as introductions or conclusions to scenes, or whole sections, of the gospel, or as transitional or explanatory notes.

Not only *when* the exposition is given but *how much* exposition is given has a determinative effect upon the kind of response a narrative evokes from its readers. A narrator may tell the reader all the vital information, or the reader may be required to figure things out as the story progresses. The narrator may have only limited insight into the story or may supply privileged information which no ordinary observer of the action would have, in which case the narrator is to a greater or lesser degree "omniscient." "Omnicommunicative" narrators tell what they know; others deliberately suppress vital information. Each narrator has a different effect upon the reader. An "unreliable" narrator may mislead and thereby alienate the reader by giving false or misleading information or by suppressing vital information. On the other hand, the narrator may win the reader's trust by giving reliable exposition early in the narrative.

The Johannine narrator is neither unreliable nor deliberately suppressive, but rather begins the narrative with an overview of the identity of the central figure and the course of action to follow (John 1:1–18). From the beginning, the narrator shares his omniscient vantage point with the reader, so the reader is immediately given all that is needed to understand the story. Later, distributed comments reinforce the initial exposition. Like the narrator, therefore, the reader knows more than any of the characters who interact with Jesus and is never in danger of mistaking "the Syracusan for the Ephesian." Trollope's philosophy echoes that reflected in John: "Our doctrine is that the author and the reader should move

---

[14] *Expositional Modes,* pp. 98–99.

along together in full confidence with each other."[15] The effect of this narrative pattern on the reader will be considered in more detail later.

POINT OF VIEW

Both Gérard Genette and Boris Uspensky have proposed distinctions which help to clarify and define the related matters of narrator and point of view. Genette has distinguished between the two by showing that point of view, or "focalization," the term he prefers, is determined by whether the story is told from within by the main character or an omniscient author or from outside by a minor character or an author who has taken the role of an observer. The identity of the narrator is determined by whether the narrator is the voice of the author or a character within the story. He adapts the following table from Cleanth Brooks and Robert Penn Warren to make his point.[16]

	Internal analysis of events	Outside observation of events
Narrator as a character in the story	1. Main character tells his own story	2. Minor character tells main character's story
Narrator not a character in the story	4. Analytic or omniscient author tells story	3. Author tells story as observer

Within this schematic of four terms, "the vertical demarcation relates to the 'point of view' (inner and outer), while the horizontal bears on voice (the identity of the narrator). . . ."[17] Accordingly, 1 and 4 present a point of view within the story ("internal"), while 2 and 3 define an external point of view. The point of view from which the story is told may remain consistently internal or external as the story progresses, or it may change from scene to scene, or different positions may be used simultaneously.[18] A narrator may also give inside views of some characters but not of others, thereby creating a difference in the reader's sense of distance from the various characters.

---

[15] Anthony Trollope, *Barchester Towers*, chap. 15; quoted by Sternberg, *Expositional Modes*, p. 259.

[16] Genette, *Narrative Discourse*, p. 186, who cites Cleanth Brooks and Robert Penn Warren, *Understanding Fiction*, p. 589.

[17] Genette, *Narrative Discourse*, p. 186.

[18] Boris Uspensky, *A Poetics of Composition*, pp. 83–96; Genette, *Narrative Discourse*, pp. 189–90.

Uspensky has contributed further significant conceptual refinements to the discussion of point of view by identifying five "planes" in which point of view may be expressed: the ideological (evaluative norms), the phraseological (speech patterns), the spatial (location of the narrator), the temporal (the time of the narrator), and the psychological (internal and external to the characters).[19] These concepts enable us to define the point of view of the narrator in John more accurately. We have already observed that the Johannine narrator is undramatized, intrusive, and omnicommunicative. It is also readily apparent that the narrator in John usually speaks in the *third person,* as one outside the action, thereby providing the effect of the voice of an observer.[20] This pattern is not maintained uniformly, however, since the first person plural, "we," is used in John 1:14, 16; and 21:24 (cf. 3:11).

Psychological point of view: omniscient. A narrator's psychological point of view is determined by whether or not he or she is able to provide inside views of what a character is thinking, feeling, or intending. Narrators are omniscient to the degree that they are able to give the reader inside views which no observer would have. Through an omniscient narrator, ". . . the author tells us what no one in so-called real life could possibly know."[21] Omniscience in narrators is not a monolithic quality, however. There are various types of omniscience, since the source and extent of a narrator's knowledge may vary. Omniscient narration may be linked, for example, with a temporally retrospective point of view so that the narrator looks back on events which happened at some time in the narrator's past. In this case, it is as if the narrator "narrates experiences which took place some time ago, and has since had time to puzzle things out *post factum,* and can reconstruct the internal state of the people, imagining what they must have experienced."[22] We may now ask what the narrator in John knows, and how he knows what he tells us.

It is pointless to speculate about what the narrator does not know or knows but does not tell us. The extent of the narrator's knowledge can only be assessed from what the reader is told. The Johannine narrator knows that in the beginning the Word was with God and knows what is

---

[19] *A Poetics of Composition,* p. 6 and *passim.*

[20] Frank Kermode, *The Genesis of Secrecy,* p. 117: "The advantage of third-person narration is that it is the mode which best produces the illusion of pure reference. But it *is* an illusion, the effect of a rhetorical device."

[21] Booth, *The Rhetoric of Fiction,* p. 3. The whole sentence reads: "Whatever our ideas may be about the natural way to tell a story, artifice is unmistakably present whenever the author tells us what no one in so-called real life could possibly know."

[22] Uspensky, *A Poetics of Composition,* p. 96.

going to happen in the story before it happens. The narrator informs the reader that Jesus knew all things (2:24) and tells us at various points what Jesus was thinking and what he meant by what he said. John 1:43, a notoriously difficult verse, states that "he"—presumably Jesus—intended to go to Galilee. Since the narrator does not say that Jesus said he wanted to go to Galilee or that he seemed to want to go to Galilee, the narrator is apparently giving the reader an inside view. Other verses provide clearer examples of inside views of Jesus' mind:

4:1	Now when the Lord knew that the Pharisees had heard, . . .
5:6	When Jesus saw him and knew that he had been lying there a long time, . . .
6:6	This he said to test him, for he himself knew what he would do.
6:15	Perceiving then that they were about to come and take him by force to make him king, . . .
6:61	But Jesus, knowing in himself that his disciples murmured at it, . . .
6:64	For Jesus knew from the first who those were that did not believe, and who it was that would betray him.
11:5	Now Jesus loved Martha and her sister and Lazarus.
11:33	When Jesus saw her weeping, he was deeply moved in spirit and troubled, . . .
11:38	Then Jesus, deeply moved again, came to the tomb; . . .
13:1	Now before the feast of the Passover, when Jesus knew that his hour had come to depart out of this world to the Father, . . . he loved them to the end.
13:11	For he knew who was to betray him, . . .
13:21	When Jesus had thus spoken, he was troubled in spirit, . . .
16:19	Jesus knew that they wanted to ask him, . . .
18:4	Then Jesus, knowing all that was to befall him, . . .
19:28	After this Jesus, knowing that all was now finished, . . .

These verses demonstrate that the narrator is able to interpret Jesus' thoughts and emotions, but as Booth has observed, "Narrators who provide inside views differ in the depth and axis of their plunge."[23] How deeply does the narrator take us into Jesus, and what is the "axis of his plunge"? As numerous as the references are, the plunge is not deep. We are told that Jesus knew "all things" (2:24). We are also told that Jesus knew his betrayer, the time of his death, and various things about other people. What the narrator says Jesus knew about others gives us a reliable inside view of them as well. Yet, while the narrator exercises a privilege which is clearly artificial by providing us with an inside view of Jesus' mind,[24] a measure of verisimilitude is preserved by the limited depth of the plunge and by coupling omniscience with retrospection, an aspect of the narrator's point of view we will discuss shortly.

---

[23] "Distance and Point of View," p. 77.
[24] Booth, *The Rhetoric of Fiction*, p. 3.

The question to be asked now is whether the narrator takes us inside other characters as well, and if so, how these "plunges" compare with the inside view of Jesus. We may work outwards from Jesus, considering first the disciples, then neutral characters, then his opponents. First there are references to the disciples as a group:

2:11	. . . and his disciples believed in him.
2:17	His disciples remembered that it was written, . . .
2:22	When therefore he was raised from the dead, his disciples remembered that he had said this; and they believed the scripture and the word which Jesus had spoken.
4:27	Just then his disciples came. They marveled that he was talking with a woman, but none said, "What do you wish?" or, "Why are you talking with her?"
12:16	His disciples did not understand this at first; but when Jesus was glorified, then they remembered that this had been written of him and had been done to him.
13:28	Now no one at the table knew why he said this to him.
13:29	Some thought that, because Judas had the money box, Jesus was telling him, . . .
20:9	. . . for as yet they did not know the scripture, that he must rise from the dead.
21:4	. . . yet the disciples did not know that it was Jesus.

Again one can see that while the excursions inside the disciples are fairly numerous, they are also rather shallow. The kind of knowledge about the disciples that is revealed by the narrator is closely tied to his retrospective point of view and may be credibly, if not entirely, accounted for as insight gained after the fact.

Surprisingly, there are very few inside views of individual disciples. We never know what Peter, Andrew, or Thomas are thinking unless they tell us themselves, and the only inside view of the Beloved Disciple comes at 20:8, ". . . and he saw and believed." Judas is the only disciple of whom we get a significant inside view, and even then it is shallow and sketchy:

12:4	But Judas Iscariot, one of his disciples (he who was to betray him), . . .
12:6	This he said not that he cared for the poor but because he was a thief, and as he had the money box he used to take what was put into it.
18:2	Now Judas, who betrayed him, also knew the place; for Jesus often met there with his disciples.

These three notes are meager. They leave unanswered the most important question about Judas: Why did he betray Jesus? Nevertheless, they confirm before the fact that Judas is the betrayer (cf. 6:71) and turn the reader's sympathy against him. With the possible exception of 12:6, retrospection could again account for this inside information. The narrator takes pains to explain how Judas knew where Jesus met with the disciples. John 13:2 could be added to this list but should probably be taken as an inside view of the Devil rather than Judas.[25]

Not only Jesus and the disciples but some of the minor characters as well are open to the narrator:

The official	4:53	The father knew that was the hour when Jesus had said to him, "your son will live"; and he himself believed, and all his household.
The lame man	5:13	Now the man who had been healed did not know who it was, . . .
Jesus' brothers	7:5	For even his brothers did not believe in him.
The parents	9:22	His parents said this because they feared the Jews, . . .
Pilate	19:8	When Pilate heard these words, he was the more afraid, . . .
Joseph	19:38	. . . Joseph of Arimathea, who was a disciple of Jesus, but secretly, for fear of the Jews, . . .
Mary Magdalene	20:14–15	. . . but she did not know that it was Jesus. . . . Supposing him to be the gardener, . . .

As these verses show, the narrator does not make profound or prolonged plunges into any of these characters. Most of the comments are aesthetically or rhetorically motivated; they involve disclosures which establish characters and explain responses. The healing of the official's son depends on his recognition of the connection between the time of Jesus' pronounce-

---

[25] John 13:2 contains textual problems that derive from an ambiguous idiom and the possibility of contradicting 13:27. The witnesses cluster in two groups:

I. The devil put it into Judas' heart
    A. "of Judas, son of Simon of Iscariot" A, Θ, f[1], f, q, the received text;
    B. "of Simon of Iscariot" f[13], c, pbo;
    C. "of Judas, son of Simon from Cariot" D, e
II. The devil put it into his (i.e. his own) heart
    A. "(that) Judas, son of Simon, the Iscariot" p[66], ℵ, B, (W);
    B. "(that) Judas, son of Simon of Iscariot" L, Ψ, 0124, 1241pc.

C. K. Barrett, *The Gospel According to St. John*, p. 439, adopts the text of II. He translates the verse "The devil had already made up his mind," and calls I. "a simplifying gloss." In support of the currency of this idiom he cites Job 22:22 and 1 Sam. 29:10. Rudolf Bultmann, *The Gospel of John*, p. 464, n. 2, argues that the sense of II. would require βεβλημένον instead of βεβληκότος: "The original text can only be that of D etc. (. . .). B's text will be a correction made in the attempt to avoid the contradiction with v. 27." Lindars and Brown adopt a mediating position: the text of II. and the sense of I. Barnabas Lindars, *The Gospel of John*, p. 449, concludes: ". . . John intends what the *received text*, smoothing out the grammar, actually says." Raymond E. Brown, *The Gospel According to John*, vol. 2, p. 550, translates it "The Devil had already induced Judas, son of Simon, the Iscariot, to betray Jesus." Barrett's solution is the most satisfying in that it recognizes the idiom, is based on the preferable text, and avoids contradiction with 13:27. The received text is probably an attempt to make sense of an unrecognized idiom.

ment and the time of his son's recovery. The brothers of Jesus are characterized by their unbelief, and the strange response of the blind man's parents is explained by their fear. Joseph is identified as a disciple, although how the narrator knew he was a disciple is unclear since we are told that he was a secret, or unconfessing, believer. Retrospection could again be invoked here, but need not be. The drama of Mary's recognition of Jesus depends on the narrator's statement that she thought he was the gardener. In general, the inside views are shallow, brief, and credible in the light of the narrator's retrospective point of view, but they are still a rhetorical device.

The last characters to be examined are "the Jews" and "the crowd."

5:16	And this was why the Jews persecuted Jesus, because he did this on the sabbath.
5:18	This was why the Jews sought all the more to kill him, because he not only broke the sabbath but also called God his own Father, making himself equal with God.
7:15	The Jews marveled at it, saying, . . .
8:27	They did not understand that he spoke to them of the Father.
8:30	As he spoke thus, many believed in him.
11:45	Many of the Jews . . . believed in him; . . .
12:9	When the great crowd of the Jews learned that he was there, they came, not only on account of Jesus but also to see Lazarus, . . .
12:10	So the chief priests planned to put Lazarus also to death,
12:11	because on account of him many of the Jews were going away and believing in Jesus.
12:18	The reason why the crowd went to meet him was that they heard he had done this sign.
12:42	Nevertheless many even of the authorities believed in him, but for fear of the Pharisees they did not confess it, lest they should be put out of the synagogue.
12:43	For they loved the praise of men more than the praise of God.

If not exhaustive, this list is at least adequate to show that the narrator uses shallow inside views of "the Jews" and "the crowd" to characterize them, explain their actions, and draw attention to the division that develops as some believe while others plot Jesus' death. It may be merely incidental, but there does not seem to be a clear case of an inside view of the Pharisees, while there are several inside views of "the Jews."

Omniscience is, of course, not limited to the privilege of providing inside views of the various characters. At times the narrator tells us what none of the characters could easily convey to the reader. As Sternberg notes,[26] Fielding once apologized for his direct statements, saying: "This, as I could not prevail on any of my characters to speak, I was obliged to

---

[26] *Expositional Modes*, p. 293, quoting *Tom Jones*, 3. 7.

declare myself." The evangelist has no such sensitivity about the role of
the narrator, who is free to tell the reader whatever is vital for the progress
of the story. In general, however, it should be said that the narrator's point
of view is external but that he frequently provides a brief inside view of
one of the characters. These inside views tend to be limited rather than
detailed and shallow rather than profound. The evangelist shows no interest in exploring the more complex psychological motivations of his
characters.[27]

Spatial point of view: omnipresent. Distinguishable from omniscience
but related to it is what is often called the omnipresence of the narrator.
Chatman defines omnipresence as "the narrator's capacity to report from
vantage-points not accessible to characters, or to jump from one to another, or to be in two places at once."[28] The Johannine narrator is not
confined to a particular locale or group of characters but is free to move
about from place to place to provide the reader with an unhampered view
of the action. The narrator is at the well when only Jesus and the woman
are present, in the Samaritan village when she announces Jesus, and
simultaneously (4:31) at the well to report Jesus' conversation with the
disciples. He travels toward Capernaum with the official (4:51ff.) and
goes with the lame man to report to the Jews (5:15). On the morning after
the feeding he reports the movement of the crowd of 5,000 across the lake
(6:22–25). He is present in the various interrogations in chapter 9, which
take place away from Jesus and the disciples, and is able to report the
plotting of the Jews in chapter 11. He is present in the courtyard when
Peter faces the servant girl and in the praetorium when Pilate questions
Jesus. He can be any place he is needed and more than one place at the
same time when necessary. While this freedom diminishes the narrative's
verisimilitude, any threat which it poses is offset by the added authority it
gives the narrator, and by implication the narrative.[29] By telling us what
no historical person could know (e.g., conversations where only two per-

---

[27] Compare the description of the narration of the story of David and Bathsheba in
Robert Scholes and Robert Kellogg, *The Nature of Narrative*, p. 166.

[28] *Story and Discourse*, p. 103; cf. p. 212.

[29] Sternberg, *Expositional Modes*, p. 295: "A narrator's omniscience is an established convention, and as such it is not amenable to the usual canons of probability. Not being one of the fictive agents, such a narrator may safely share the
infallible awareness of the all-knowing immortals, in terms of whose superior
nature alone his superhuman attributes can indeed be conceived of at all. His
unlimited knowledge, in short, is by definition motivated in terms that are quasi-
mimetic (godlike) but flagrantly lacking in verisimilitude." Verisimilitude may
not be as threatened by such a narrator in scripture as it is in modern fiction. In
scripture, or a work written to be used with scriptural authority, the "godlike"
effect of an omniscient narrator may be employed quite deliberately.

sons were present), the narrator exposes the story to the question of how anyone could know these things. On the other hand, the authority of the narrator is elevated by the fact that he knows everything relevant for the story, and the story's verisimilitude is recovered by other means, one of which (as we have just seen) is the limitation of inside views to brief, shallow plunges which can generally be explained as retrospective insight.

The spatial point of view of the narrator may be further defined. Generally the narrator assumes the position of one who observes Jesus and the disciples, but one who is also free to interpret their minds when necessary. The narrator, in his omnipresence, does not limit himself to the position of the disciples, however, and his third-person references to them serve to place them at a distance. He never refers to himself and the disciples as "we." In John, the first person plural seems to refer to a group or community which gathered around the Beloved Disciple (21:24–25). So, while the narrator's point of view at times approximates that of the disciples, he does not claim that position. At most, the narrative gives the impression that the narrator is a part of the group around Jesus because much of it deals with events that occurred within that group. In short, the story is presented by an omniscient observer.

The spatial point of view of the narrator does not define his geographical position, however. The issue is complicated by the ambiguity of the Greek verb ἔρχεσθαι, which is used frequently in John and may mean either "to come" or "to go." It is therefore difficult to tell where the narrator stands. We may take a clue from the repeated use of ἐκεῖ and ἐκεῖθεν, which mean "there" and "from there" respectively. Ἐκεῖ occurs 22 times and ἐκεῖθεν twice in John. Among the places that are "there" are: Cana (2:1), Capernaum (2:12), Judea (3:22), Aenon near Salim (3:23), Sychar (4:6, 40), the pool of Bethesda (5:5), the mountain "across" the Sea of Galilee (6:3, 22, 24), "across" the Jordan (10:40, 42), Bethany (12:2, 9), and the garden (18:2, 3). Even granting that some of these references are dictated by narrative factors other than distance from the narrator, the pattern is still significant. All the references listed above are part of the narration. In contrast, ὧδε ("here") occurs only five times, and all of them are in dialogue. To the narrator, therefore, everywhere is "there" and nowhere is "here." This leaves the impression that the narrator stands at some distance from all the locations mentioned in the narrative. The location of the narrator does not necessarily give any clue to the location of the author, however, and John does not fix its narrator in any specific place.

Temporal point of view: retrospective. Already we have noted that the narrator speaks retrospectively. His temporal point of view and its effects may now be considered in more detail. A narrator may either be limited to the temporal point of view of a character, in which case he knows no more about the future than the character; he may tell the story retrospectively, telling the reader what will happen before the fact and before the characters know; or he may employ some combination of these perspectives. His sense of time may be that of one of the characters, or it may be his own.[30]

The retrospective point of view of the narrator is illustrated by such statements as "For the Spirit was not yet given because Jesus had not yet been glorified" (John 7:39). More specifically, the Johannine narrator tells the story of Jesus' ministry from the temporal perspective of a group, "we," which advocates belief in Jesus after his resurrection. The narrator therefore speaks from some point in the future within the narrative world and interprets Jesus as no contemporary observer would have been able to do.[31] The references to what the disciples did not know at the time but discovered after Jesus' resurrection (2:22; 12:16; 13:7; and 20:9) suggest that the perspective of the believing community—should we say the Johannine community—is presented as absolutely necessary if one is to have an adequate understanding of Jesus. By employing the device of a narrator who speaks retrospectively, the author shows that he is not attempting to record "history" without interpreting it, for to do so would mean that the reader might miss its significance. As Northrop Frye perceptively notes, in contrast to the historian who tries to put his reader in the past,

> The apostle feels that if we had been "there," we should have seen nothing, or seen something utterly commonplace, or missed the whole significance of what we did see. So he comes to us, with his ritual drama of a Messiah, presenting a speaking picture which has to be, as Paul says, spiritually discerned.[32]

The author's understanding of scripture and his interpretation of the meaning of Jesus' death probably conditioned his view of the past. John 12:16 provides a helpful clue to part of the process which conditioned the retrospective view which the author adopted for his narrator:

> His disciples did not understand this at first; but when Jesus was glorified, then they remembered that this had been written of him and had been done to him.

---

[30] Uspensky, *A Poetics of Composition,* pp. 65–66.

[31] See Wead, *The Literary Devices in John's Gospel,* pp. 1–11. Uspensky, *A Poetics of Composition,* p. 67, describes this temporal position as follows: "When the author stands outside his characters, however, within his own time, he adopts a retrospective view, looking from the future back into his characters' present. He knows what the characters cannot know. Then his point of view is external to the ongoing narration."

[32] "The Critical Path," pp. 146–47.

The reference emphasizes the role of memory and the study of scripture. As the narrator tells the story he occasionally refers to passages of scripture which the author apparently found to be relevant for interpreting particular elements in the story about Jesus. The comment that the disciples remembered that these things were written about him must be elliptical. The disciples are presented by the narrator as perceiving that passages being applied to the expected Messiah had been fulfilled by Jesus, or, more likely, that they noticed what could be taken as veiled allusions to what they remembered Jesus had done. Their perspective is therefore characterized as one informed by memory of an earlier time and the interpretation of scripture, which they formulated subsequently. As Wolfgang Iser observed: "Whenever something is remembered, it changes according to the circumstances under which it is remembered, but the resultant change in the past becomes a past itself which, in turn, can be remembered and changed again."[33] In John 12:16 and in fact throughout most of the narrative, memory and scripture are blended and reinterpreted. Memory provokes interpretation of scripture, and the latter overlays memory and gives it a new focus so that the story the narrator tells is set in a perspective no "on the scene" reporter would have.

John 12:36b–43 provides a further illustration of this blending of memory and interpretation as it tells of Jesus' withdrawal and his rejection by the Jews. The narrator explains that these things occurred because they were prophesied by Isaiah. What the narrator adumbrated in 12:16 receives further application when the events are explained in the light of interpretation of Isaiah 53:1 and 6:10. These verses in turn are explained on the basis of the assertion that in his vision Isaiah had seen the glory of the *logos*.[34] The response of the Jews which follows in 12:42 reflects later developments in the conflict between the Johannine community and the synagogue in the future of the story world. The narrator reflects on what occurred both before and after the events he narrates.

This perspective calls for a broadening of the concept of point of view along the lines proposed by Robert Weimann:

The New Critics believed that the novel had to be described and evalu-

---

[33] *The Implied Reader,* p. 144. Earlier (p. 104) he makes the following observations regarding Sir Walter Scott's presentation of the past which are suggestive for our own discussion: "If the past has been kept alive, this is primarily due to the structural pattern through which the events are conveyed to the reader: the effect is gained by the interplay between the implied author who arranges the events, and the narrator who comments on them. The reader can only gain real access to the social reality presented by the implied author, when he follows the adjustments of perspective made by the narrator in viewing the events described."

[34] See A. T. Hanson, *The New Testament Interpretation of Scripture,* pp. 103, 163.

ated in terms of its intrinsic categories. Their primary methodological contention about point of view in fiction was that it had to be derived from the text alone. In suggesting that, these critics overlooked the obvious, which is the historical connection of the text: namely, that the texts themselves derive from, and act upon, contexts. . . . In the act of telling his story, the teller of the tale is faced, not simply with a series of technical problems and not only with the rhetorical task of communication, but with a world full of struggle and change where the writer, in order to transmute his experience into art, has constantly to reassess his relations to society as both a social and an aesthetic act. . . . this relationship itself is the basis on which representation and evaluation are integrated through point of view.[35]

In this broad sense, the Johannine narrator, who presumably expresses the perspective of the author, tells the story from a point of view which in its retrospection is informed by memory, interpretation of scripture, the coalescing of traditions with the post-Easter experience of the early church, consciousness of the presence of the Spirit, a reading of the glory of the risen Christ back into the days of his ministry, and an acute sensitivity to the history and struggles of the Johannine community.[36] But with this observation we have moved to the narrator's ideological or evaluative point of view, and there is yet one more factor to consider regarding his temporal point of view.

While the story is told retrospectively, there are occasional departures from this perspective which move the reader from the time of the telling to the time of the story. These are signaled by the use of present tense verbs, "historical presents," in the narration. The imperfect tense is a half step between the aorist (or simple past tense) and the present tense in that it causes the reader to see past action in progress.[37] A survey of the early chapters of the gospel reveals a fairly well defined pattern in the appearance of historical presents. Whenever the narrator is providing a transition from one scene to another, his normal mode is the aorist or imperfect tense. The narrator uses a present tense verb in the introduction to a scene, however, when describing physical phenomena still present in his own time: 4:5—"a city of Samaria, called Sychar"; 5:2—"Now there is in Jerusalem by the Sheep Gate a pool, in Hebrew called Beth-zatha, which has five porticoes." At other places where the narrator departs from the past tenses, we may suspect a polemical interest. The most significant of these departures in the first six chapters occurs at 4:1—"Now when the

---

[35] *Structure and Society in Literary History*, pp. 236, 237.

[36] Cf. Amos N. Wilder, *Early Christian Rhetoric*, pp. 69–70.

[37] Uspensky, *A Poetics of Composition*, pp. 74–75.

Lord knew that the Pharisees had heard that Jesus was making and baptizing more disciples than John. . . ." Is the choice of the present tense for
these verbs motivated by a desire to affirm or imply that Jesus was still
making and baptizing more disciples than the followers of John the Baptist? The use of the present tense for John's testimony about Jesus in 1:15
fits the pattern also.

Quite commonly we find the present tense in narration within scenes
rather than between them or at the beginning of a scene. The effect of this
switch to the present tense is to move the reader into the scene so that even
though it is told in the course of narrating the past, readers feel that they
are in the scene. By far the most commonly used historical present is λέγει
("he says").[38] Even when the present tense is not used consistently in a
particular scene, it serves to stop the movement of time. The story of the
wedding at Cana illustrates the pattern. In the introduction to the scene
(2:1–2) two aorist tense verbs (ἐγένετο and ἐκλήθη) and one imperfect
(ἦν) are used. Past tense verbs are used to describe the scene (2:6) and
move the action along (2:9), but the dialogue is consistently introduced by
λέγει (2:3, 4, 5, 7, 8, 9 [φωνεῖ] "he calls," 10). The transitional summary
which follows the scene reverts to verbs in the aorist tense. Uspensky
interprets this pattern by means of analogy:

> This particular kind of narrative construction may be compared to a
> slide show, where the individual slides are linked together sequentially
> to form a plot. When a slide is shown, narrative time stops; in the
> intervals between the slides, narrative time is accelerated and moves
> very rapidly.[39]

This pattern is again evident in the conversation with the Samaritan
woman, but not in the dialogue in the synagogue in chapter 6. We may
conclude, therefore, that although the pattern is not uniform, the historical presents in John are often used to place the reader within scenes, and

---

[38] See O'Rourke, "The Historic Present in the Gospel of John," pp. 585–86, for a
list of the 151 historic presents in John. Λέγει occurs 112 times, and λέγουσιν 7
times. The remaining 32 historic presents involve 21 different verbs (19 different
stems). Christian P. Casparis, *Tense without Time*, traces the use of the historical
present to Herodotus (pp. 138–39) and notes that "by far the most common
group of hist. Pres. formulae is the one connected with *verba dicendi*, especially
the verb *to say*. . . . The accumulated occurrence of these formulae is notably
restricted to colloquial or vulgar oral narrative situations. Situations in which the
eyewitness narrator is bent upon creating the impression of reproducing a dialogue or monologue word for word. He may resort to this technique for various
reasons: to authenticate his tale (. . .); to point out the importance, . . . of what
has been said in his presence; to kindle by his own involvement the wonder or
compassion of his audience" (pp. 116–17).

[39] *A Poetics of Composition*, p. 71.

occasionally to score a polemical point. While they are not as important as the narrator's retrospective point of view, their effect should not be overlooked.

Ideological point of view: reliable and stereoscopic. We have held back this aspect of the narrator's point of view in order to get these other matters in place first. The most important function of the narrator in the Gospel of John is bound up in what Uspensky calls his "ideological" or evaluative point of view.[40] No narrator can be absolutely impartial; inevitably a narrator, especially an omniscient, omnipresent, omnicommunicative, and intrusive one, will prejudice the reader toward or away from certain characters, claims, or events and their implications.[41] More than that, no story can be very meaningful unless the readers are introduced to its value system or provided with some way of relating it to their own.[42] Nor is there any evidence that the Johannine narrator attempts to maintain any neutrality toward his story: his function is to facilitate communication of the implied author's ideological or evaluative system to the reader.

For this purpose the narrator is established not only as omniscient and omnicommunicative but also as entirely *reliable.* All limits on our sense of his reliability are lifted by so structuring the narrative that the reader is elevated to the narrator's Olympian perspective on the characters and events, given this information at the outset and as necessary throughout the narrative, and then shown how the narrator's perspective is in fact borne out by the action and character development that follows.[43] We soon trust him implicitly and completely. The Johannine narrator is entirely reliable in that "he speaks in accordance with the norms of the work (which is to say, the implied author's norms). . . ."[44] The reliability of the narrator (as defined by Booth and used as a technical term by literary critics) must be kept distinct from both the historical accuracy of the narrator's account and the "truth" of his ideological point of view. "Reliability" is a matter of literary analysis, historical accuracy is the territory of the historian, and "truth" is a matter for believers and theologians. While readers may be oblivious to the first and disinterested in the second, they cannot escape the narrator's challenge with reference to the third:

---

[40] *A Poetics of Composition,* p. 8.

[41] Booth, *The Rhetoric of Fiction,* p. 78.

[42] Booth, *The Rhetoric of Fiction,* p. 112.

[43] Regarding a reader's predisposition to trust a narrator, see Sternberg, *Expositional Modes,* p. 270; Kermode, *The Genesis of Secrecy,* p. 113; Chatman, *Story and Discourse,* p. 227.

[44] Booth, "Distance and Point of View," p. 72.

"but these things have been written in order that you may believe that Jesus is the Christ the son of God . . ."(20:31).

J. M. Lotman has perceptively noted something else about the Gospel of John that is as significant as it is obvious: "All of the speeches add up to one of two views: the 'correct' (coinciding with that of the text as a whole) and the 'incorrect' (opposed to it)."[45] From this he concludes:

> Although several characters and groups of characters figure into the text, its very structure allows only three positions: that of truth, that of untruth, and that of transition from one to the other ("revelation" and "apostasy"). That is, only two points of view are possible—the true and the untrue.[46]

We shall return to this conflict between ideological points of view in Chapter 4. At that time we can define more precisely the implied author's attitude toward various characters and groups. We have already noted that the narrator speaks from the temporal and ideological position of the Johannine community, which is defined by the gospel as a whole and by various references within it. All of the topics which are usually treated in discussions of the theology of the Gospel of John are, in fact, aspects of the implied author's ideological point of view as it is conveyed through Jesus and the narrator. One aspect of the narrator's ideological point of view merits special attention, however.

For want of a better term, the narrator's point of view on Jesus and his story may be called *stereoscopic*. The dictionary defines a stereoscope as an optical device with two eyeglasses which creates the illusion of solidity and depth by "assisting the observer to combine the images of two pictures taken from points of view a little way apart."[47] The term is appropriate, for the narrator views Jesus and his ministry from the twin perspectives of his "whence" and his "whither," his origin as the pre-existent *logos* and his destiny as the exalted Son of God. Only when these perspectives are combined can Jesus be understood. This stereoscopic perspective conditions not only what the narrator says but the gospel's entire characterization of Jesus.

John 13:1–6, the gospel's most majestic scene introduction, illustrates this stereoscopic perspective. First, it does the required: it sets the time, the place, and the characters involved in the ensuing action. Beyond that, it sets the footwashing and the farewell discourse in the context of Jesus' awareness of his origin and his destiny. That which has been explained to

---

[45] "Point of View in a Text," p. 342.

[46] "Point of View in a Text," pp. 342–43; cf. p. 352.

[47] *Webster's New Collegiate Dictionary*, 6th ed., s.v. "stereoscope."

the reader by the narrator and shown by the action and dialogue of the narrative is now said to be self-conscious in Jesus. He had come from the Father, and he was going to be exalted and glorified. The hour had come for him to go from this world to the Father.

This introduction shows that the narrator, who shares Jesus' knowledge of himself, knows that Jesus is the divine, pre-existent *logos* who was responsible for creation. The gospel narrative therefore portrays Jesus as the one who continued the creative work of the divine *logos* by creating eyes for a man born blind, restoring the dead to life, and breathing spirit into spiritless disciples. The narrator also knows that Jesus will be exalted to the Father, so he prepares the reader to understand Jesus' death as exaltation rather than humiliation. These entrance and exit points, which are subjects of concern repeatedly in the gospel, condition the Johannine narrator's stereoscopic view of the ministry of Jesus.

Relationships Within the Text

Up to this point we have been considering the identity of the narrator primarily as it is defined by his point of view, but the narrator may also be identified in terms of the way he relates to other figures in the narrative context: the characters (especially Jesus), the implied author, and the implied reader. The latter relationship will be discussed in Chapter 7. The narrator may be more or less identified with, sympathetic with, or distant from each of the other figures, and the cumulative effect of these relationships defines in large measure the nature of the narrator's role.[48]

The narrator and Jesus. A great deal has already been said about the narrator's relationship to Jesus. The narrator knows who Jesus is and what he knows. They both know "all things." The narrator, however, serves as an authoritative interpreter of Jesus' words.

In John 11:11, Jesus tells the disciples that Lazarus has fallen asleep. The disciples miss Jesus' metaphor and therefore misunderstand. The narrator clarifies Jesus' statement for the reader: "Now Jesus had spoken of his death, but they thought that he meant taking rest in sleep. Then Jesus told them plainly, 'Lazarus is dead.'" Here, in a calculated way, the author presents the narrator as the one who understands Jesus' words even when the disciples do not. The importance of the narrator's role as interpreter becomes obvious when one skips the narration and reads only

---

[48] See Booth, *The Rhetoric of Fiction*, pp. 155–59; Sternberg, *Expositional Modes*, pp. 259–60.

the dialogue. Without the narration the dialogue in this passage loses most of its significance. John 11:11–14 is not an isolated case; the narrator serves as the authoritative interpreter of Jesus' words in the following verses:

2:21 But he spoke of the temple of his body. Cf. 2:22.

6:6 This he said to test him, for he himself knew what he would do.

6:71 He spoke of Judas the son of Simon Iscariot, for he, one of the twelve, was to betray him.

7:39 Now this he said about the Spirit, which those who believed in him were to receive; for as yet the Spirit had not been given, because Jesus was not yet glorified. Cf. 19:30; 20:22.

8:27 They did not understand that he spoke to them of the Father.

12:33 He said this to show by what death he was to die.

13:11 For he knew who was to betray him; that was why he said, 'You are not all clean.'

18:32 This was to fulfill the word which Jesus had spoken to show by what death he was to die.

21:19 This he said to show by what death he was to glorify God.

21:23 The saying spread abroad among the brethren that this disciple was not to die; yet Jesus did not say to him that he was not to die, but, "If it is my will that he remain until I come, what is that to you?"

Even when the interpretation does not occur in the immediate context of the saying, it is clear that the narrator is the authoritative interpreter of Jesus' words. For example, in John 5:44 Jesus asks the Jews, "How can you believe, who receive glory from one another and do not seek the glory that comes from the only God?" The narrator's words about the Jewish authorities at the end of chapter 12 return to this statement: "For they loved the glory of men more than the glory of God" (12:43). The implication is that the narrator understands Jesus' words and knows how they are to be interpreted. In addition to Jesus' words, the narrator also interprets the words of the parents of the blind man (9:22), Caiaphas (11:51–53), Judas (12:6), and Isaiah (12:41). Then, in John 21:23, the narrator corrects the misunderstanding that was current among "the brothers" regarding the coming of the risen Lord before the death of the Beloved Disciple. By this point it has long been clear to the reader that the narrator is the authoritative interpreter of Jesus' words and therefore his interpretation has authority over any other interpretations. Actually, of course, the narrator interprets only a few statements. But what Jesus says, and the gospel as a whole, represents a massive, daring re-interpretation of Jesus. The narrator is only part of the larger whole. Yet the aura of reliability which is infused around the narrator goes a long way toward disposing the reader to accept the gospel's interpretation of Jesus.

In order to define further the relationship between the narrator and

Jesus it is necessary to compare aspects of their points of view. John, 13:31–17:26 is generally referred to as the farewell discourse, although technically chapter 17 is a parting prayer. In this discourse, as elsewhere, Jesus has a distinctive point of view from which he interprets his mission, his departure and return, and the disciples' relationship to him. Since the narrator intrudes in a significant way only once during the farewell discourse (16:17, 19; see also 13:31; 17:1, and possibly 17:3), a comparative analysis of Jesus' point of view in the farewell discourse with the narrator's should provide a classic test for determining the relationship between the two and consistency of point of view throughout the gospel. The question may be put this way: Does the farewell discourse reflect the same point of view as the narrator's voice elsewhere in the gospel, or do these two—narration and discourse—offer different perspectives on Jesus?

The following paragraphs will show that Jesus' point of view, as it may be inferred from the farewell discourse, corresponds remarkably to that of the narrator. Both Jesus and the narrator are omniscient, retrospective, and ideologically and phraseologically indistinguishable.

Jesus' omniscience may be inferred from what he says. Jesus knows when the disciples do not want to ask him the meaning of what he said (16:19). He knows that Peter will deny him three times that night (13:38). He explains to the disciples that his Father's house has many resting places and that he is going to prepare a place for them (14:2). He is entirely aware of his unique relationship to the Father (14:7, 9, 10, 11, 24; 15:1; 16:15; 17:11). He knows that the hour is coming when they will all abandon him (16:32), and that the ruler of this world is coming (14:30). Beyond that, the "little while" will pass (16:16, 20, 22), and they will see him again. In short, the farewell discourse shows that Jesus knows the spiritual orientation of the disciples (15:19; 17:16) and the world, the hearts and minds of the disciples, his own origin, mission, destiny, and relationship to the Father, and significant future events. Finally, just before the prayer in chapter 17, the author drives home the fact and significance of Jesus' omniscience by having the disciples say: "Now we know that you know all things, and need none to question you; by this we believe that you came from God" (16:30; cf. 2:24–25).

The temporal perspectives of the farewell discourse are notoriously difficult to sort out. In chapter 17 especially one finds retrospective statements:

17:4   I glorified thee on earth, having accomplished the work which thou gavest me to do, . . .

17:6   I have manifested thy name to the men whom thou gavest me out of the world, . . .

17:11   And now I am no more in the world, . . .

With such pronouncements Jesus speaks from the position of the risen and exalted Lord: they characterize the significance of Jesus' life.

Although there are a few similar statements in the farewell discourse proper (e.g., 14:9), their prominence in chapter 17 is distinctive. In the earlier chapters the author presents Jesus as speaking proleptically about the events which were yet to occur: "And now I have told you before it takes place, so that when it does take place, you may believe" (14:29; cf. 13:7; 16:4). Among the things he discusses beforehand one may list: his departure, the coming of the Paraclete, their joy when they see him again (16:22–23), the greater works the disciples will do (14:12), the persecution they will experience (15:21), their expulsion from the synagogue (16:2–4), and Peter's death—though the reference in 13:36 is veiled. It is commonly thought that the author was in the midst of these events when he wrote. Therefore, while the narrator views Jesus retrospectively in the rest of the gospel, in the farewell discourse Jesus speaks proleptically of the life situation of the fictional narrator, which probably corresponds to that of the author himself. The link between Jesus and the later time is thereby maintained in the farewell discourse by Jesus' proleptic speech. It is the counterpart of the narrator's retrospective point of view, and it was the only narrative device open to the author for maintaining this linkage once he chose to place the material in the form of discourse from the mouth of Jesus.

The temporal point of view of the farewell discourse is, therefore, correlative to that of the narrator. By means of this linkage in perspective the author presents the significance of Jesus for the author's own time. The author's objective is transparent when Jesus says, "But I have said these things to you, that when their hour comes you may remember that I told you of them" (16:4).

An even clearer comparison between the point of view of the narrator and the farewell discourse can be drawn from Jesus' repeated references to his origin and his destiny. The parade example of this emphasis is John 16:28—"I came from the Father and have come into the world; again, I am leaving the world and going to the Father." The disciples respond by acclaiming Jesus' omniscience and professing that it is sufficient basis for believing that he has come from God (16:29–30). The importance of Jesus' eternal whence and whither in the farewell discourse is clearly illustrated by its recurrence in the following statements:

14:12 ... I go to the Father.
14:28 You heard me say to you, 'I go away, and I will come to you.' If you loved me, you would have rejoiced because I go to the Father; ...
16:5 But now I am going to him who sent me; yet none of you asks me, 'Where are you going?'

16:10   . . . because I go to the Father, and you will see me no more; . . .
17:11   . . . and I am coming to thee; . . .
17:13   But now I am coming to thee; . . .
17:18   As thou didst send me into the world, so I have sent them into the world.
17:24   Father, I desire that they also, whom thou has given me, may be with me
         where I am, to behold my glory which thou hast given me in thy love for me
         before the foundation of the world.

The one instance where the narrator intrudes significantly in the farewell discourse (with the possible exception of 17:3) occurs after Jesus' statement about the "little while," which concludes "because I go to the Father" (16:17). Immediately, the narrator tells us that the disciples spoke to one another and Jesus knew they wanted to question him (16:17, 19). Overcoming the disciples' ignorance of Jesus' origin from above and return to the Father was consequential enough to justify this break in the flow of the discourse. The intervention of the narrator further confirms the emphasis given to Jesus' whence and whither in the discourse and fits the pattern established by the prologue and the stereoscopic perspective of the narrator elsewhere in the gospel.

The striking congruence in the points of view of the narrator and the farewell discourse, especially since the narrator remains silent through virtually all of these chapters, is significant for establishing the perspective from which the reader is to view Jesus' life and death. Both Jesus and the narrator are omniscient and speak in retrospect—or prospect as discussed above—from the life situation of the Johannine community, while viewing Jesus' life in the context of his origin and destiny in glory. This consistency with respect to point of view in disparate elements of the gospel demonstrates the remarkable unity of perspective throughout John. The implication is that unless the readers see Jesus in the light of the narrator's temporal and ideological point of view, they cannot understand who Jesus was.

Commentators have identified numerous parallels to the discourse material among the pronouncements of Jesus elsewhere in the gospel, but it is more difficult to assess the relationship between the narrator's speech and the discourse material he reports. Nevertheless, it is worth asking whether there is a difference in idiom or speech patterns (i.e., Uspensky's phraseological plane) between Jesus and the narrator. The author controls both. If there is any convergence between the idioms of these two distinct and disparate narrative elements, it is significant for the interpretation of the gospel. In addition to the verses cited above (p. 35) in which the narrator interprets the words of Jesus or another character, there are interpretative statements which are not related to a specific saying:

7:30   So they sought to arrest him; but no one laid hands on him, because his hour had not yet come.

8:20   . . . but no one arrested him, because his hour had not yet come.

12:16 His disciples did not understand this at first, but when Jesus was glorified, then they remembered that this had been written of him and had been done to him.

The correlation of the narrator's explanatory comments with the themes of the farewell discourse is surprising. The comments deal with Judas (6:71; 12:6; 13:11), Jesus' hour (7:30; 8:20), his glorification (7:39; 12:16), the giving of the Spirit (7:39), exclusion from the synagogue (9:22; 12:42), the Father (8:27), the significance of Jesus' death (11:51–53), and the manner of his death (12:33; 18:32). Missing are statements related to Jesus' going away and the unity and mutual love of the disciples. With these exceptions, the narrator's explanatory or interpretative comments deal with virtually all of the main themes of the farewell discourse, and with only one or two exceptions (11:13 and perhaps 12:41) every point at which the narrator intervenes to interpret a statement is related to concerns dealt with by the farewell discourse. Many of the themes of the farewell discourse, therefore, are foreshadowed by the narrator.

The interpretative comments also function as vehicles of plot development. Their effect is to focus the reader's attention on the betrayal, death, and glorification of Jesus and thereby build dramatic interest in how these events will occur. In this area the author is particularly skillful: he never shows his hand all at once, but he never leaves the impression that he is holding back on the reader.

In tracing the narrator's foreshadowing of the events related to Jesus' death, one sees that Jesus and the narrator share the same vocabulary and use terms with the same veiled or double meaning. The development cannot be traced here, but John 7:39 illustrates the pattern. In this verse, the verb δοξάζω, with which John advances his distinctive interpretation of Jesus' death and resurrection, appears for the first time in the gospel. It will subsequently occur nine times in the farewell discourse and is always on the lips of Jesus except in 12:16 and 21:19, where the narrator speaks.[49] The narrator explains that the Spirit had not yet been given because Jesus had not yet been glorified. This linking of the coming of the Spirit to the death of Jesus receives substantial development later in the gospel, and in the farewell discourse in particular. In 7:30 and 8:20 the narrator explains the failure of the officials to arrest Jesus by saying, "his hour had not yet come." The mysterious significance of his hour was

---

[49] C. H. Dodd, *The Interpretation of the Fourth Gospel*, p. 396.

introduced by Jesus in 2:4. The narrator, who of course understands its importance, refers to it now in the context of the attempts by the Jews to arrest Jesus. The reader therefore begins to grasp its meaning. In 12:23 (and 17:1) Jesus ties the "hour" to his glorification. The narrator then introduces chapter 13 by saying that Jesus knew that the hour had now come. In similar fashion, the narrator refers five times to the one who will betray Jesus (6:64, 71; 12:4; 13:2, 11) before Jesus himself finally alludes to his betrayer in 13:21. The reader is given a piece at a time, and slowly the pieces fit together, unveiling the course and meaning of coming events.

These examples show that the narrator uses or introduces most of the significant terms related to Jesus' death which figure prominently in the farewell discourse:

	Narrator	Farewell Discourse
ὥρα (hour)	7:30; 8:20; 13:1	16:32; 17:1; cf. 16:2
δοξάζω (glorify)	12:16	13:31, 32; 14:13; 15:8; 16:14; 17:1, 4, 5, 10
πνεῦμα (spirit)	7:39; cf. 11:33; 13:21	14:17, 26; 15:26; 16:13
ἀποσυνάγωγος (out of the synagogue)	9:22; 12:42	16:2

This sample of the evidence shows how the author has tied the farewell discourse to the gospel narrative by using the narrator to introduce some of its key terms earlier in the narrative. Moreover, the narrator and Jesus deal with the same themes and use the same key terms in the same ways. The death of Jesus is of such enormous significance that it is carefully foreshadowed and interpreted by both the narrator and the discourse material.

In the farewell discourse, and indeed in the gospel generally, there is a remarkable uniformity in the idiom of the narrator and Jesus. There is certainly the theoretical possibility that the author has adapted the speech of his narrator to Jesus' idiom, but it is more likely that Jesus' speech is "contaminated" by authorial speech patterns. In John, the "phraseological points of view," or speech characteristics, of the narrator and Jesus are so close that the narrator's phraseological point of view seems to be imposed on Jesus.[50] The difference between the idiom of the Johannine Jesus and the synoptic Jesus, on the one hand, and the similarity between this idiom

---

[50] Uspensky, *A Poetics of Composition*, p. 52, makes the following relevant observations: "The less differentiation there is between the phraseology of the described (the character) and the describing (author or narrator), the closer are their phraseological points of view. The two opposite poles are: the faithful representation of the specifica of the character's speech (the case of maximum differentiation), and the narrated monologue (the case of the minimal differentiation)."

and the language of the Johannine epistles, on the other hand, confirms that when Jesus, the literary character, speaks, he speaks the language of the author and his narrator.[51]

The ideological and phraseological planes of the narrator's point of view, which correspond so closely to Jesus' point of view, subtly influence the presentation of Jesus and the other characters throughout the narrative. This influence can be seen most clearly when dialogue is created by, grows out of, illustrates, or is influenced by narration. For example, a new word is introduced in John 6:41 when the narrator explains that the Jews were "murmuring" ($\dot{\epsilon}\gamma\acute{o}\gamma\gamma\upsilon\zeta o\nu$, a vividly onomatopoetic word) about Jesus. The word is carefully chosen because it evokes the murmuring of the Israelites against Moses (Exod. 16:7–9, 12; 17:3; Num. 11:1; 14:27, 29; 16:41; 17:5; Ps. 59:5; 106:25). By describing the Jews' response to Jesus with this word, the narrator has led the reader to view the action in the light of the Exodus events. This context has already been established by the dialogue in 6:31–32. Jesus immediately picks up the narrator's description of what was taking place: in 6:43 Jesus says, "Do not murmur ($\gamma o\gamma\gamma\acute{\upsilon}\zeta\epsilon\tau\epsilon$) among yourselves." Later, the narrator tells us that Jesus' perception of what was happening even among the disciples corresponds to his own: "But Jesus, knowing in himself that his disciples murmured ($\gamma o\gamma\gamma\acute{\upsilon}\zeta o\upsilon\sigma\iota\nu$) at it . . ." (6:61). Since the narrator's description corresponds exactly with Jesus', the reader is all the more inclined to accept the narrator as a reliable guide to the meaning of Jesus' life. Other passages fit this pattern also. In John 1:32, the narrator uses a characteristically Johannine word, "and John bore witness. . . ." John's own words echo this description immediately: "And I have seen and have borne witness that this is the Son of God" (1:34). Here again, the narrator's interpretation of the meaning of an event is carried over into the dialogue.

Because of the similarity in Jesus' and the narrator's speech patterns, and because of the narrator's influence on dialogue, it is impossible to tell when Jesus or John the Baptist stops speaking in chapter 3 and when or if the narrator speaks. The identity of the speaker in 3:13–21 (or 3:16–21) and 3:31–36 is a well-known problem.[52] The author often allows charac-

---

[51] On the substitution of points of view, see *A Poetics of Composition,* p. 119.

[52] D. Moody Smith, *The Composition and Order of the Fourth Gospel,* p. 126, comments on 3:13–21 and 31–36: "Both may be understood as commentary of the evangelist rather than words of Jesus and John the Baptist respectively." Brown, *John,* vol. 1, pp. 159–60, treats 3:31–36 as "an isolated discourse of Jesus" which "has been attached to the scenes of ch. iii as an interpretation of those scenes," but (p. 149) he rejects the notion that there is a change of speakers in 3:13 (or 16): "Of course the evangelist has been at work in this discourse, but his work is not of the type that begins at a particular verse. All Jesus' words come to us through the channel of the evangelist's understanding and rethinking, but the gospel

ters to fade from the narrative without notice, but does not normally change speakers without telling the reader. It is certainly not clear that a change of speakers is intended in these passages. The temporal perspective, terminology, and content of 3:13–21, 31–36 vary in appropriateness for Jesus (or John) and the narrator. It appears to be a classic instance of the blending of the narrator with Jesus' voice. There are numerous parallels between these verses and the prologue and the farewell discourse. There is also a change of temporal point of view in verses 13 and 14. The imposition of one time on another, one voice on another, requires the reader to hear Jesus speaking to the reader's time through the narrator and hence the gospel. Chatman observes that when it is not possible to decide whether the words are a character's or the narrator's it may well be intended:

> The implication is "It doesn't matter who says or thinks this; it is appropriate to both character and narrator." The ambiguity may strengthen the bond between the two, make us trust still more the narrator's authority. Perhaps we should speak of "neutralization" or "unification," rather than ambiguity. . . . Such statements imply that character and narrator are so close, in such sympathy, that it does not matter to whom we assign the statement. . . . A feeling is established that the narrator possesses not only access to but an unusual affinity or "vibration" with the character's mind. There is the suggestion of a kind of "in"-group psychology: . . .[53]

This suggestive analysis could be applied to the gospel's portrayal of the Beloved Disciple, a matter we will consider shortly.

The over-all effect of the similarity between the narrator's and Jesus' points of view, the relationship between narration and the farewell discourse, the narrator's influence on dialogue, and the blending of voices in chapter 3 point to a complex relationship between Jesus and the narrator. Both narrator and character, of course, can be vehicles for the implied author's ideology. In the gospel it appears as if the narrator is adopting Jesus' point of view ideologically and phraseologically, but this is just the impression the reader has of the situation. Actually, the author, who was

---

presents Jesus as speaking and not the evangelist." Dodd, *The Interpretation of the Fourth Gospel*, p. 308, comments on 3:31–36: "It is doubtful how far it is possible, here or elsewhere in this gospel, to draw a clear line between reported dialogue or discourse and the evangelist's reflections." Rudolf Schnackenburg, *The Gospel According to St. John*, vol. 1, pp. 360–63, develops an elaborate theory of the origin of these verses, which he calls "kerygmatic exposition of the evangelist."

[53] *Story and Discourse*, pp. 206–07.

probably informed by tradition handed down within the Johannine community, fashioned the character, Jesus, as he wrote and interpreted Jesus through both Jesus' dialogue and the narrator's interpretive comments. It is therefore not a matter of the narrator's speech being conformed to Jesus', but of both reflecting the author's speech patterns and expressing his ideological point of view. The consonance between Jesus and the narrator is a result of the author's expression of his point of view through both his central character and the narrator. The character is not as objective or removed from the narrator as the unsuspecting reader may think. As a result, the narrator is an absolutely reliable guide to what Jesus meant to the author, a view, or better, a belief which the author sought to convey to the reader.

The narrator and the implied author. Another of the narrator's significant relationships is to the author, or implied author. The distinction between the two may help to highlight the aesthetic and rhetorical choices which the "real" author made in writing the gospel, but there is no reason to suspect any difference in the ideological, spatial, temporal, or phraseological points of view of the narrator, the implied author, and the author. Because of the peculiar character of the gospel, the relationships among these entities are best approached by looking further at the three figures which have interpretive roles in the gospel: the narrator, the Paraclete, and the Beloved Disciple. Implicitly or explicitly the authority of each is emphasized. The omniscient narrator tells about Jesus retrospectively with the effect that the reader is led to trust his account. Jesus speaks of the future role of the Paraclete, the Spirit of Truth, who will teach the disciples all things, remind them of what Jesus said (14:26), and bear witness concerning him (15:26). The Beloved Disciple has borne witness (19:35; 21:24-25), and the narrator confirms that his witness is true. A strong, complementary relationship among these three Johannine interpreters of the Jesus tradition is therefore evident.

Previously I have argued that the similarity in the functions of the Paraclete and the Beloved Disciple within the Johannine community suggests that the community formed its understanding of the Spirit as Paraclete in the light of reflection on what the Beloved Disciple had done in their midst.[54] I shall not pursue that relationship further here. The key references for discussion of the relationship between the Beloved Disciple, the narrator, the implied author, and the author are John 19:35 and 21:24-25. Discussion of these verses has generally been concerned with their place within the gospel's composition history: was 19:35 written by

---

[54] *The Johannine School*, pp. 266-70.

the evangelist or the redactor? Perhaps new insights can be gained by starting from the observation that it is the narrator who makes these comments.

Such a reading of John 19:35 reveals that it fits appropriately into the narration of the gospel. The narrator, who speaks about Jesus retrospectively, here relates something which happened subsequent to the crucifixion: namely, "the one who saw these things," presumably the Beloved Disciple, bore witness to them. Then the narrator, who like the Paraclete knows all about Jesus, affirms that the Beloved Disciple's witness is true. The narrator, therefore, is not the Beloved Disciple but speaks as one who knows what is true, knows the mind of the Beloved Disciple, and knows that what the Beloved Disciple said is true. It is difficult to go further on the basis of this verse alone. The Beloved Disciple may be just another character through whom the author's point of view is communicated, or he may be an idealized representation of the author (hence a dramatic approximation of the implied author), or an accurate characterization of the author himself.

Before turning to the crucial, concluding verses of the gospel it will be helpful to review what the Beloved Disciple knows and what he tells in the course of the narrative. It may well be that the unidentified companion of Andrew in 1:35–40 is the Beloved Disciple. If so, as one of the first two disciples, he was with Jesus from the beginning of his ministry, the beginning of the story. There is some cogency in identifying both this disciple and Peter's unnamed companion in 18:15 with the Beloved Disciple. The explicit reference to the Beloved Disciple as "the other disciple" in 20:4 adds to the likelihood of this identification, but the narrative stops short of making it certain. The Beloved Disciple is introduced for the first time at the last supper. There, he is the one closest to Jesus. Jesus reveals to him the identity of the betrayer (13:25–26) through the dipping of the morsel. If the Beloved Disciple understands what Jesus means, he does not reveal Jesus' secret to Peter or any of the others before its time.[55] At the empty tomb the Beloved Disciple sees the grave clothes and believes (20:8), but does not tell Peter or any of the others what he understood. News of the resurrection reaches them through Mary Magdalene (20:18). The Beloved Disciple's silence about the empty tomb fits the pattern of the last supper scene and his seeing the water and the blood at the cross. He understands but does not bear witness until later. Luke would have said he "kept all these things, pondering them in his heart."

Virtually every part of John 21:24 is open to multiple interpretations

---

[55] Cf. Marinus de Jonge, *Jesus,* pp. 211–13.

except "this disciple," who must be the Beloved Disciple (cf. 21:20–23).[56] What are "these things" to which he has borne witness: John 21:23 and its immediate context (as C. H. Dodd argued), John 21, or the gospel as a whole?[57] Does ὁ γράψας mean "who wrote (these things)" or "who caused (these things) to be written"?[58] Who is denoted by "we," and what was their relationship to the Beloved Disciple?

Without needlessly multiplying entities, John 21:24–25 is open to interpretations involving one, two, or three persons. The one-person theory claims that the Beloved Disciple, the author, identified himself here after implying that the community should not expect him to live until the parousia. This view founders upon four considerations: (1) John 21 seems to be an appendix added after the gospel reached its penultimate form; (2) it is more likely that 21:23 implies that the Beloved Disciple has died; (3) the writer identifies himself with the "we" over against "this disciple"; and (4) it is unlikely that anyone would refer to himself as "the Beloved Disciple." One version of the two-person theory would say that 21:24–25 was written by the evangelist (the author of the rest of the gospel) and that the evangelist attributed his work to the Beloved Disciple, who may have been his mentor and the source of his material. Assuming this version of the two-person theory, the author at the end writes as a member of the group that has received the gospel written by the Beloved Disciple and attests to its truth. If this is the case, the Gospel of John is a pseudonymous writing in which the author subverts any suspicion that he has written it by attributing the gospel to the Beloved Disciple. A more common version of the two-person theory maintains that these verses are the work of an editor who identified the gospel's real author, the Beloved Disciple. This view is usually coupled with the assumption that the gospel's depiction of the Beloved Disciple is historically accurate. The three-person theory distinguishes the Beloved Disciple, the evangelist, and the editor as three separate persons. John 21:24–25 comes from an editor who attributed the gospel to the Beloved Disciple, the community's founding father, when in reality the Beloved Disciple was merely the source of the evangelist's material. If, as seems probable, John 19:35 comes from the evangelist, he

---

[56] For a good, brief discussion of the problems involved in interpreting John 21:24–25 see: Stephen S. Smalley, *John: Evangelist and Interpreter*, pp. 80–81.

[57] C. H. Dodd, "Note on John 21, 24," pp. 212–13. Dodd's view of this verse has not been widely accepted. Cf. Bultmann, *John*, p. 717, n. 4; Brown, *John*, vol. 2, pp. 1123–24; Barrett, *John*, p. 588.

[58] Brown, *John*, vol. 2, p. 1123, follows G. Schrenk, *"Graphō," TDNT*, vol. 1, p. 743, in adopting the weakened, causative, meaning. On the other hand, Barrett, *John*, p. 587; Lindars, *John*, p. 641; and de Jonge, *Jesus*, p. 221, n. 28, favor the more direct sense, "who wrote."

too acknowledged the gospel's dependence on the Beloved Disciple.[59] Regardless of whether the Beloved Disciple was the evangelist, or wrote parts of the gospel or its source material, or just inspired its writing, the narrator's retrospective point of view may derive from his influence on the gospel. The debate over these alternatives, however, has not given much attention to the role of the narrator in the gospel. What difference does it make if these verses are taken as an integral part of the narration, that is, as the words of the narrator?

First, the appearance of the narrator speaking in the first person at the end of the narrative should be seen as a common literary convention, not as something extraordinary or problematic. Uspensky has explored the function of framing in literature and pictorial art. Both present a strange new world which the viewer or reader must enter to comprehend it and then leave to re-enter the "real" world. In literature there are various devices which facilitate this transition from an external to an internal point of view at the beginning and from an internal to an external point of view at the conclusion. Among these are references to the narrator in the first person and the reader in the second person. John fits the pattern perfectly. The only clear references to "we" (omitting, for example, 3:11; 4:22) are at the beginning (1:14, 16) and at the end (21:24), and the reader is referred to directly with the second person plural in what is generally taken to be the original conclusion of the gospel (20:30–31). Uspensky did not have John in mind, but might well have, when he wrote:

> We have presented examples from folklore, but the same principle is evident in literature. Thus, for example, it is typical for some narratives that a first-person narrator who did not appear earlier in the story suddenly appears at the end. In other cases, this first-person narrator appears once at the beginning of the story, and then disappears. . . . his function . . . is only to provide a frame for the story.
>
> Exactly the same function may be attributed to the unexpected address to a second person which occurs at the end in some narrative forms—that is an address to the reader, whose presence had been completely ignored until that moment.[60]

Uspensky also notes that the death of "the dominant representative of the authorial point of view in the story" is a device which effects a shift to the external point of view and produces what Frank Kermode called "the

---

[59] Smith, *The Composition and Order of the Fourth Gospel*, p. 233; Brown, *John*, vol. 2, p. 1127.

[60] *A Poetics of Composition,* p. 147.

sense of an ending."[61] The death of the Beloved Disciple is implied by John 21:23. In all these respects, the conclusion of the gospel fits well established patterns for framing a narrative.

The relationship between the narrator and the Beloved Disciple can be clarified further if one takes the view that the Beloved Disciple is an idealized characterization of an historical figure. Insofar as there is a consensus among Johannine scholars, it is that there was a real person, who may have been an eyewitness to events in Jesus' ministry, and who was later the authoritative source of tradition for the Johannine community. The witness of this Beloved Disciple was probably also understood to be an expression of the work of the Paraclete. Because of his significance for the community, the Beloved Disciple was idealized by the author and given a role at the last supper, the crucifixion, the discovery of the empty tomb, and the appearance in Galilee. There is no corroborative evidence for his role, however, and he does not bear witness until after the resurrection and therefore does not affect events in the story.

On such a reading, the narrator finally identifies, or better, characterizes the implied author as the Beloved Disciple: "This is the disciple who is bearing witness to these things, and who has written these things" (21:24). Booth's definition of the implied author as the literary image of the artist should be recalled: "This implied author is always distinct from the 'real man'—whatever we may take him to be—who creates a superior version of himself, a 'second self,' as he creates his work."[62] Not only does the evangelist create a superior version of himself as he writes, but the editor identifies this superior self ("who has written these things") as the Beloved Disciple. When the narrator dramatically pulls the curtain on the implied author in the closing verses of the gospel, the reader recognizes that the Beloved Disciple fits the image the gospel projects of its implied author as one who knows Jesus intimately, shares his theological perspective, and can interpret reliably, that is, "his witness is true." The reader is thus given yet another reason for believing the gospel: its implied author is the Beloved Disciple. The narrator is presented as a member of the group ("we") which knows that the testimony of the Beloved Disciple is true. In the last verse the narrator adds that there are many other things which are not written here and comments that there is no end to the books that could be written.

In John 21:24, therefore, the editor characterizes the implied author (the superior self of the evangelist reflected in John 1–20, i.e., "he who has written these things") as the Beloved Disciple (the gospel's idealized por-

---

[61] Uspensky, *A Poetics of Composition*, p. 148; Kermode, *The Sense of an Ending*.
[62] *A Rhetoric of Fiction*, p. 151.

trayal of the evangelist's mentor). This conclusion not only assumes a
three-person theory but relates it to the role of the narrator throughout the
gospel. As a variation of the three-person theory it must also assume that
the editor: (1) did not know the evangelist, or (2) was guided in his identification primarily by the internal evidence of John 1-20 rather than personal or community knowledge, or (3) used ὁ γράψας in its weakened,
causative sense, or (4) deliberately sought to increase the authority of the
gospel and honor the memory of the Beloved Disciple by this identification. These alternatives, which are not mutually exclusive, are listed in
order of ascending probability. The last fits the evidence of John 21:24,
the careful buttressing of the gospel's authority, and the idealization of the
Beloved Disciple in John. The separation of the narrator from the implied
author, which is without a parallel in ancient literature, probably came
about, therefore, as a result of the idealizing of the Beloved Disciple and
the comment of an editor rather than as a sophisticated ploy by an individual author.

Since the gospel is so daring in its perspective, its authority is established on the witness of the Beloved Disciple (an eyewitness), the reliability of the narrator, and the words of Jesus about the Paraclete. The
narrator is not only omniscient but also omnicommunicative and gives
ample preliminary exposition in the prologue, which is confirmed by the
story itself. All of these narrative devices incline the reader toward accepting the author's understanding of Jesus. In fact, the gospel makes use of
virtually all of the devices available for heightening the credibility and
authority of a narrative: appeal to tradition, a reliable narrator, inspiration (the Paraclete), eyewitness testimony, the authority of an esteemed
figure (the Beloved Disciple), and the approval of a community.[63] Inter-
nally, the provision of historical, geographical, and descriptive detail
which is either demonstrably true or verisimilar serves to confirm the

---

[63] Scholes and Kellogg, *The Nature of Narrative*, pp. 246–47, describe the use of
authority-establishing techniques in antiquity: "By the end of Roman times
virtually all the possibilities for establishing the authority of a narrative had been
employed in one way or another. A writer dealing with the past could adopt any
of a number of postures: he could be a historian (Tacitus), the inspired bard
(Vergil, Ovid) or something in between (Lucan). A writer dealing with more
recent times could present a personal eye-witness account in his own name
(Augustine), a fictional account in a character's name (Petronius), or something
in between (Apuleius). A writer more concerned with fictional than traditional,
historical, or mimetic representation could offer a story with no justification
(Xenophon of Ephesus' *Ephesian Tale*), one which carried its own esthetic and
didactic justification (Longus' *Daphnis and Chloe*), or one which leaned toward
eye-witness testimony (Achilles Tatius' *Leucippe and Cleitophon*)." See also pp.
242–43, 265–66.

claims the narrative makes for itself.[64] There is no chance that the reader will miss the seriousness of the gospel's claim that it has the potential for a life or death effect on its readers. Such deliberate construction of credibility suggests a context of controversy in which John's distinctive stereoscopic Christology, the claim that Jesus was the pre-existent *logos* and exalted Son of God, was the divisive issue. It suggests further that one of the major purposes of the Fourth Gospel was to present a corrective view of Jesus. The disciples did not understand Jesus or his words during his ministry (12:16; 13:7). Only later did they understand. So any account, whether written or oral, from an apostle or a prophet, which was not informed by the retrospective ideological point of view of this gospel could not present Jesus or his words in their true light.

Although the wizard has refused to give his name, we have heard his whisper. Our study of the role of the narrator, his point of view, and his relationship to Jesus and the implied author has at least established the contours of his identity. His effect on the reader has been noted repeatedly, but this is a matter to which we shall return after discussion of the time of the narrator's story, its plot, and its characters.[65]

---

[64] Kermode, *The Genesis of Secrecy,* pp. 109, 118.

[65] While it is not my purpose to attempt to clarify further the gospel's composition history, this chapter may have certain implications for that task. The narrator's intrusive and interpretive comments cannot easily be attributed to an editor unless the editor is given a significant formative role in the gospel's composition or is virtually indistinguishable from the evangelist in his perspective. There is no evidence that they are later (or scribal) glosses, for they express a consistent point of view. Moreover, the correspondence in point of view between the narrator and the farewell discourse may be a significant indicator of a common origin for the farewell discourse and narrative material in the gospel. At least it renders problematic any theory which attributes either type of material to a source drawn from outside the Johannine community. In its present form, if not in its origin, the gospel must be approached as a unity, a literary whole.

Chapter Three

NARRATIVE TIME

When any extraordinary Scene presents itself (as we
trust will often be the Case), we shall spare no Pains
nor Paper to open it at large to our Reader; but if whole
Years should pass without producing anything worthy
of his Notice, we shall not be afraid of a Chasm in our
History, but shall hasten on to matters of Consequence
and leave such Periods of time totally unobserved. . . .
My Reader, then, is not to be surprised if in the Course
of this Work he shall find some Chapters very short,
and others altogether as long; some that contain only the
Time of a single Day, and others that comprise Years;
in a Word, if my History sometimes seems to stand still
and sometimes to fly.

Henry Fielding
Tom Jones

One characteristic of the Gospel form is thus its combination of two distinct functions of religious narrative:
the reenactment of the past and the leading into the
future.

William A. Beardslee
Literary Criticism of the New Testament

Time passes, and we sense its passing; but only in the most artificial sense can we "measure" or "tell" time. When we read a story, we sense the passage of time, though we may become so absorbed in the passage of time within the story that we lose all awareness of the time we have spent reading. The handling of time in a narrative is a fascinating topic, and one through which other characteristics of the Gospel of John can be seen more clearly.

First, it is necessary to distinguish "narrative" from "story." For terminological clarity this chapter will use the pioneering, yet highly acclaimed, work of Gérard Genette, *Narrative Discourse.*[1] The "narrative" is the text (the signifier, the discourse, or the "how") which conveys the "story" (the signified, the content, or the "what").[2] Narrative time may then be distinguished from story time. For our purposes story time is the passage of time during the ministry of Jesus as John records it. The relationship between story time and real or historical time, or whether Jesus' ministry actually

---

[1] Frank Kermode applauds Genette's accomplishment: "in a foreword Jonathan Culler rightly observes that this is 'the most thorough attempt we have to identify, name and illustrate the basic constituents and techniques of narrative'" ["Figures in the Carpet," p. 297]. Seymour Chatman, *Story and Discourse,* p. 63, adds his own accolade: "Gérard Genette's elegant analysis of the time-relations between story- and discourse-time must form the basis of any current discussion."

[2] This distinction can be traced back to the *fabula* and *sujet* of the Russian Formalists. Chatman's terminology may be more refined than Genette's, since he employs three concepts: narrative text, discourse, and story (*Story and Discourse,* p. 19). "Story" means the same for Genette and Chatman, but Chatman uses "narrative text" as the signifier of the story (the "what") and the discourse (the "how"). Chatman's scheme has the advantages of having a category which unites story and discourse, and of allowing the interpreter to use "discourse" to describe how the "narrative" conveys the "story." On the other hand there are disadvantages to using Chatman's terms here: (1) "narrative" and "discourse" are not easily separated; (2) "discourse" has overtones of monologue and dialogue for Johannine scholars (as in "the farewell discourse" and Bultmann's "discourse source"); and (3) to adopt Chatman's use of the terms at this point would mean that Genette's definitions of terms we will use throughout this chapter would have to be adjusted constantly, and perhaps confusingly. Hence, while we will recognize that at times "narrative" can be used for the text and at other times for the form or the "how," Genette's terms will be used consistently. For further comparison, see Meir Sternberg's four-way distinction of story, plot, *fabula,* and *sujet* in *Expositional Modes and Temporal Ordering in Fiction,* pp. 8–14.

lasted some two and a half years, is not a question we will pursue here. That is the length of Jesus' ministry in John's story. Narrative time, on the other hand, is determined by the order, duration, and frequency of events in the narrative. It may correspond more or less closely to story time, but the two are never equal. We can read the narrative of Jesus' ministry in a few hours, the sequence of events in the narrative is often not the same as the sequence in the story (order), some parts of the story are told more quickly than other parts (duration), and some events in the story may be repeated several times in the narrative (frequency). Each of these elements of narrative time concerns the interpreter of the Fourth Gospel.

ORDER

The order of events in the gospel provides a beginning point. Genette labels as anachronies "the various types of discordance between the two orderings of story and narrative."[3] The identification of anachronies can proceed by comparing the order in which events are presented in the narrative with the sequence in which they occur in the story. The order of events in the story can be inferred with varying degrees of accuracy from clues in the narrative or from external data. At times the narrative breaks the story sequence to refer to events which occurred in the past or events which are yet to occur. For example, John 1:19 states: "And this is the testimony of John (A), when the Jews from Jerusalem sent (B) priests and Levites to ask (C) him, 'Who are you?'" John's response follows immediately. From this verse, with its sequence of three events, it is clear that the story order was (B) sending, (C) asking, (A) testifying. Although very simple, this example illustrates how anachronies occur in narrative order. The order in which the narrative tells of the events is not the same as the order in which they occur in the story.

When references to events are presented in direct discourse (dialogue or monologue), the problem is complicated. The narrative may be presenting the discourse in sequence, but the discourse itself may refer to other events in the story anachronically. To illustrate this feature of the text we turn to John 1:19–34. The story begins here *in medias res,* relating the testimony of John on two successive days. John's testimony and the narration refer to a great many events which occur before or after these two days in the story. In order to compare the sequence of the narrative with the sequence of the story, references to events will be assigned a letter in alphabetical order as they occur in the narrative:

---

[3] *Narrative Discourse,* p. 36.

1:19		the testimony of John	A
		the Jews sent	B
	Q1	to ask him	C
1:20	A1	he confessed	D
1:21	Q2	they asked	E
	A2	He said	F
	Q3	[They asked]	G
	A3	he answered	H
1:22	Q4	They said	I
		Let us have an answer	J
		those who sent us	B
1:23	A4	He said	K
		Isaiah the prophet said	L
1:24		they had been sent	B
1:25	Q5	They asked him	M
1:26	A5	John answered them	N
		I baptize	O
		Among you stands one whom you do not know	P
1:27		he who comes after me	Q
1:28		John was baptizing	O
1:29		The next day he saw Jesus coming	
		toward him, and said	R
		who takes away the sins of the world	S
1:30		I said, after me comes a man	Q
		he was before me	T
1:31		I myself did not know him	U
1:32		John bore witness	A
		I saw the Spirit descend	W
1:33		I myself did not know him	U
		he who sent me . . . said	X
		he who baptizes with the Holy Spirit	Y
1:34		I have seen	W
		and have borne witness	A

From these twenty-five references in the narrative the following slightly simplified sequence in the story may be reconstructed:

1.	He was before me	T
2.	Isaiah said	L
3.	He who sent me said	X
4.	I came baptizing	V, O
5.	I did not know him	U
6.	I saw the Spirit descend	W
7.	The Jews sent	B
8.	The testimony of John (two days):	
	five questions C, E, G, I, M	
	five answers D, F, H, K, N	
9.	Among you stands one	P
10.	After me comes a man	Q
11.	John's announcement upon seeing Jesus	R
12.	the priests and Levites give an answer	J
13.	he takes away the sin of the world	S
14.	he baptizes with the Holy Spirit	Y

This example reveals how anachronic is the order in which the narrative presents the events of the story. The story time is no more than two days, but the narrative of those two days gives the reader an overview of much of the story to be presented in the rest of the narrative. Jesus actually preceded (i.e., was before) John (1). Isaiah prophesied prior to John also (2). John himself was sent with a specific commission (3) and came baptizing (4). At first he did not know Jesus (5), but identified him when he saw the Spirit descend upon him (6). Some time later, the Jews sent priests and Levites to question John (7). John's testimony is contained in his answers to their questions (8), and in these he refers both to Jesus' anonymity (9) and to his imminent coming or public appearance (10). When Jesus does come, John announces him (11), and in some sequence relative to these events the priests and Levites will report to those who sent him (12). Still further into the future, Jesus will take away the sin of the world (13) and baptize his followers with the Holy Spirit (14). The reader is left to arrange the story, but only part of the sequence is determined. For example, does 3 precede or follow 4 or 5? Does 6 precede or follow 7? Not only the sequence but also the interval between the events is left ambiguous at points. The reply of the priests and Levites (J) to the Jews in Jerusalem is not taken up later in the narrative, so the reader is never told whether the reply was given, when, or what its effect was. Similarly 13 and 14 are anticipations, or prolepses, of events which will be related later in the narrative, but the reader is not told when they will occur or whether they will occur simultaneously or in succession.

These early verses are important, however, because they are so rich in allusions to previous and coming events that they quickly communicate a great deal of story content while leaving readers with unanswered questions to stimulate their interest. The allusions to previous events may be identified more precisely as "analepses," which Genette defines as "any evocation after the fact of an event that took place earlier than the point in the story where we are at any given moment."[4] Similarly anticipations of coming events are called "prolepses," that is, "any narrative maneuver that consists of narrating or evoking in advance an event that will take place later."[5] Further precision is attained by labeling as "external" those analepses and prolepses which refer to events which occur entirely before or after the time of the narrative. Since the first eighteen verses are exposition, the narrative proper begins with John the Baptist's testimony and extends through the resurrection appearances. External analepses may therefore be illustrated by 1, 2, 3, 5, 6, and 7 in John 1:19–34. These

---

[4] *Narrative Discourse,* p. 40.
[5] *Narrative Discourse,* p. 40.

events occurred before John's testimony. There are no external prolepses in these verses, that is, no references to events which take place after the post-resurrection appearances. Analepses and prolepses which call to mind events which occur within the narrative may then be called "internal," that is, events 10–14 in the example above are internal prolepses, although one might argue that 13 and 14 belong in the next category. "Mixed" analepses begin prior to the narrative and continue into it (e.g., event 4), and "mixed" prolepses allude to events which begin within the time of the narrative and continue beyond it (e.g., possibly events 13 and 14).[6] All the events referred to in the narrative are part of the story and are to be placed at their proper points in story time.

Armed with these concepts we can turn to the structure of the narrative as whole, realizing that detailed analysis on such a scale is not possible. We will treat as external analepses all references to events which occur prior to the testimony of John. One could argue that the prologue requires the interpreter to extend narrative time back to "the beginning," but since the narrator does not take up the story in detail until John's testimony in 1:19, it is better to treat the prologue as exposition which prepares the reader for the narrative which begins with John's testimony.

A survey of the external analepses in John reveals that they fall into two distinct categories, which we shall call "historical" and "pre-historical," though the gospel does not make this distinction. The historical analepses recall moments in the history of Israel. The analepses we shall call "pre-historical" refer to events which did not occur in human history but in the relationship between Father and Son in the indefinable past of the incarnate *logos*. The following references illustrate this category: "the Father, . . . has given all things into his hand" (3:35), "for I have come down from heaven" (6:38), and ". . . as the Father taught me" (8:28). These analepses are so closely tied to the functions of the Father and the identity of Jesus that they are best left for consideration in Chapter 5. Their importance may be merely noted at this point: they convey Jesus' special knowledge concerning his identity, origin, and mission. The narrator shares this knowledge with the reader, and in the story Jesus attempts to convey it to others.

The historical analepses recall particular events which occurred prior to the ministry of John the Baptist. Rarely does the narrative itself enable the reader to arrange these events in any fixed order, though from external information we may give some order to the events recalled by John's historical analepses. All things were created through the Word (1:3). The devil was a murderer from the beginning (8:44). Abraham saw Jesus' day

---

[6] *Narrative Discourse,* pp. 49, 68.

and rejoiced (8:56; cf. 8:40, 58). From the seed of Abraham came the Jewish people (8:33; cf. 8:52, 53). Jacob dug a well in the region he gave to Joseph (4:5-6, 12). The Jews began to celebrate Passover (2:13; 6:4), ate manna in the wilderness, and died (6:31, 49). Moses gave the Law (1:17; 7:19) and circumcision (which really came from the Patriarchs; 7:22), and lifted up a serpent in the wilderness (3:14). Moses also wrote about Jesus (1:45; 5:46). Bethlehem was David's village (7:42). Elijah is mentioned (1:21). Isaiah saw Jesus' glory and spoke concerning him (12:41; cf. 1:23). The Samaritan fathers worshiped on Mt. Gerizim (4:20), and although both Jews and Samaritans expected a Messiah (4:25), all messianic claimants who came before Jesus were "thieves and robbers" (10:8). Work was begun on the temple forty-six years prior to Jesus' appearance in it (2:20), and when Peter was younger he used to gird himself and go wherever he wished (21:18). To these might be added the historical analepses already identified in 1:19-34. The list could be further expanded by seizing on references to scripture, feasts, and customs which might imply a practice or expectation which had its origin in the past; but the list is sufficiently complete and the references sufficiently explicit to support the observation that historical analepses in John enrich the narrative by extending it back to the beginning of time and by tying it to the central events in the larger biblical story. They also recall events in the Jewish past, thereby locating the story squarely within the history and scriptural heritage of the Jewish people.

The internal analepses are generally the yeomen of the gospel's temporal references. They often serve no more glamorous functions than providing an identification, recollection, or transition which allows the narrative to proceed smoothly. This necessary but rather insignificant service is performed by references like: ". . . he who was with you beyond the Jordan, to whom you bore witness, . . ." (3:26), "you sent to John, and he has borne witness to the truth" (5:33), and "I did one deed, . . ." (7:21). Genette calls analepses such as these "repeating analepses," since they serve to recall earlier portions of the narrative.[7] Often these references are to statements or events within the scene in which they are recalled; but even when they refer to earlier scenes their temporal position within the story can easily be determined by the reader, since they refer to events which have been narrated previously. The purpose of repeating analepses is generally to clarify, recall for further interpretation, or emphasize.

The more interesting internal analepses are those which refer to events which have already occurred but which have not been narrated. Readers suddenly learn that something has happened along the way of which they

---

[7] *Narrative Discourse*, p. 54.

had not been informed: "For his disciples had gone away into the city" (4:8; cf. 5:13). Genette calls these "completing analepses," since they "fill in, after the event, an earlier gap in the narrative."[8] It is sometimes difficult to distinguish between a repeating analepsis which places a new interpretation on an event (e.g., ". . . he spoke to them of the Father," 8:27, or "I manifested thy name to the men whom thou gavest me out of the world," 17:6) and a completing analepsis which presents a new fact about a situation mentioned earlier in the narrative (e.g., "Before Philip called you, when you were under the fig tree, I saw you," 1:48). The farewell discourse contains several such difficult references because of its peculiar temporal point of view. Nevertheless, we may still isolate a relatively short list of completing analepses which present important information about events which were omitted from the narration. A surprising number of these deal with the calling and commissioning of the disciples:

4:38   I sent you to reap that for which you did not labor; others have labored, and you have entered into their labor.

6:70   Did I not choose you, the twelve, . . .

15:15   . . . I have called you friends, for all that I have heard from my Father I have made known to you.

15:16   I chose you and appointed you. . . . (cf. 13:18; 15:19)

17:18   . . . I have sent them into the world.

These verses are peculiar because they point to a calling and commissioning scene (like Mark 3:13–19) which is omitted from John. The choosing of the twelve begins in the first chapter, but it is not completed, and their commissioning does not come until 20:21–23. Even in chapter 1 John the Baptist sends two of the disciples after Jesus, Andrew finds Peter, and Philip calls Nathanael; the process of "calling" is not as explicit as it is in the synoptic gospels. While it is less direct, it is more like the way in which believing readers of the gospel probably came to believe in Jesus. Even if 4:38 may be explained in part by 4:35, and even if 17:18 may be explained in part as a displaced reference to 20:21–23, they retain an anachronic force through their location in the narrative and cumulatively point to a scene of appointment and commissioning which has been omitted. That Jesus called those so appointed "friends" appears only in 15:15. Why is the appointment scene omitted? The question will have to be raised with reference to the characterization of the disciples.

Other completing analepses refer to actions which "the Jews" have taken "off stage."

9:22   . . . for the Jews had already agreed that if any one should confess him to be Christ, he was to be put out of the synagogue.

---

[8] *Narrative Discourse*, p. 51.

> 11:57   Now the chief priests and the Pharisees had given orders that if any one
> knew where he was, he should let them know. . . .

We are not told precisely when the decisions were made, only that they had occurred prior to the point at which they are introduced. Communication of the information in analepses is economical for it obviates the necessity to create a scene away from Jesus and those around him. It also adds intrigue in that Jesus' opponents may, by implication, be doing other things the reader is unaware of.

The more interesting completing analepses merit discussion:

> 10:41   John did no sign. . . .
> 11:2   It was Mary who anointed the Lord with ointment and wiped his feet with
> her hair. . . .
> 13:2   [Lit.] . . . the Devil having already put it into his heart that Judas Iscariot,
> son of Simon, should betray him. (cf. the RSV)
> 16:11   . . . because the ruler of this world is [Lit. "has been"] judged.
> 20:30   Now Jesus did many other signs in the presence of the disciples. . . .

John 10:41 supplies a piece of information which sets John's ministry in contrast to Jesus' and elevates the credibility of Jesus' words. John 11:2 is one of the well-known anomalies of the gospel. In form it is an internal analepsis which has the appearance of being a repeating analepsis inserted to re-introduce Mary, but the anointing is not narrated until the following chapter. In other words, it is a misplaced analepsis which functions as a prolepsis since it alludes to the anointing, which is yet to come. This apparent misplacement raises questions regarding the possibility of editorial rearrangement of the text or of appeal to tradition known by the reader. The devil's decision (13:2) and his defeat (16:11) are conveyed by analepses, since there is no easy way in which they could be described. The reference to "many other signs" in 20:30 completes the impression the narrative gives that the signs were typical of Jesus' ministry and leaves it to the reader to assume that they occurred during the gaps in the narrative, gaps to which we shall return shortly.

John's recollection of the baptism of Jesus has been treated above as an external analepsis since it occurred prior to John's testimony. The very fact that the author chose to begin with John's testimony rather than the baptism of Jesus is important. By this maneuver he has moved the baptism into a secondary position, thereby reducing its importance (cf. its importance in Mark), and introduced it by means of John's speech rather than the narrator's. John himself, therefore, is made to bear witness to Jesus' superiority.

The mixed analepses, those which allude to events which begin prior to the beginning of the narrative and continue into narrative time, serve the important function of tying the story to the events referred to in the exter-

nal analepses, events in the history of Israel and in the relationship between the Father and the Son:

3:13   No one has ascended into heaven. . . .

5:37   And the Father . . . has himself borne witness to me. His voice you have
       never heard, his form you have never seen. . . .

5:45   . . . it is Moses who accuses you, on whom you set your hope.

8:33   We are descendants of Abraham, and have never been in bondage to any
       one.

9:32   Never since the world began has it been heard that any one opened the eyes
       of a man born blind.

Undoubtedly it is significant that the mixed analepses deal with both historical and pre-historical events; the effects of both are felt throughout the
narrative.

Clearly, some analepses are difficult to classify as mixed or internal,
completing or repeating. It has not been our purpose to insist on a definitive classification or to offer exhaustive lists of each type but to illustrate
the functions of these narrative elements in the Gospel of John. These are
by no means all the analepses in John. In general, the text proceeds in a
straightforward manner from one event to the next, ties the various events
together by internal analepses and prolepses, and binds the story to past
events—historical and pre-historical—by means of external and mixed
analepses. There are no extended analepses which recount whole scenes
in detail. Instead, the evangelist uses only brief references to evoke earlier
events.

Prolepses, references to events which have not yet occurred at the point
in the narrative at which they are foretold, may also be classified according to whether the events will occur within narrative time. Internal prolepses refer to events which occur prior to the narrative's conclusion, while
external prolepses refer to events which will occur following the end of the
narrative.[9] The internal prolepses may be defined according to whether
the events they refer to will be narrated in due course (repeating prolepses) or not (completing prolepses).[10] Generally we are concerned with
the more or less explicit references to coming events as opposed to suggestive allusions which only acquire their significance in retrospect or
upon re-reading the gospel,[11] but the two are often difficult to distinguish
in the Gospel of John. Mixed prolepses are those which tell of events
which will begin prior to the end of the narrative and continue past its
ending. Many of the prolepses in John defy precise classification, how-

[9] *Narrative Discourse*, pp. 68, 77.

[10] *Narrative Discourse*, pp. 71, 73.

[11] *Narrative Discourse*, pp. 75–76.

ever, because they are metaphorical ("night comes, when no one can work," 9:4), allusive ("my hour has not yet come," 2:4), subject to multiple meanings ("so must the Son of man be lifted up," 3:14), or tied to events which are only partially or symbolically accomplished within the narrative ("the hour is coming, and now is, when the dead will hear the voice of the Son of God, and those who hear will live," 5:25; cf. 11:43–44). Whether these prolepses should be treated as explicit references or suggestive allusions is related to the identity of the implied reader (cf. Chapter 7). Still, some of the prolepses and their distinctive functions stand out clearly.

The completing prolepses, not surprisingly, are hardly ever ambiguous or metaphorical. They supply information about coming events which will not be narrated, and hence they must do so clearly. Only the following examples fit this pattern completely:

> 3:24   For John had not yet been put in prison.
> 19:27   And from that hour the disciple took her to his own home
> [a mixed prolepsis].

John 3:30, "He must increase, but I must decrease," might be added, but it is very general in its reference. Likewise, John 14:2, "I go to prepare a place for you," is subject to differing interpretations: when does he go? Is the place in this world or with his Father? The scarcity of completing prolepses shows that the evangelist presents all the events that are important for the story and is given more to repetitive references to key events than to allusion to incidental events. In this respect, John is a very focused narrative. One also notices that in John the completing prolepses have little or no dramatic significance in contrast to advance mentions and repeating prolepses.

It is pointless to force a distinction between suggestive allusions and explicit repeating prolepses; both are used for plot development and dramatic intensity. There is a perceptible development toward greater explicitness, however, as one moves through the gospel. While there are exceptions, most of the early prolepses are ambiguous:

> 1:50   You shall see greater things than these.
> 2:4   My hour has not yet come. (cf. 7:6, 8, 30; 8:20)
> 3:14   . . . so must the Son of man be lifted up. (cf. 8:28)
> 3:17   . . . that the world might be saved through him.
> 6:27   . . . the food which endures to eternal life, which the Son of man will give to you. . . .
> 6:64   . . . and who it was that would betray him. (cf. 6:71)
> 7:34   . . . you will seek me and you will not find me. (cf. 7:35–36; 8:21)
> 7:38   Out of his heart shall flow rivers of living water.

More explicit prolepses do occur in 2:22; 6:51, 71; 7:39. If a transition point can be located, after which the prolepses are generally explicit, it is roughly chapters 10 and 11. There are no prolepses in chapter 9, except 9:4. John 10 contains two important prolepses (10:15, 17–18), and from the end of chapter 11 on, there is no doubt about the course of coming events:

10:15	. . . I [will] lay down my life for the sheep.
10:17	. . . because I lay down my life, that I may take it again. (cf. 10:18)
11:51	. . . that Jesus should die for the nation. . . .
11:57	. . . so that they might arrest him.
12:4	Judas . . . (he who was to betray him). . . .
12:7	. . . let her keep it for the day of my burial.

The way in which the coming events are made clear and the role of the narrator in this process will be left for consideration at a later point. Here it is enough to conclude that the internal prolepses have an important role in building dramatic intensity by anticipating events which are not clearly defined but gradually come into focus as the narrative proceeds.

Mixed prolepses abound in the farewell discourse. Generally these define the nature of Jesus' relationship to the disciples following his death and the role of the Spirit during this period. Most of the mixed prolepses are progressive: the conditions for their fulfillment are established by the end of the narrative, but their fruition lies beyond it.

14:16	And I will pray the Father, and he will give you another counselor [Paraclete], to be with you for ever. . . .
14:17	. . . for he dwells with you, and will be in you.
14:18	I will not leave you desolate; I will come to you.
14:19	Yet a little while, and the world will see me no more, but you will see me; . . . you will live also.
14:20	In that day you will know that I am in my Father, and you in me, and I in you.
14:21	. . . and I will love him and manifest myself to him.

One problem in defining these prolepses precisely arises from the ambiguity of the point at which Jesus "goes to the Father." John 20:17 is the *locus classicus* of this difficulty. In spite of occasional exegetical ambiguities, it is still clear that the mixed prolepses do not serve to build dramatic intensity like the repeating internal prolepses. On the contrary, their function is to tie the experience of the intended readers (who we will later argue are Christians) to the final events in the ministry of Jesus. By this means the readers' experience is authorized by the story, and the enduring significance of Jesus' ministry is at least partially specified. Like the mixed analepses, the mixed prolepses in John have a linking function. The mixed analepses link Jesus to Israel; the mixed prolepses link Jesus to the church. Jesus therefore stands (temporally) between Israel and the church, simultaneously linking and separating them.

The external prolepses, references to events which will occur following the end of the narrative, may be divided into two basic types: historical prolepses, those which refer to events which will occur among the disciples and later believers, and eschatological prolepses, those which refer to "the last day," the end of time. With John's emphasis on "realized eschatology" it is not surprising that its historical prolepses outnumber its eschatological prolepses. Again, a developmental pattern is apparent. Eschatological prolepses are relatively numerous early in the gospel; but, although there are some ambiguities and exegetical difficulties, one encounters only historical prolepses following John 14:3. This progression indicates the direction of John's argument: that which was traditionally expected at the end has already been experienced, at least in part. The following are clearly eschatological:

5:28-29   . . . for the hour is coming when all who are in the tombs will hear his voice and come forth, those who have done good, to the resurrection of life, and those who have done evil, to the resurrection of judgment.

6:40   . . . and I will raise him up at the last day. (cf. 6:39, 44, 54)

12:48   . . . the word that I have spoken will be his judge on the last day.

14:3   . . . I will come again and will take you to myself, that where I am you may be also. [This reference to parousia expectation is severely modified in the remainder of John 14.][12]

The relationship or sequence of resurrection, coming, receiving, and judging is not established, nor is it John's purpose to clarify their sequence.[13] John 16:22, 23, and 25 could possibly be added to this list, but they are better taken as mixed prolepses referring to the period which begins with the resurrection and continues through the history of the church.[14] John 1:51 is also a candidate for this list, but should probably be taken as a metaphorical reference to the revelation which occurred during Jesus'

---

[12] Jürgen Becker, "Die Abschiedsreden Jesu im Johannesevangelium," pp. 226–28, argues convincingly that John 14 substitutes in polemical fashion a Christology and eschatology of the presence of Christ for that of the future return of Christ which is contained in the *Traditionsstück* in 14:2f.

[13] Lodewijk van Hartingsveld, *Die Eschatologie des Johannesevangeliums,* pp. 145–51, suggests that the fulfillment of John's eschatological expectations might occur in three phases: (1) the gathering of Diaspora Jews in Palestine, (2) the gathering of believers who are already in the holy land and the messianic reign, and (3) the resurrection and the judgment. He proceeds, however, to show that such a sequence is untenable, and in rejecting any periodization of eschatological expectations he is surely correct. Some ordering of events may be possible, but John makes no attempt to provide the reader with a sequence.

[14] Cf. Raymond E. Brown, *The Gospel According to John,* vol. 2, pp. 640, 722.

ministry. That it refers in its present form to a specific experience, like John 12:28, and is hence a completing internal prolepsis, can safely be discounted, since we have already observed that John rarely uses completing internal prolepses and surely would not do so for a significant event. John 6:37 might also be considered here, but again the eschatological nuance seems to be secondary.

The historical prolepses can be divided into those which have occurred by the time the narrator tells the story and those which are to occur in the story's future. This division is little more than theoretical, since there is hardly a single historical prolepsis in John which refers to an event which has not occurred by the time the narrator tells the story. At most, relationships and processes begun previously may be assumed to continue between the time of the narrator and "the last day," but no new events are expected. There is therefore a blank in this period within John, which is surprising for at least two reasons. First, it stands in striking contrast to the common apocalyptic practice of predicting cataclysmic events between the time of a writing and the end time; and second, this is the time of the reader, at least insofar as it can be distinguished from the time of the narrator or the author. This departure from the apocalyptic genre is further proof of John's distinctive emphasis on "realized" elements of traditional, even traditional Christian, eschatological expectations. One small group of prolepses may fill this blank period in John's story time. It is comprised of references to the gathering of "the flock," the "children of God," or "all men":

10:16   And I have other sheep, that are not of this fold; I must bring them also, and they will heed my voice. So there shall be one flock, one shepherd.

11:52   . . . but to gather into one the children of God who are scattered abroad.

12:32   . . . And I, when I am lifted up from the earth, will draw all men to myself.

The chief danger here is that of imposing on John a later Christian perspective regarding church unity. It is also not certain that the three verses refer to the same event or the same groups. The latter two references are clearly related to the effects of Jesus' death. The first two speak of gathering those who have been scattered (cf. 10:12; 16:32), but the identity of the scattered and the form and time of the gathering are all unclear and hotly debated. At least five alternative interpretations have been proposed in recent discussions of these passages: (1) the drawing together of Jewish and Gentile believers,[15] (2) present and future believers,[16] (3) Johannine

---

[15] C. K. Barrett, *The Gospel According to St. John*, p. 376; Brown, *John*, vol. 1, pp. 396, 442; cf. his *The Community of the Beloved Disciple*, p. 90; C. H. Dodd, *The Interpretation of the Fourth Gospel*, p. 282; Rudolf Schnackenburg, *The Gospel*

and non-Johannine (or Petrine) Christians,[17] (4) the gathering of the Jews of the dispersion,[18] and (5) the gathering of Jewish Christians scattered by their exclusion from the synagogues.[19] Nothing demands a monolithic interpretation of these verses, and there is some danger in imposing judgments formed regarding one verse on the others. John 10:16 is set in the context of discussion following the blind man's exclusion from the synagogue and therefore (while other interpretations may not be excluded) the contention that it refers to the gathering of Jewish Christians excluded from the synagogues is favored by the narrative context. The terms in John 11:51–52, as shown by Severino Pancaro, must be interpreted in relation to a people of God composed of both Jews and Gentiles. Admittedly, however, John shows no specific concern for the unity of Jews and Gentiles such as one sees in Luke and Paul. In 12:32 such distinctions have already ceased to be significant. The conclusion that these verses express concern for the unity of believers, whatever the precise meaning of each verse, is further warranted by Jesus' petition in chapter 17, which is voiced repeatedly following the reference to those who will come after the disciples and believe on account of their word (17:20), "that they may be one just as we are one" (vv. 21, 22, 23). The unity of believers is grounded in the unity of Father and Son, but remains unfulfilled. There is a strong futuristic emphasis in all these verses, and C. K. Barrett's comment on this point is, as usual, judicious: "The unity of the Church thus constituted on earth is to be fully consummated in heaven; John retains this eschatological hope."[20] But it would be wrong to limit the fulfillment of this hope to the eschaton. The gathering in chapter 10, the prayer that the believers may be one in chapter 17, and the concern for the relationship between Peter and the Beloved Disciple (and by implication their followers) in chapter 21 point strongly toward a concern for unity both among Johannine Christians and between them and other believers. While complete unity may not be realized until "the last day," the time between the writing of the gospel and the eschatological future is filled by an agenda with one overriding item: unity—"that they may be one just as

---

According to St. John, vol. 2, pp. 299, 350; S. Pancaro, "'People of God' in St. John's Gospel," p. 129.

[16] Mark L. Appold, *The Oneness Motif in the Fourth Gospel,* pp. 264, 275.

[17] Brown, *The Community of the Beloved Disciple,* p. 90; cf. R. Alan Culpepper, "The Pivot of John's Prologue," pp. 30–31.

[18] J. A. T. Robinson, "The Destination and Purpose of St. John's Gospel," p. 127; W. C. van Unnik, "The Purpose of St. John's Gospel," pp. 394, 403, 407; van Hartingsveld, *Die Eschatologie des Johannesevangelium,* pp. 94–98.

[19] J. Louis Martyn, *The Gospel of John in Christian History,* pp. 117–20; cf. H. B. Kossen, "Who were the Greeks of John XII 20," pp. 106–7.

[20] *John,* pp. 407–8.

we are one." That is the agenda for the church in John's story, even if it is Christ who draws and gathers.

The historical prolepses are important for attempts to reconstruct significant moments in the history of the Johannine community. The assumption at work in this reconstruction is that what the narrator presents as Jesus' words to the disciples about future events in the story has indeed found life and therefore reflects the situation of the evangelist and his intended readers at the time of writing. We may look first at the retrospective comments of the narrator which function as external prolepses:

2:22   When therefore he was raised from the dead, his disciples remembered that he had said this; and they believed the scripture and the word which Jesus had spoken.

12:16   His disciples did not understand this at first; but when Jesus was glorified, then they remembered that this had been written of him [Zech. 9:9; Isa. 35:4; 40:9] and had been done to him (cf. 13:7).

20:9   . . . for as yet they did not know the scripture, that he must rise from the dead.

These retrospective comments reflect a period of recollection (memory) informed by the study of the sacred writings for allusions to what had occurred in Jesus' death and resurrection. This process and the narrator's perspective on it were examined in the last chapter.

In the epilogue the deaths of Peter and the Beloved Disciple are foreshadowed, though the latter is not an explicit prolepsis:

21:18   . . . but when you are old, you will stretch out your hands, and another will gird you and carry you where you do not wish to go. (This he said to show by what death he was to glorify God.)

21:23   The saying spread abroad among the brethren that this disciple was not to die; yet. . . .

The greatest concentration of external prolepses, however, is found in the farewell discourse. Many of these are rather general in nature (14:21; 15:16) and assure the disciples of the Lord's continuing presence with them (14:23; 15:10, 11) through prayer (14:13; 15:7; 16:26) and the work of the Paraclete (14:26; 15:26; 16:7-8, 13–14). What specific prolepses there are in the farewell discourse point toward ostracism, hostility, and exclusion from the synagogue:

15:18   If the world hates you. . . .

15:20   . . . they will persecute you. . . .

15:21   But all this they will do to you. . . .

16:2   They will put you out of the synagogues; indeed, the hour is coming when whoever kills you will think he is offering service to God.

16:3   And they will do this because. . . .

16:4   But I have said these things to you that when their hour comes you may remember. . . .

It is conceivable, of course, that these events were not taking place when the evangelist wrote but appeared imminent. There is no theoretical way to exclude this possibility; but the gospel's treatment of these matters suggests that banishment from the synagogue was a distressing reality, not just a dark possiblity that loomed on the evangelist's horizon.

The references just cited have the effect of collapsing or compressing narrative time. That which was expected in the future of the story may have already occurred in the reader's past. In a sense, therefore, not only the eschatology of the Johannine community but also its history is "realized" in the gospel story. The exclusion of the readers from the synagogue could therefore be seen as a fulfillment of Jesus' prediction (16:2) and a continuation of the events which began in Jesus' ministry (see 9:22; 12:42).[21] By setting the persecution within the story of Jesus' triumph and glorification, the gospel provides its readers with a new context for understanding their experience. While these prolepses may tell us something about the history of the Johannine community, interpreters should remember that they actually tell us about the future of John's story world, which may or may not correspond to any historical reality.

We may now return to a point adumbrated earlier: John's departure from the commonplaces of apocalyptic genre which are so prevalent in early Christian literature. Complete as the departure appears to be, interesting comparisons can be made between the way the Fourth Gospel and apocalyptic writings relate past, present, and future:

(1) In neither John nor the apocalypses does the narrator stand in the narrative's present. In John the narrator looks back on past events; in apocalyptic literature the narrator stands in the past and tells of future events.

(2) John uses the past to clarify the reader's present; apocalyptists use the future to clarify the present, though the future is presented as having been foreseen in the past. Correspondingly, John's source of hope lies in the past, whereas the apocalyptists look to the future for hope.

(3) John emphasizes the similarity or continuity of the past (Christ's ministry) and the present; the apocalyptist emphasizes the discontinuity of present and future.

---

[21] J. Louis Martyn, *History and Theology in the Fourth Gospel*. This collapsing of narrative time supports Louis Martyn's theory that the Johannine narrative relates not only what occurred in the ministry of Jesus but also what was occurring in the Johannine community.

(4) John compresses or collapses the distance from past to present
    (Martyn argues that he superimposes the two); the apocalyptist
    may compress but never collapse or superimpose present distress
    and future vindication.

(5) Consequently, salvation is present for John (at least potentially);
    for the apocalyptist it is imminent.[22]

Our survey of the anachronies between narrative time and story time in
the Gospel of John has shown that there are varieties of analepses and
prolepses, each of which performs a distinct narrative function in filling
out story time. I have omitted from the discussion what we might call
"potential" prolepses, those which refer to what might happen. These may
be illustrated by verses which refer to what a group or character intended
to do (6:15), or a hypothetical possibility (6:62 "Then what if you were to
see . . ." or 15:6 "If a man does not abide in me . . ."). Each analepsis and
prolepsis may be defined by its "reach," that is, the temporal distance
between the point at which it is inserted in the narrative and the event(s)
to which it refers.[23] We have found anachronies which point to previous or
coming events within the narrative (internal analepses and prolepses),
those which point to events which lie outside narrative time (external),
and those which point to events or processes which lie both within and
outside the temporal limits of the narrative (mixed). In effect, the anachronies in the Gospel of John establish five periods in its story time
(summarized in chart on p. 70). John's story time, which moves in
grand—almost epic—fashion from "the beginning" to "the last day,"
spans the breadth of cosmic time. To summarize, the external analepses
refer to events in both the pre-historical and historical pasts. Mixed
analepses serve the yeoman function of providing narrative flow, clarity,
emphasis, and subsequent interpretation; while internal prolepses have

---

[22] The Johannine interpretation of the present through the past is hardly unique;
most of the "historical" writings of the period have this as their purpose. The
Martyrdom of Isaiah, a pseudepigraphical work, part of which at least is
generally dated in the second century B.C., provides a particularly transparent
example of this use of the past. It recounts the apostasy of Israel and "the princes
of Judah" (4:11) as a result of the work of Beliar, "the ruler of this world" (2:4),
in the time of Manasseh, the flight of the prophets to "a mountain in a desert
place" (2:8), and the courageous martyrdom of the faithful prophet, Isaiah. One
suspects that the story is told in such a way that its readers would have seen a
reflection of their own time in the events of Manasseh's reign and "the lawless-
ness which was spread abroad in Jerusalem" (2:4). They would consequently
interpret their own situation accordingly and be inspired to greater faithfulness
by the account of Isaiah's martyrdom. See R. H. Charles, *The Apocrypha and
Pseudepigrapha of the Old Testament in English,* pp. 155–162.

[23] Genette, *Narrative Discourse,* p. 48.

the more exciting task of heightening dramatic intensity by anticipating coming events. Internal anachronies may also fill gaps in the narrative,

narrative past		narrative present	narrative future	
		internal analepses and prolepses		
mixed analepses			mixed prolepses	
external analepses			external prolepses	
pre-historical past	historical past		historical future	eschatological future
'in the beginning'	Israel	the ministry of Jesus from John's testimony to the post-resurrection appearances	the Johannine community	'the last day'

but they seldom have this function in John. Mixed prolepses link the ministry of Jesus to the intended readers and vice versa. Finally, a few of the external prolepses are eschatological, but their relative scarcity is a distinctive mark of the contrast between John and the rest of the corpus of early Christian literature. More numerous are the external prolepses which allude to events which had probably already occurred by the time the gospel was written. The narrator, who probably speaks for the author, stands between the experience of the gospel's readers and the eschatological future and tells the story from this temporal perspective.

DURATION

The second factor related to narrative time which Genette exposes to analysis is the relationship of the length of the narrative to the length of the story. The relationship is relative at best. As is well known, three Passover festivals are mentioned in John (2:13; 6:4; 13:1). The gospel, therefore, covers a period of about two and a half years in twenty-one chapters, since the narrative includes the testimony of John and the gathering of disciples before the first Passover and the appearances following the third Passover. Yet, the evangelist, like Henry Fielding's ingenious traveler, does not jog "with equal Pace through the verdant Meadows or over the barren Heath," but "always proportions his Stay at any Place to the Beauties, Elegancies, and Curiosities which it affords."[24]

---

[24] Henry Fielding, *The History of Tom Jones*, vol. 2, book XI, chapter 9, pp. 612–13; quoted by Sternberg, *Expositional Modes*, p. 15.

In the Gospel of John there is considerable variation in the "speed" of the narrative as it relates the events of Jesus' ministry. Genette defines the speed of a narrative "by the relationship between a duration (that of the story, measured in seconds, minutes, hours, days, months, and years) and a length (that of the text, measured in lines and pages)."[25] The passages in which the length of the narrative most nearly approximates the duration of the story are *scenes,* which consist almost exclusively of dialogue or monologue. The narrative covers story time more rapidly in *summaries,* which provide only essential facts or a characterizing description. The distinction between scenes and summaries is not always indisputable, since scenes in which the dialogue is abbreviated in favor of narration may not differ greatly from relatively detailed summaries. In what follows, a passage is generally called a scene if it provides more than minimal details about a series of events which occurred at a particular time. A passage is called a summary if it characterizes a period or serves primarily as a transition between scenes. When the narrative leaves a gap, we may say there is an *ellipsis* at that point. Ellipses and summaries may cover (or skip) a definite or an indefinite period of time, and ellipses may be either explicitly noted in the text or left more or less implicit. Genette labels the fourth possible type of text as "descriptive pauses," that is, passages which mark no advance in story time but give an extended description of a setting, character, or emotion.[26] For all its realism, John is noticeably free of descriptive *pauses.* At best there are the narrator's introductions to scenes (5:2-5; 11:18-19) and his interpretive comments (especially 12:37-43), the epilogues in 3:16-21 and 3:31-36, and Jesus' "soliloquy" in 12:44-50. These intrusions slow the narrative down, but strictly speaking they should probably not be called descriptive pauses. Still, there is a perceptible slowing of the speed of the narrative in chapter 12, with 12:37-50 acting as a rhetorical "brake." The narrative, therefore, slows down as it approaches the awesome "hour" of Jesus' glorification.

A survey of the use of scenes, summaries, and ellipses in John is difficult to present succinctly but sets in relief the rhythm and flow of the narrative. The temporal structure of the gospel consists of scenes connected to each other by summaries or explicit ellipses. This oscillation between scenes, which generally involve confrontation, and summaries of periods of withdrawal gives the narrative a rhythm as it progresses and distracts attention from the disparity between the story with its presumed continuity and the narrative with its great gaps.

Progress may be made by identifying the major scenes and gaps in the

---

[25] Genette, *Narrative Discourse,* pp. 87-88.
[26] For Genette's definitions of these terms see *Narrative Discourse,* pp. 94-95.

narrative. The three Passovers (2:14–3:21; 6:5–65; 13:1–19:42) provide annual intervals within which the rest of the narrative is structured. Allowing some time for the events prior to the first Passover and following the last, the story covers a period of roughly two and a half years. A year's time is covered between the Passover week of 2:14–3:21 and the mention of the next Passover in 6:4. In this period we are told of "some time" in 3:22–24, a brief testimony in 3:25–36, three days in Samaria (4:4–42), two days following Jesus' arrival in Galilee (4:47–53), a journey to Jerusalem and perhaps a week at an unnamed feast there (5:1–47), and a return to Galilee. The scenes which are presented during this year occupy about two weeks, and the rest of the year is either passed over in silence or conveyed in brief generalizing summary statements. The whole year occupies only about 116 verses (3:22–6:2).

The second year is described in more detail: 295 verses (6:66–12:50). The passage of time is also marked more clearly than during the first year; John 7:1–8:59 (and perhaps 9:1–41) may be placed around the feast of Tabernacles in late September or early October, and 10:22–39 at the feast of Dedication in late December. The scenes from this second year cover roughly a month (7:1–8, a day; 7:14–8:59, a week; 9:1–41, a day or two; 10:1–18, a day; 10:22–39, a day; 11:1–53, a week; 12:3–50, a week). The rest of the year is related in brief summaries or passed over in silence. John 12–20 covers a two-week period, and chapters 13–19 are devoted to the events of a single twenty-four hour period. The "speed" of the narrative reduces steadily, therefore, until it virtually grinds to a halt at the climactic day. In order to give the narrative continuity, the most extended ellipses are all indefinite (e.g., six months pass between 6:65 and 7:2, and three months pass between 8:59 [or 9:41] and 10:22). These lengthy gaps are so well hidden they are often difficult to locate precisely. Sometimes they are filled by brief discourses or summaries. At other times there is nothing to mark a passage of months which must have occurred at about a given point in the narrative (e.g., between 8:59 and 9:1). The minor ellipses, on the other hand, are usually definite ("the next day"), and the longest definite ellipsis is only a week (20:26). These brief, definite ellipses give the narrative added realism and movement, while the longer, indefinite ellipses, which are often implicit, mask its gaps.

If one were to complete the calculation of time covered by the scenes (omitting the summaries and ellipses), it would become evident that the scenes can be fitted into about two months of the two-and-half-year period covered by the narrative. So, only a small fraction of the story is actually told. This calculation will be important for analysis of the gospel's plot development because it shows how episodic the gospel is.

As one looks more closely at the main episodes in chapters 2–12, a further characteristic of Johannine composition may be observed. The miracle stories of the synoptic gospels are exploded into major episodes, and there is a progressive conjunction between sign and discourse material. The first and second signs (2:1–11 and 4:46–54) are about the length of synoptic miracle accounts and not greatly dissimilar from them. The next three miracle stories (5:2–9; 6:2–21; 9:1–7) each have extended discourses attached to them (5:10–16, 17–47; 6:22–65; and 9:8–41). Within these discourses some technical development is clear. John 9 with its seven scenes,[27] marks a new level of literary achievement as it ties the discourse material to the sign and weaves the whole into a delightful ironic and dramatic unit. With the last sign, the raising of Lazarus, the progressive conjunction of sign and discourse reaches its zenith: the two cannot be separated successfully. The dialogue advances the action and delays the sign, thereby building dramatic interest. By now, the evangelist is the master of his material.[28]

FREQUENCY

The third aspect of narrative time treated by Genette is frequency. Under this rubric he explores the alternative of narrating once an event that happened once (the singulative narrative), narrating repeatedly an event that happened once (repetitious), narrating repeatedly events that happened repeatedly (repetitive), and narrating once events that happened repeatedly (iterative).[29]

It is immediately apparent that John moves in a relatively straightforward manner, and does not narrate repeatedly (i.e., repetitiously) events that happened once. This does not mean, as we have seen, that he does not frequently employ repeating analepses and prolepses to call the reader's attention again to events he narrates in detail only once.

Of more interest is the way the narrative deals with events that happened repeatedly and how these are related to the gaps in the narrative. We must first recognize, as Genette does, that in a strict sense no event can occur repeatedly.[30] We are really talking about similar events, or events of

---

[27] John 9 contains seven distinct scenes: 9:1–7, the healing of the blind man; 9:8–12, neighbors question the man; 9:13–17, Pharisees question the man; 9:18–23, Pharisees question the parents; 9:24–34, Pharisees question the man again; 9:35–38, Jesus questions the man; 9:39–41, Pharisees question Jesus.

[28] Dodd, *The Interpretation of the Fourth Gospel*, p. 363. This progressive development of technique suggests that these chapters reached their definitive shape in roughly the order in which they appear in the gospel.

[29] *Narrative Discourse*, pp. 114–16.

[30] *Narrative Discourse*, p. 113.

a particular type or category, which recur frequently in the story. There is further the possibility that given the iterative sense of the Greek imperfect tense we should investigate every occurrence of verbs in the imperfect tense which could reasonably be taken as denoting events that occurred repeatedly. No doubt such a study would be interesting, but cannot be undertaken here.

The Gospel of John makes great use of repetitive narrative, that is, repeated references to events that happened repeatedly. Jesus does a series of signs, has extended (and often repetitious) discourses, goes to the Jewish festivals in Jerusalem, and withdraws from these scenes of confrontation. The interchange of these activities provides the material for the story, and the repetition of vocabulary, themes, activities, and settings serves to create the impression that these were characteristic of Jesus' ministry.

If the scenes are highly repetitive, so are the summaries which fill gaps (as opposed to the summaries which provide an introduction for the next scene and those which appear to be scenes summarized briefly by the narrator). The summaries are both iterative and repetitive in that each summary tells once of events that happened repeatedly and together the summaries tell of the same kind of events repeatedly. The following activities recur most frequently in the summaries: Jesus abides ($\mu\acute{\epsilon}\nu\epsilon\iota\nu$) in a certain region or others abide with him (1:39; 2:12; [3:22]; 4:40; 7:9; 10:40; 11:6, 54; [18:1–2; 19:31]), others come to believe in him (2:23; 4:41; 7:31; 10:42; 11:45; 12:11, 42; [20:31]), Jesus does signs (2:24; 6:2; 20:30 and probably also 4:45; 5:16; 11:45; 21:25), the Jews persecute Jesus (5:16, 18; 7:11, 30; 11:57; [12:10]), and crowds follow him (6:2; 10:41; 12:9, 11; [11:45]). The summaries also interrelate these activities: where Jesus abides or where he does signs, people believe in him (2:23–24; 4:40–41; 10:40–42; 11:45; 20:30–31), and where some believe others persecute (7:30–32; 11:45–46). All of these activities, of course, occur repeatedly in the scenes, so we do not feel that we have missed anything when we are given a summary because we have already read about such activities and can fill in the story for ourselves. We are thereby also led to fill the gaps (ellipses) with these characteristic activities. In this way, the gaps are masked by iterative summaries and repetitive scenes. This pattern of masking or filling the gaps complements the scarcity of completing analepses and prolepses which we observed earlier. Nothing significant takes place in the gaps. Even if Jesus "did many other signs in the presence of the disciples, which are not written in this book" (20:30), which the reader must locate in the time of the summaries and gaps, we do not see their omission as a problem because we have been led to assume that we have been given a full account of both the characteristic events and the highlights of Jesus' ministry. The fact that the reader senses no logical difficulty in this assumption and is willing to accept the signs and discourses as somehow both the ordinary stuff of Jesus' ministry and its crucial moments is due in large measure to the author's use of iterative references, summaries, and implicit ellipses. Logically they could hardly be both ordinary and crucial, characteristic and pivotal. In reality, the reader is accepting an impression created by the author. Yet, by the end of the narrative the reader is satisfied that the author has told as much of the story as possible, and all that is necessary. This, of course, does not mean that there is not more to the story (cf. 21:25), but it means that the author has handled story time skillfully in his narrative. He has done his job well.

Our exploration of the temporal aspects of the gospel has exposed many features of its narrative rhetoric which will be taken up in the following chapters. Not the least of these is the relationship between time and plot in the gospel.

Chapter Four

PLOT

Real incidents, not fictionalized by an author, make a story. A Plot is wholly an artistic creation.

Boris Tomashevsky
"Thematics"

The most important causality in stories, then, does not lie simply in the sequence of events, but rather in how the sequence of events stimulates a sequence of emotion in the reader.

Kieran Egan
"What is a Plot?"

It is the genius of the Fourth Evangelist to have created a gospel in which Jesus as representative of the world above visits and really lives in this world without depriving life here of its seriousness.

D. Moody Smith
"The Presentation of Jesus in the Fourth Gospel"

The whispering wizard of our second chapter, the narrator, tells a strange story. What is his story, though, and what makes it that story and not another?[1] Whatever else must be said about it, it is the story of a central character of enormous proportions. In an often-quoted line, Henry James asks, "What is character but the determination of incident? What is incident but the illustration of character?"[2] Even beyond this interrelationship between plot and character, the two blend almost inseparably in the Gospel of John. Here and in the next chapter, the shape of each and the bond between them is examined.

Before these matters can be taken up, significant problems must be acknowledged even if they cannot be resolved here. What is a "plot"? Does a gospel have a plot? Are "plot" and "characters" relevant for interpreting an account of the life of a historical personage?

WHAT IS A PLOT?

"Plot" is one of those terms everyone understands but defines differently. The following is a representative sample of current definitions.

Robert Scholes & Robert Kellogg:	an outline of events
	an articulation of the skeleton of narrative
	the dynamic, sequential element in narratives[3]
R. S. Crane	. . . the plot, considered formally, of any imitative work is . . . not simply a means—a "framework" or "mere mechanism"—but rather the final end which everything in the work, if that is to be felt as a whole, must be made, directly or indirectly, to serve.[4]

---

[1] Derek Brewer, "The Gospels and the Laws of Folktale," p. 42.
[2] "The Art of Fiction," p. 597.
[3] *The Nature of Narrative,* pp. 12, 207.
[4] "The Concept of Plot," p. 241.

Frank Kermode   The clock's *tick-tock* I take to be a model of what we
                      call a plot, an organization that humanizes time by
                      giving it form. . . .[5]

E. M. Forster: A plot is also a narrative of events, the emphasis
                      falling on causality. "The king died, and then the
                      queen died" is a story. "The king died, and then the
                      queen died of grief" is a plot. The time-sequence is
                      preserved, but the sense of causality overshadows it.[6]

Kieran Egan: A plot is a set of rules that determines and sequences
                      events to cause a determinate affective response.[7]

M. H. Abrams: The plot in a dramatic or narrative work is the
                      structure of its actions, as these are ordered and
                      rendered toward achieving particular emotional and
                      artistic effects.[8]

Abrams' definition is a concise synthesis of most of the elements of the
other definitions. From these one may judge that the central features of
"plot" are the sequence, causality, unity, and affective power of a narrative.

It is no surprise that these four constitutive features closely resemble
Aristotle's "essential characteristics of a plot": order, amplitude, unity,
and probable and necessary connection (*Poetics* 1450b–1451b). "Order"
requires that the plot have a beginning, a middle, and an end: "Well
ordered plots, then, will exhibit these characteristics, and will not begin or
end just anywhere" (*Poetics* 1450b).[9] Aristotle further delineated three
types of *mimesis* in tragedy which can be extended to other types of narrative as well: "the *mimesis* of the actions, the plot, by which I mean the
ordering of particular actions," the *mimesis* of "the moral characters of the
personages," and the *mimesis* of "their intellect" (*Poetics* 1450a). The
objects of *mimesis* are "people doing things," people who are good or bad.
The characters may be morally better, worse, or the same as are found in
the world (*Poetics* 1448a). *Mimesis* of character is later explained as "that
which makes plain the nature of the moral choices the personages make,

---

[5] *The Sense of an Ending*, p. 45.
[6] *Aspects of the Novel*, p. 87.
[7] "What is a Plot," p. 470.
[8] *A Glossary of Literary Terms*, p. 127.
[9] Quotations from Aristotle's *Poetics* are taken from D. A. Russell and M. Winterbottom, eds., *Ancient Literary Criticism*.

so that those speeches in which there is absolutely nothing that the speaker chooses and avoids involve no *mimesis* of character" (*Poetics* 1450b). Aristotle attributed much of the attraction of tragedies to *peripeteiai* (twists and reversals) and *anagnorisis* (discovery or recognition).[10] The latter is particularly significant in John: "Recognition is, as its name indicates, a change from ignorance to knowledge, tending either to affection or to enmity; it determines in the direction of good or ill fortune the fates of the people involved" (*Poetics* 1452a). The least artistic species of recognition is "recognition by visible signs." Recognition may also be based on memory and reasoning, but the best kind is "that which arises from the actions alone" (*Poetics* 1454b–1455a). These judgments not only provide conceptual tools for analyzing the Fourth Gospel but correlate remarkably well with its focus on recognizing the *logos* enfleshed and its judgment on faith that is based on signs.

Aristotle's influence has been so profound that the formal analysis of literature is described as "poetics," and it is possible to speak of some contemporary literary critics as Neo-Aristotelians. Crane classifies plots in three categories derived from the *Poetics:* plots of action (in which there is a change in the protagonist's situation), plots of character (in which there is a change in his moral character), and plots of thought (in which there is a change in his thoughts or feelings).[11] A plot requires a change of some kind, and its peculiar affective power is produced by the hopes and fears, desires and expectations it imposes on the reader as it unfolds the change from beginning to end.[12] By the end of the story the reader has been led to a particular emotional or volitional response: catharsis, satisfaction, outrage, anxiety, or belief. Seymour Chatman has found six plot types inherent in Aristotle's *Poetics,* three fatal and three fortunate:

1. An unqualifiedly good hero fails: this is shockingly incomprehensible to us, since it violates probability.
2. A villainous protagonist fails; about his downfall we feel smug satisfaction, since justice has been served.

---

[10] Geoffrey F. Nuttall, *The Moment of Recognition,* p. 9, comments on F. L. Lucas, *Tragedy in Relation to Aristotle's Poetics,* p. 95: "I prefer F. L. Lucas' understanding of *peripeteia* as error, a false step taken in blindness, with its attendant irony . . . ; and of *anagnorisis* as what he calls 'the realization of the truth, the opening of the eyes, the sudden lightning-flash in the darkness.'" *Anagnorisis* often includes "recognition of someone to whose identity previously one was blind."

[11] "The Concept of Plot," p. 239.

[12] "The Concept of Plot," pp. 240–41; Norman Friedman, "Forms of the Plot," pp. 154–55.

3. A noble hero fails through miscalculation, which arouses our pity and fear.

4. A villainous protagonist succeeds; but this causes us to feel disgust, because it violates our sense of probability.

5. An unqualifiedly good hero succeeds, causing us to feel moral satisfaction.

6. A noble hero . . . miscalculates, but only temporarily, and his ultimate vindication is satisfying.[13]

Norman Friedman extends Crane's system of three types of plot further by suggesting the following classifications within each type: *Plots of fortune:* (a) the action plot, (b) the pathetic plot, (c) the tragic plot, (d) the punitive plot, (e) the sentimental plot, (f) the admiration plot. The last he describes as

> a change in fortune for the better which is caused by a sympathetic protagonist's nobility of character. . . . he gains primarily in honor and reputation and, it may be, even in spite of a loss of some sort in his material welfare. Our long-range hopes are fulfilled, as in the sentimental plot, but with the difference that our final response is respect and admiration for a man outdoing himself and the expectations of others concerning what a man is normally capable of.[14]

Plots of character are classified as: (a) the maturing plot, (b) the reform plot, (c) the testing plot (". . . a sympathetic, strong, and purposeful character is pressured in one way or another, to compromise or surrender his noble ends . . ."),[15] and (d) the disillusionment plot.[16] From the analysis later in this chapter it will become apparent that John's plot has affinities with the admiration and testing plots. While such classifications may help to categorize the gospel, they hardly satisfy as a characterization of the "uniqueness, complexity, and power" of the work, which is the criterion suggested by Philip Stevick for the use of "plot" in critical discussion.[17]

Northrop Frye has made the most ambitious effort to date to extend Aristotle's categories into a grammar of literary types. On the basis of Aristotle's character types, Frye establishes five categories: myth (the hero is a divine being, "superior in *kind* both to other men and to the environment of other men"), romance (the hero is "superior in *degree* to other men and his environment. . . . The hero of romance moves in a world in

---

[13] *Story and Discourse,* p. 85.
[14] "Forms of the Plot," p. 160.
[15] "Forms of the Plot," p. 162.
[16] "Forms of the Plot," pp. 157–62.
[17] *The Theory of the Novel,* p. 140.

which the ordinary laws of nature are slightly suspended"), high mimetic (the hero is "superior in degree to other men but not to his natural environment"), low mimetic (the hero is "superior neither to other men nor to his environment"), and ironic (the hero is "inferior in power or intelligence to ourselves").[18] Frye observes that in the course of its history fiction "has steadily moved its center of gravity down the list."[19] Later, Frye postulates four basic categories or *mythoi* into which literary genres may be grouped ("the romantic, the tragic, the comic, and the ironic and satiric").[20] Each of the four has six phases which shade into the phases of the neighboring *mythoi*. Although there are elements of comedy, tragedy, and irony in the gospels, they approximate most closely the *mythos* of romance. Typically, the romance presents a successful quest with three main stages: " . . . the preliminary minor adventures; the crucial struggle, usually some kind of battle in which either the hero or his foe, or both, must die; and the exaltation of the hero."[21] Frye continues:

> We may call these three stages respectively, using Greek terms, the *agon* or conflict, the *pathos* or death-struggle, and the *anagnorisis* or discovery, the recognition of the hero, who has clearly proved himself to be a hero even if he does not survive the conflict.[22]

The hero embodies all the reader's values. As romance inclines towards myth the hero may possess attributes of divinity, but the conflict "takes place in, or at any rate primarily concerns, *our* world."[23] The relevance of a *mythos* so described is obvious. In the Gospel of John, Jesus, who has descended from the world above, is unrecognized except by a privileged few. As he strives to fulfill his mission, preliminary minor "adventures" (i.e., signs and conflicts with opponents) begin to reveal his identity. He is faced with a crucial struggle, his own death, which he accepts and thereby finishes his task successfully: "It is finished" (19:30). Although triumph takes the form of apparent defeat, he is recognized by his followers as "my Lord and God" (20:28).

---

[18] *Anatomy of Criticism*, pp. 33–34. Later (p. 325), Frye comments: "For most readers, myth, legend, historical reminiscence, and actual history are inseparable in the Bible; and even what is historical fact is not there because it is 'true' but because it is mythically significant. . . . When we apply this principle to the gospels, with all the variations in their narratives, the descriptive aspect of them too dissolves. The basis of their form is something other than biography, just as the basis of the Exodus story is something other than history."

[19] *Anatomy of Criticism*, p. 34.

[20] *Anatomy of Criticism*, p. 162.

[21] *Anatomy of Criticism*, p. 187.

[22] *Anatomy of Criticism*, p. 187.

[23] *Anatomy of Criticism*, p. 187.

The classification of John, or any of the gospels, as "romance" has only limited value, however. The fit is certainly not perfect. The gospels are clearly very different from other members of this genre or *mythos*. Only when the general shape of the *mythos* is considered somewhat abstractly do the gospels begin to fit it. In specifics, John is quite different from *Peer Gynt, The Faerie Queene*, or *Don Quixote*. The "fit," such as it is, is due in part to the influence of the gospels on both the authors of the later romances and on Frye himself. In John, moreover, Jesus' most intense period of struggle comes before his death (John 12:27–13:30), and *anagnorisis* permeates the plot rather than serving merely as a device of the concluding scene, though it is important there too. The whole story is a death struggle over the recognition of Jesus as the revealer, so *agon, pathos,* and *anagnorisis* are blended throughout the gospel. Although Frye's analysis is perceptive and suggests a basic, almost primordial, form for the gospels, we must press further to find a satisfactory characterization of their "uniqueness, complexity, and power."

Amos Wilder's characterization of the gospels as "wholes [which] must be seen formally as cult-histories representing a unique mythological genre" is suggestive and more precise than Frye's but stops short of defining the "unique mythological genre."[24] As a methodological principle one may suggest that if an adequate characterization is forthcoming it will not depend on preconceptions about the general class of literature to which the gospels belong but will emerge from study of the gospels themselves. Frye looks at the gospels through a wide-angle lens which sets them in the context of the literature of western culture. We are interested in the sort of picture one gets at closer range.

DOES A GOSPEL HAVE A PLOT?

Various events, perhaps even the general shape of the story, were already set for the evangelists in the traditions they received. Yet, the evangelists still had to fashion these materials into a coherent whole. To do so, they had to impose a meaning on the events and convince the reader that this meaning was implicit in the events all along.[25] Whereas we can only guess at the meaning of events we actually experience, events in a narrative have a definite meaning because they are part of a story which has an ending.

---

[24] *Early Christian Rhetoric*, p. 120. See also William A. Beardslee, *Literary Criticism of the New Testament*, pp. 16, 27–28; Charles H. Talbert, *What is a Gospel?*

[25] Hayden White, "The Value of Narrativity," p. 23.

The plot, with its ending, gives the events what Hayden White calls "the odor of the ideal." He adds: "This is why the plot of a historical narrative is always an embarrassment and has to be presented as 'found' in the events rather than put there by narrative techniques."[26] The ending brings a closure which is acceptable—or even better, inevitable—when the entire story is reviewed. The plot, therefore, interprets events by placing them in a sequence, a context, a narrative world, which defines their meaning. The events are then secondary to the story or message which gives them meaning. As Derek Brewer put it: "The relationship of the narrative is primarily to the message about the hero, only secondarily to actual events. What happens is that such events as there were generated the message, but the message then shapes the telling of the events."[27] To establish internal coherence and convey the significance of the story, the evangelists selected, shaped, and arranged material so that its sequence established a certain progression and causality. Action and dialogue were used to establish various themes or motifs which recur throughout the gospels, and the narrator and characters were made to cooperate in conveying the meaning of the story.

Each of the evangelists tells essentially the same story, but the plots and emphases of the gospels differ greatly. The difference is due not only to the vigorous creativity of the evangelists but to the peculiar social and religious struggles of their intended readers. The story and its roots in the religious and cultural heritage of both Jews and Gentiles were complex and fertile enough to allow for a great variety of themes, emphases, ironies, and implications. The fluidity of the gospel traditions was also such that the evangelists were able to shape them into different plot structures. Where each evangelist chose to begin and end his gospel and which conflicts receive the most attention tell a great deal about their plots. Mark focuses on how the secret of Jesus' messianic identity is revealed and the developing and decaying relationship between Jesus and the disciples.[28] Matthew begins with a genealogy, linking Jesus with Abraham and David, and the birth of Jesus as Emmanuel (Matt. 1:23). It ends on the same note after having explored the relationship between old and new in the ministry of Jesus; the connections between his teachings, mighty works, and death; and the significance of the story for a church of Jewish Christians sharing their faith with Gentiles. Luke begins within the chrysalis of Judaism and traces the life of Jesus to Jerusalem, the point at

---

[26] "The Value of Narrativity," p. 24.

[27] "The Gospels and the Laws of Folktale," p. 45.

[28] See Werner H. Kelber, *Mark's Story of Jesus,* and David Rhoads and Donald Michie, *Mark as Story.*

which the disciples are ready to begin the work of the church, which will culminate in the gospel being preached "openly and unhindered" (Acts 28:31) to the Gentiles, which is the story of the book of Acts.[29] Luke's gospel therefore focuses on the emergent movement in Jesus' ministry and how it was possible for it to continue after his death.[30] Likewise, it relates that movement back to its beginnings in Jesus' ministry. The dawning awareness that Jesus will be killed and rising hostility toward him provide major sources of drama for the gospels, but each develops a distinctive plot and different themes.

Not only do the gospels have plots, but the plot is, in a sense, the evangelist's interpretation of the story, and none of them could avoid—or for that matter wanted to avoid—interpreting it. They wrote precisely in order to propound their interpretations of the gospel story. Plot and characterization are both means by which they fulfilled this task and requirements imposed upon every writer of narrative literature. Analysis of these components of the medium should expose the unique design of each gospel more clearly.

What is John's Plot?

Conscious plotting of the narrative is more obvious in John than in the synoptics, even if its structure is no tighter than theirs. Several literary features point to the shaping of John's plot. First, events are put in a different order from the synoptic accounts. Jesus moves back and forth between Judea and Galilee, and the confrontation in the temple is his first public act rather than his final provocation, as it is in the synoptics. Although it is far from certain that the evangelist altered traditional material in which there was a set sequence which corresponded to that of the synoptic gospels, it is at least probable that he is responsible for the sequence of events established in the gospel. Second, John's dialogues are noticeably more contrived and less realistic than those of the synoptics.[31] Although John is not entirely devoid of realistic, life-like exchanges (cf. 2:9–10) and there is evidence of manipulation of discourse material for thematic and theological reasons in the synoptics (cf. Matt. 5–7), the point remains. There is evidence of the shaping of a plot in John. The dialogue is often impelled by misunderstanding, inept questions, and double en-

---

[29] Frank Stagg, *The Book of Acts.*
[30] Cf. Erich Auerbach, *Mimesis,* pp. 43–44.
[31] Wilder, *Early Christian Rhetoric,* p. 48; Hans W. Frei, *The Eclipse of Biblical Narrative,* p. 16.

tendre. Both Jesus and his opponents speak in the Johannine idiom, and the same themes recur repetitively. The more repetition there is in a work the more evident it is that the author is using repetition to make a point, and there is a great deal of repetition in John.[32] Images, terms, themes, signs, confrontations over the Law and Jesus' identity, appearances at feasts in Jerusalem, and dialogues with followers and opponents are repeated throughout. Together these features point unmistakably to the careful crafting of a unified sequence and a logic of causality which is developed through the repetition of scenes and dialogues in the gospel.[33]

What, then, is the plot of the Fourth Gospel? The beginning, ending, repeated material, tasks of the characters, and nature of the conflicts all provide clues. The gospel begins with an extended introduction of Jesus, and the plot clearly revolves around him. The prologue not only introduces Jesus as the divine *logos* but also provides clues to the gospel's plot. John 1:11–12 has often been regarded as a summary of the gospel: "He came to his own home, and his own people received him not. But to all who received him, who believed in his name, he gave power to become children of God." Verse 14 characterizes the significance of Jesus' ministry: "And the Word became flesh and dwelt among us, full of grace and truth; we have beheld his glory. . . ." Jesus' task is stated more precisely in other verses:

1:18   . . . the only Son, who is in the bosom of the Father, he has made him known.

1:29   Behold, the Lamb of God, who takes away the sin of the world!

17:4   I glorified thee on earth, having accomplished the work which thou gavest me to do.

17:6   I have manifested thy name to the men whom thou gavest me out of the world. (cf. 17:26)

---

[32] Beardslee, *Literary Criticism of the New Testament*, p. 25; John Painter, *John*, p. 11.

[33] Wolfgang Iser, *The Implied Reader*, p. 93, comments on Sir Walter Scott's work: "Truth, as they say, is stranger than fiction—and in this case, fiction prevents the truth from seeming too strange. . . . this fictitious consistency ensures that the past will be comprehensible. . . ." His description of Scott's technique (pp. 92–93) permits interesting comparisons with John: "The facts are true, but they are made probable by means of fiction, and it is only this fiction that enables Scott to produce the illusion of historical reality. In the epilogue to *Waverly*, he himself comments on this form of illusion: '. . . for the purpose of preserving some idea of the ancient manners of which I have witnessed the almost total extinction, I have embodied the imaginary scenes, and ascribed to fictitious characters, a part of the incidents which I then received from those who were actors in them. Indeed, the most romantic parts of this narrative are precisely those which have a foundation in fact' [*Waverly*, p. 554]. In transforming eye-witness accounts of historical facts into fiction, Scott ensures that the highly romantic-seeming situations retain their basis of fact, for they would seem incredible were it not for the fictitious characters that authenticate them."

18:37   For this I was born, and for this I have come into the world, to bear witness
         to the truth.

To manifest the Father's name (17:6, 26) is to make him known (1:18).
These authoritative statements about Jesus' mission, the success of which
is the substance of John's plot, suggest that Jesus' task is multi-faceted. In
the face of opposition of cosmic proportions, his task is to reveal the Father
by bearing witness to the truth (which ultimately is personal rather than
propositional) and take away the sin of the world. Are the two synony-
mous, or related? Is the latter (taking away sin) a consequence of the
former (revealing the Father)? The revelation of the Father seems to be
the distinctive Johannine contribution which has been imposed on the
traditional interpretation of Jesus' role (taking away sin). John 16:8–9
characterizes "the sin of the world" as unbelief. For John the two seem to
be related. Sin is "taken away" when one recognizes the *logos,* and recognition comes only to those who believe. Both facets of Jesus' task culminate at his death. The cross is his glorification, which finally reveals his
glory for all to see. The more Jesus announces his redemptive mission the
more clearly his identity is revealed and the more intense the hostility
toward him becomes. The hostility in turn dramatizes the radical difference between those who believe and those who do not. Finally, the apparent triumph of Jesus' opponents is in fact the awesome fulfillment of
his mission. Jesus' death is John's *peripeteia,* the falsification of expectation; "the end comes as expected, but not in the manner expected."[34] The
crucifixion is part of Jesus' glorification.

The rising hostility toward Jesus and the dawning awareness that he
will be killed provide major sources of drama. The plot of the Gospel of
John, however, revolves around Jesus' fulfillment of his mission to reveal
the Father and authorize the children of God ($\tau\acute{\epsilon}\kappa\nu\alpha\ \theta\epsilon o\hat{v}$).[35] The plot is a
plot of action in the sense that Jesus achieves his goals while his fortune
apparently changes for the worse. It is a plot of character only in the sense
that it is bound up with his moral character and the threats to it, for Jesus
is a static character. There is no change or development. All that is essential to his character is revealed to the reader before Jesus ever makes his
appearance in the narrative, but his identity is repeatedly demonstrated,
confirmed, and given richer tones by the signs and discourses.

Plot development in John, then, is a matter of how Jesus' identity
comes to be recognized and how it fails to be recognized. Not only is Jesus'

---

[34] Kermode, *The Sense of an Ending,* p. 53.
[35] See R. Alan Culpepper, "The Pivot of John's Prologue."

identity progressively revealed by the repetitive signs and discourses and the progressive enhancement of metaphorical and symbolic images, but each episode has essentially the same plot as the story as a whole. Will Nicodemus, the Samaritan woman, or the lame man recognize Jesus and thereby receive eternal life? The story is repeated over and over. No one can miss it. Individual episodes can almost convey the message of the whole; at least they suggest or recall it for those who know the story. The prologue gives each of these episodes an ironic background in that the reader has already been taken into the confidence of the narrator and knows who Jesus is. We are therefore made to feel superior to the characters Jesus confronts, because in contrast to them we know that Jesus is the incarnate *logos* revealing the Father. For us to question this understanding would mean that we would have to give up our privileged position and be no more perceptive than the characters we are able to look down upon. This literary dynamic pushes the reader to embrace the ideological point of view of the author, that is, the confession that Jesus is "the Christ, the Son of God" (20:30). The ignorance, or "blindness," of "the Jews" gives the story a continuing dramatic force that ties the various episodes together and maintains the tension while various characters accept or reject Jesus. The challenging profusion of metaphorical imagery also serves to maintain our interest and prevent the repetitions from becoming monotonous.

PLOT DEVELOPMENT IN JOHN

The development of John's plot can now be analyzed in more detail. The prologue introduces Jesus as the incarnation of the divine *logos* which was active in creation. His mission is to reveal the Father. It also establishes the antithetical norms which will be in conflict throughout the narrative: light and darkness, belief and unbelief, grace and truth and the law. The prologue, however, would probably never be convincing to the reader were it not for the rest of the narrative.[36] Confession ultimately depends upon story for its credibility.

The first section of the gospel, through 2:11, provides a dramatic introduction to Jesus and his work. He is acclaimed by John the Baptist and some of the disciples and then reveals his glory to the disciples through the

---

[36] Cf. Scholes and Kellogg, *The Nature of Narrative*, p. 209: "The epic plot is to a certain extent bespoken by epic characterization. The plot is inherent in the concept of the protagonist, but that concept is not realized in the narrative until this character is expressed through action."

sign at Cana (2:11; cf. 1:14). In this section, opposition is at most implied in the references to the priests and Levites sent by the Jews in Jerusalem to interrogate John the Baptist and in Jesus' initial allusion to his "hour" (2:4). The first chapter is very optimistic. Jesus is majestically introduced, John fulfills his role as a witness, and immediately various individuals, most notably an Israelite, begin to follow him. Revelation is taking place, and there is the promise of even greater things to come (1:50).

The second chapter of John both clarifies and complicates the narrative. The plot emerges more clearly with Jesus' dramatic opposition to the abuse of temple. Jerusalem is established as the locus of Jesus' sharpest conflict with unbelief which has been hardened by misunderstanding of the scriptures, institutions, and festivals of Judaism. The faith of the disciples is established beyond question (2:11), and the value of seeing the signs, remembering, and believing in scripture and the words of Jesus is affirmed (2:17, 22). The latter verse is the first indication the uninitiated reader would have that Jesus will die and be raised from the dead, but it is no more than a passing reference. The reader is also given a problem to work out: why did Jesus not accept the many who believed "in his name" (2:23–24)? The problem is posed not by Jesus but by the narrator. What is the difference between these believers and the disciples (cf. 2:11)? Is it that faith is acceptable only when it leads to an open commitment to follow Jesus?[37] This problem gives the second chapter a less optimistic ending than the first. Jesus' death has been foreshadowed (2:21–22), and there are some to whom Jesus will not entrust himself even though they believe in his name.

In John 3 there is still no real opposition to Jesus, but the reader is given further guidance in understanding the meaning of acceptable faith and the ramifications of believing or refusing to believe. Jesus begins to make an impression on a representative of Jewish leadership. Simultaneously, the author clarifies that the real conflict is not between Jesus and the Jews or their official leadership but between Jesus and those who refuse to accept the revelation he brings. Unbelief is the real opponent. It belongs to "flesh" and this world, which is opposed to "spirit" and the world above, from which Jesus comes (3:6, 12–13, 31). The conversation with Nicodemus, like each succeeding sign, dialogue, and discourse, introduces new images and gives a richer texture to the gospel's interpretation of Jesus. There is a dark reference to the Son of Man being lifted up (on a

---

[37] Zane C. Hodges, "Problem Passages in the Gospel of John," pp. 139–52. On the representation of various types of faith in the opening chapters see F. J. Moloney, "From Cana to Cana (Jn. 2:1–4:54) and the Fourth Evangelist's Concept of Correct (and Incorrect) Faith."

pole? to the world above?), but, like the reference to Jesus' hour in the previous chapter, it is left unexplained (3:14). Jesus' influence increases (3:23, 30), and his following grows.

In John 4 there is again little opposition to Jesus. The chapter opens with an allusion to the threat posed by the Pharisees (4:1, 3). There is a proleptic reference to Jesus' rejection in 4:44 (cf. 1:11), but the rest of the chapter is positive. Jesus is making more disciples than John (4:1). The Samaritan woman hails him as the Christ, and many in her village say he is "the savior of the world" (4:29, 39–42). He is received in Galilee (4:45) and brings an official to faith by means of his second sign (4:46–54). There is therefore no more than token opposition in the first four chapters and a foreshadowing of more to come. These chapters have a powerful "primacy effect," that is, they firmly establish the reader's first impression of Jesus' identity and mission.[38] The reader is led to accept the evangelist's view of Jesus before the antithetical point of view is given more than passing reference. It is hardly possible after these chapters for the reader to be persuaded by another view of Jesus.

John 5 brings a fresh development. The conflict over Jesus' identity intensifies sharply. The Jews become important for the first time, and the basis of the conflict is explained. The issue is the locus of revelation— Jesus or the Law? Those who hold the absolute authority of Torah claim that Jesus has violated the sabbath and committed blasphemy. To them, these offenses disprove his claims for himself. The narrator drives home the issue in 5:18—"This was why the Jews sought all the more to kill him, because he not only broke the sabbath but also called God his own Father, making himself equal with God." The Jews represent the only clear alternative to the disciples' belief in Jesus. Jesus himself speaks of his role as Son of Man (5:25–47) and attests his claims by citing witnesses (the Father, John the Baptist, the works, the scriptures, Moses). The dramatic power of the rest of the gospel is built around this conflict.

The conflict with unbelief escalates in chapter 6. There are no other significant conflicts in John, no conflict with demons or nature, no conflict with himself, and little sustained conflict with the disciples. The walking on the water may not involve the stilling of a storm at all. Its significance, which is hardly developed, lies in its reenactment of the exodus and its character as an epiphany. Whatever conflict there is with the disciples follows in part from the necessity that their faith be incomplete until after the completion of Jesus' work at his death. The evangelist shows how the Jews' refusal to believe reveals that in fact they have not understood the

---

[38] For a discussion of "primacy effect" see: Meir Sternberg, *Expositional Modes and Temporal Ordering in Fiction,* pp. 102–4.

Torah, Moses, or the exodus. The misunderstanding motif in John extends equally to Jesus' words and the Torah. Both can be a cause of offense, yet both can convey a deeper meaning to those who can perceive it. Jesus' fulfillment of the role of Moses in the exodus and his claim to provide a bread of life more durable than manna cause division and disagreement among the Jews. At first the Jews "murmur" (6:41). Later the narrator tells us they quarrel with one another (6:52). They ask the question which becomes typical of earthly, literal, superficial understanding: "how?" (cf. 3:4, 9; 4:9; 6:42, 52; 7:15; 8:33; 9:10, 15, 16, 19, 21, 26; 12:34; 14:5). The disturbance among the Jews spreads to the disciples as well. They begin to murmur (6:60–61), some of them do not believe, and one will betray him (6:64). John 6:66–71 looks very much like a doublet of 6:60–65. Many of the disciples disassociate themselves from the movement (6:66), signaling a sharp change in Jesus' fortunes. The optimism of the early chapters collapses, and there is cause for real doubt as to whether Jesus will be able to execute his mission successfully. If it were not for the prologue and the early chapters, the reader would be fearful that the forces of unbelief were on their way to complete victory. The twelve seem to be not those who were especially selected and appointed but those who remained after this mass defection (see however 6:70; 13:18; 15:16). "The twelve" appear only here (6:67, 70, 71) and in 20:24. Only two are named, Judas and Thomas. One believes, one does not. There is good reason, however, to suspect that the other named disciples belonged to the twelve. Not only is Jesus reduced to twelve followers, but one of them will betray him.

In John 7 the opposition hardens and begins to mobilize itself. The Judean Jews seek to kill Jesus (7:1, 19, 25), and repeatedly attempt to arrest him. Even Jesus' brothers do not believe in him (7:4–5). There is simultaneous movement in two directions. While disbelief spreads from the crowds to the disciples, the twelve, and even Jesus' brothers; dissension spreads to the crowds (7:12) because some believe. Those who contemplate belief now have cause to fear the Jews (7:13; cf. 9:22; 19:38; 20:19). The efforts to arrest Jesus are thwarted because his hour has not yet come (7:30), so the hour is connected with his arrest. This is a delaying device which builds drama while implying that Jesus' hour is the hour of his trial or death. Another scenario is offered in 7:33–36. Jesus says he will go to the one who sent him and they will not be able to find him. Does this mean that Jesus will elude his opponents by returning to the Father, or will Jesus flee to the diaspora? Whose plan will be fulfilled? For the reader who does not know the outcome, the veiled language is a source of drama; for the informed reader it is a source of ironic enrichment. John 7:39 links the giving of the Spirit to Jesus' glorification but does not ex-

plain what that glorification will entail. If there is any doubt about the
outcome of the conflict, there is none about the weakness of the arguments
of those who refuse to accept Jesus. The crowd charges that Jesus has a
demon (7:20; cf. 8:48, 49, 52; 10:20–21) because he thinks they seek to kill
him (cf. 7:1). They think Jesus cannot be the Messiah because they know
where he is from (7:27), because the Messiah will come from Bethlehem
(7:42), because no prophet has come from Galilee (7:52). For the discerning reader these charges expose the ignorance and misunderstandings
of Jesus' opponents.

In John 8 the verbal exchange between Jesus and the Jews reaches its
most hostile and strident tones.[39] Many of the themes and arguments of
the previous chapters are repeated, but the central issue is paternity. The
Jews, who presumably had heard of unusual circumstances surrounding
Jesus' birth, charge ironically that they do not know who Jesus' father is
(8:19). They also claim a privileged status as children of Abraham (8:33).
Jesus responds that the Jews are not acting like children of Abraham
(8:39–40). As an implicit slur on Jesus, they retort that *they* were not born
of fornication but have one father, God. Jesus says that since they reject
him and seek to kill him they show that their real father is the devil (8:44).
They shout back "Samaritan!" "Demoniac!" (8:48). The scene ends with
Jesus claiming to be older than Abraham (and hence superior to him) and
the Jews attempting to stone him (8:59). There is no longer any hope of
reconciliation.

In many respects chapter 9 and the first part of chapter 10 form an
interpretive interlude. The pitch of the hostility seems to drop, and the
maneuverings to arrest Jesus make little progress. In turn the thematic
development is clear. Jesus, who announced he was the light of the world
(8:12), now gives sight to a man born to darkness. Gradually the blind
man receives spiritual insight as well, and the blindness of the Pharisees is
simultaneously revealed (9:39–41). The Jews methodically attempt to
gather evidence of sabbath violation, and the narrator alludes, almost in
passing, to an agreement that anyone confessing Jesus as the Christ
should be banished from the synagogue (9:22). This allusion adds further
justification for the crowd's fear of the Jews (7:13; cf. 12:42; 16:2). The

---

[39] Iser, *The Implied Reader*, p. 153, refers to the definition of dramatic monologue
by Roman Ingarden, *Das literarische Kunstwerk*, pp. 408–9: "A conversation
between two people is rarely a matter just of communication; it is concerned with
something of much more vital importance—the influencing of the person to
whom the words are addressed. In all 'dramatic' conflicts, such as are developed
in the world presented by the play, the speech addressed to a character is a form
of action on the part of the speaker, and basically it only has any real importance
for the events depicted in the play if it actually brings about a genuine advance in
the action that is developing."

relationships among Jesus, the Jewish leaders, and the crowds are then interpreted by the parabolic statements in chapter 10. The section closes with Jesus' declaration that he will lay down his life and take it up again. No one will take it from him. Since this assertion comes at the end of five chapters of escalating hostility, it adds intrigue while limiting the power of the opposition. There is again division among the Jews (10:19) and debate over whether Jesus is demon possessed. Jesus' claim to unity with the Father in 10:30 provokes another attempt to stone him (10:31) and a repetition of the charge of blasphemy (10:33). Again the attempt to seize him is unsuccessful (10:39), however, and he withdraws from Jerusalem.

The tangled relationship between life and death is exposed in John 11. Jesus returns to call a dead friend to life in spite of Thomas' prophetic perception that the mission will cost Jesus his own life. Another misunderstanding underscores the point that real death is more than just "falling asleep" (11:11–14). Life is believing, and Jesus is resurrection and life (11:25–26). The occasion brings Jesus face to face with his own death, his own tomb, weeping women, and the symbolic stone which defends the tomb from the living. Jesus is shaken but, through the strength of his relationship to the Father, prevails over death. Some believe, but immediately the authorities plot his death, justifying it as necessary for national security (11:48–50). The narrator cannot resist explaining the irony (11:51–53). Now there is little reason to hope that the authorities will fail again.

In many ways chapter 12 is a transitional chapter. It brings Jesus' public ministry to a close, describes the final preliminary steps toward his arrest and death, and forms a solid link between chapters 11 and 13. The opening scene is the anointing of Jesus' feet (not his head) while he reclines at table. Judas is again introduced as the one who was about to betray him, and Jesus links the event to the preparation of his body for burial (12:7). Upon his entry into Jerusalem, Jesus is hailed as king, a title that will assume significance at his trial and death. The request of Greeks to "see" Jesus triggers his inner sense that the hour of his death is at hand (12:23). After further interpreting the meaning of his death by likening himself to a seed dying to bear fruit (12:24), Jesus experiences the agony of accepting his death (12:27–28). He accepts it, however, because it will glorify the Father, overthrow "the ruler of this world," and be his exaltation from the earth. Through his death he will draw all men to himself (12:27–32). This statement suggests both the means and the meaning of his death (12:33). While Jesus withdraws into seclusion, the narrator interprets the reasons for unbelief. Jesus then offers a summarizing interpretation of his ministry in the form of a closing soliloquy.

John 13 opens with the narrator's explanation that Jesus knew that the hour for his return to the Father had arrived. The devil had already singled out Judas for the role of betrayer (13:2). Symbolically portraying the cleansing significance of his imminent death, Jesus washes his disciples' feet.[40] Shaken again, but for the last time, Jesus predicts his betrayal and, having given his betrayer the choice morsel, sends him out into the night to set in motion the dark forces which will paradoxically lead to Jesus' glorification. The disciples, who will not be able to follow him are commanded to love one another, but even Peter will deny him that night. His departure will be to their advantage. He will prepare a place for them, return to abide with them in Spirit, and send the Paraclete, who will teach, remind, and comfort them, bear witness to him, and convict the world. The disciples will face severe testing. They will be excluded from the synagogue, persecuted, and scattered, but they will have joy and peace and their distress will pass. Before leaving the table to meet his adversaries, Jesus prays for himself, his own, and those who will follow in faith later. Again Jesus recognizes that the hour has come (17:1; cf. 12:23; 13:1; 16:32) and prays that he might be glorified so that the disciples may be set apart from the world, united with the Father, and sent to carry on the work of revealing Jesus to the world (17:21–23).

With chapter 18 the waiting is over, and events begin to move quickly toward Jesus' death. Jesus is in control even while his enemies force a legal endorsement of their judgment upon him. The amassed political and religious forces which come to seize him are powerless in his presence, but he goes with them voluntarily after securing the release of his disciples. Peter, who has not understood that Jesus must die, tries to defend him with the sword and continues to be a foil for Jesus during the interrogations before Annas and Caiaphas. Inside, Jesus is saying that he has spoken boldly and publicly, challenging his accusers, and suggesting that they ask those who have heard him. Outside, Peter is attempting to remain anonymous and denying his discipleship to evade accusations. Whatever Jesus accomplished with his disciples during his ministry, it was not enough. The necessity of Jesus' death is established by the disciples' faithlessness.

Pilate's position between Jesus and his accusers is dramatized by having them remain outside, lest they defile themselves on the eve of Passover while they call for his death. Pilate goes back and forth between them and Jesus. The evangelist skillfully turns the full glare of the spotlight on Pilate. It is he who is on trial, and his judgment will be a verdict on himself as much as it is on Jesus. In the discussions between Jesus and Pilate

---

[40] Cf. James D. G. Dunn, "The Washing of the Disciples' Feet in John 13:1–20," p. 249.

the nature of authority and Jesus' kingship are clarified. Three times Pilate pronounces Jesus innocent, and in the end the title he nails to the cross, "Jesus of Nazareth, the King of the Jews," announces his recognition of Jesus' true identity. But, although he tries to deliver Jesus, the glory of men finally has a stronger claim on Pilate than the glory of God (19:12–13). When the Jews in effect commit blasphemy and renounce their heritage by claiming "we have no king but Caesar" (19:15), Pilate delivers Jesus to them. Jesus is crucified on the eve of Passover, the designated time for the slaughter of the Passover lambs. While soldiers cast lots for his garments, Jesus cares for his own by uniting his mother and the Beloved Disciple. Just before dying, the giver of living water thirsts. His only cup is a sponge. He drinks the wine, solemnly declares "It is finished," and "hands over the spirit." Before dark the soldiers pierce his side, which is interpreted as further fulfillment of scripture, and Jesus is given a lavish, kingly burial by Joseph of Arimathea and Nicodemus.

On the first day of the week Mary Magdalene discovers the tomb empty. Peter and the Beloved Disciple run to the tomb and find the grave clothes are still there (cf. 11:44). The Beloved Disciple sees and believes. Mary Magdalene meets Jesus now risen, but does not recognize him until he calls her name. She is told that he has not yet ascended to the father, but to go and tell "my brothers," meaning the disciples. The choice of this term now that Jesus' work is complete probably signals that they have in fact become "children of God," brothers of the unique "son of God." The appearances that follow authorize their continuing mission to bring others to believe. Thomas, who at first demands physical proof that what the others saw was the earthly Jesus, offers the gospel's climactic confession, "my Lord and my God." With a beatitude upon those who will believe without seeing, the gospel reaches its original ending, a conclusion which affirms that the gospel was written to lead readers (or hearers) to believe.

John 21 is an epilogue, apparently added shortly after the gospel was completed. It resolves some of the minor conflicts (the Beloved Disciple and Peter, Jesus and Peter), and brings the development of John's symbols to a climactic flourish. The characterization of Peter and the Beloved Disciple is completed by allusion to their roles in the future of the story world: Peter will die a martyr's death, but the Beloved Disciple too will bear a faithful witness. The gospel ends without an ascension, for the ascension in John is collapsed into Jesus' exaltation, his being "lifted up" on the cross and his resurrection. It is metaphorical rather than physical. Jesus is with the disciples at the end; the Paraclete will remain with them. His revelatory work will be extended through their testimony. Chapter 21 is, therefore, the necessary ending of the gospel. By alluding to the disciples' future work and the writing of the gospel, it bridges the gap between the story and the reader. The story may depict an ideal past, but the present is related to that past in such a way that the story becomes determinative for the reader's present.

CONCLUSION

The plot of the gospel is propelled by conflict between belief and unbelief as responses to Jesus. The centrality of this conflict is confirmed by the fact that almost half of the occurrences of the verb "believe" in the New Testament are found in John (98 out of 239).[41] The repetitiveness of the gospel has also been noted by various critics. Its plot is episodic, and perhaps therefore defective.[42] But the author uses the various episodes skillfully to enrich the texture of the whole. Like Fielding, the author "deprives most of these episodes of actional or propulsive value precisely in order to direct the reader to integrate them with the rest of the work not in terms of plot but of theme."[43] While the dialogues slow down the action, they intensify conflict and characterization and provide space for thematic development. John's pervasive thematic integration allows, furthermore, for readers who know the story to see its end and its meaning in each of the familiar episodes.[44]

The four constitutive features of a plot identified at the beginning of the chapter are present in John in ascending order of importance. Sequence or order, a feature which some commentators have found remarkably lacking in John, allows each episode to have a meaningful place in the story. Causality, though it is less important than thematic development, contributes to the story's unity. The affective power of the narrative, however, is the most important feature of its plot. By showing Jesus confronting a wide variety of individuals in everyday situations, the gospel dramatizes the message that the Word has become flesh and dwelt among us. At a wedding and a well, at the temple among the religious and at a pool among the wretched and lame, ordinary persons come step by step to recognize glory enfleshed. The gospel is the testimony of one who speaks for all those who recognized the Word in Jesus: ". . . and we have beheld his glory." The "we" can therefore be understood to include all the characters in the gospel who finally believe and bear witness: John the Baptist,

---

[41] Painter, *John*, p. 77.

[42] Aristotle, *Poetics*, 1451b: "Of defective plots or actions the worst are the episodic, those, I mean, in which the succession of the episodes is neither probable nor necessary. . . ."

[43] Sternberg, *Expositional Modes*, p. 169.

[44] Cf. Paul Ricoeur, "Narrative Time," p. 179.

the disciples, the Samaritans, the blind man, and the others. They have all beheld his glory, and the reader sees what they saw. The effect of this narrative structure, with its prologue followed by episodic repetition of the conflict between belief and unbelief, is to enclose the reader in the company of faith. The gospel's plot, therefore, is controlled by thematic development and a strategy for wooing readers to accept its interpretation of Jesus.

Chapter Five

CHARACTERS

[The novelist's touch] selects for literary purposes two
or three facets of a man or woman, generally the most
spectacular and therefore 'useful' ingredients of their
character and disregards all the others. Whatever fails
to fit in with these specially chosen traits is eliminated;
must be eliminated, for otherwise the description would
not hold water. . . . it takes what it likes and leaves the
rest. The facts may be correct as far as they go, but there
are too few of them; what the author says may be true,
and yet by no means the truth. That is the novelist's
touch. It falsifies life.

> Norman Douglas, quoted by E. M. Forster
> *Aspects of the Novel*

Literature must always represent a battle between real
people and images.

> A. S. Byatt, quoted by F. Kermode
> *The Sense of an Ending*

But in the novel we can know people perfectly, and
apart from the general pleasure of reading, we can find
here a compensation for their dimness in life. In this
direction fiction is truer than history, because it goes
beyond the evidence and each of us knows from his own
experience that there is something beyond the evidence.

> E. M. Forster
> *Aspects of the Novel*

Given the predilection of people to be interested in people, it is not surprising that the success of a literary work depends heavily on whether its characters are convincing, in some general sense "life-like," and interesting. Many great works draw the reader deeply into the perplexities of life as they are experienced by fictional characters who plan, decide, choose, react, and feel like real people. The reader experiences for a little while life's perplexities as they are encountered by "others," and is thereby led to wrestle with them from a different perspective. Here we shall examine John's characters. What sort of characters populate the gospel? How do they interact with one another?

CHARACTERIZATION IN CONTEMPORARY CRITICISM

It is surprising that the art of characterization has not yielded more to analysis than it has. Literary critics can draw upon relatively precise and sophisticated analyses of time and point of view, for example, but when they come to characterization they are likely to find W. J. Harvey's judgment confirmed: "Modern criticism, by and large, has relegated the treatment of character to the periphery of its attention, has at best given it a polite and perfunctory nod and has regarded it more often as a misguided and misleading abstraction."[1] Literary analysts have not been idle, however, and a brief review of work in this area will again suggest new lines of approach to the study of characters in the biblical narratives.

Aristotle proposed that writers should aim at four things in the representation of character: (a) "first and foremost, the character represented should be morally good"; (b) "the characters represented should be suitable"; (c) "they should be life-like"; and (d) "they should be consistent" (*Poetics,* 1454a). These proposals provide some basis for judging whether or not the characterization in a given work is satisfactory, but offer little assistance in the task of understanding how characters are shaped and how they function.

Contemporary approaches to characters in narrative literature fall

---

[1] *Character and the Novel,* p. 192.

roughly into two camps depending on whether characters are seen primarily as autonomous beings with traits and even personalities or as plot
functionaries with certain commissions or tasks to be fulfilled.[2] Seymour
Chatman champions the first approach, while the formalists and structur-
alists have adopted the second.[3] Attractive as Chatman's program is, it
probably has limited value for the study of the Gospel of John because
most of the characters in it appear so briefly that it is difficult to form an
impression of them as "autonomous beings." Only Jesus appears frequently or long enough to receive substantial multi-faceted development.
When any of the minor characters conveys an impression of personhood it
is usually the personification of a single trait: Thomas doubts, Pilate
wrestles with the claims of truth and political expediency, Peter is impul-
sive, the Beloved Disciple is perceptive. As Percy Lubbock observed about
Balzac's stories, "such of [the] people as appear by the way, incidentally,
must for the time being shed their irrelevant life; if they fail to do so, they
disturb the unity of the story and confuse its truth."[4] The evangelist is not
a novelist whose great concern is full-blown development of his characters. Most of the characters appear on the literary stage only long enough
to fulfill their role in the evangelist's representation of Jesus and the responses to him. As a result, one is almost forced to consider the characters
in terms of their commissions, plot functions, and representational value.[5]

E. M. Forster's deceptively simple lectures on characterization have
had a profound impact.[6] He distinguished "flat" characters, which are
types or caricatures which embody a single idea or quality, from "round"
characters, which are "complex in temperament and motivation," as difficult to describe as people in real life, and "like most people . . . capable of
surprising us."[7] Forster also observed that "characters" are different from
people: whereas people can only know each other imperfectly, characters
can be transparent.[8] The reader may be admitted to the character's mind
for an inside view or assisted by the narrator to gain a "true" view of the
character. Characters can be fully exposed; people cannot. The implication of this observation for the study of the gospels is powerful: the gospels,
in which Jesus is a literary character, can make him known to readers

---

[2] Cf. David Rhoads, "Narrative Criticism and the Gospel of Mark," pp. 417–18.

[3] *Story and Discourse*, p. 119.

[4] *The Craft of Fiction*, p. 210.

[5] Robert C. Tannehill, "Tensions in Synoptic Sayings and Stories," p. 148, notes
how this approach has worked in the study of Mark.

[6] *Aspects of the Novel*, pp. 54–84. Cf., for example, the references in M. H.
Abrams, *A Glossary of Literary Terms*, p. 21.

[7] Forster, *Aspects of the Novel*, pp. 73, 81; Abrams, *A Glossary of Literary Terms*,
p. 21. See also Meir Sternberg, *Expositional Modes*, p. 138.

[8] *Aspects of the Novel*, pp. 69–70, quoted at the beginning of the chapter.

more profoundly than he, as a person, could have been known by his contemporaries. To what extent does John seize this advantage? Much of its power derives from the fact that the central character, who by design is revealed by the narrative, is acclaimed as the creator and redeemer of mankind who came to live virtually unrecognized in this world. To those who accept its message the gospel offers the possibility of knowing their Lord more perfectly than they can know other persons.

Forster also distinguished "life by values" from "life by time." In the former the crucial, intense moments are paramount; in the latter, life is controlled more by pure chronological succession. Chronological development did not come into its own until western culture developed "a time-consciousness sophisticated enough to make the kind of temporal discrimination which this sort of characterization required."[9] In ancient literature, exemplified by Homer, characters are "invariably 'flat,' 'static,' and quite 'opaque.'"[10] Many of the biblical characters are different, however:

> The heroes of the Old Testament were in a process of becoming, whereas the heroes of Greek narrative were in a state of being. Process in Greek narrative was confined to the action of a plot. And even so, the action exemplified unchanging, universal laws; while the agents of the action, the characters, became as the plot unfolded only more and more consistent ethical types. Abraham, Jacob, David, and Samson, on the other hand, are men whose personal development is the focus of interest.[11]

In John, the character of Jesus is static; it does not change. He only emerges more clearly as what he is from the beginning. Some of the minor characters, the Samaritan woman and the blind man in particular, undergo a significant change.[12] To some extent, therefore, the Gospel of John draws from both Greek and Hebrew models of character development, but most of its characters appear to represent particular ethical types.

Another helpful distinction is that between the protagonist, the intermediate characters, especially the ficelles, and the background characters. Protagonists are the central characters, the characters whose "motivation and history is most fully established." They are also

> . . . the vehicles by which all the most interesting questions are raised; they evoke our beliefs, sympathies, revulsions; they incarnate the moral

---

[9] Robert Scholes and Robert Kellogg, *The Nature of Narrative*, p. 169.

[10] Scholes and Kellogg, *The Nature of Narrative*, p. 164.

[11] Scholes and Kellogg, *The Nature of Narrative*, p. 123.

[12] On the inward development of characters as a Christian element in narrative literature, see Scholes and Kellogg, *The Nature of Narrative*, p. 165.

vision of the world inherent in the total novel. In a sense they are what the novel exists for; it exists to reveal them.[13]

The ficelles, on the other hand, are typical characters easily recognizable by the readers. They exist to serve specific plot functions, often revealing the protagonist, and may carry a great deal of representative or symbolic value.[14] In John, Jesus is the protagonist and most of the other characters are ficelles. This observation is important for understanding the literary architecture of the gospel. Progressively, in one episode after another, the author sketches his vision of the world, but in the process the vision "decomposes and splits into various attributes which then form the structure of disparate characters."[15] Instead of isolated units, the reader finds that the characters are profoundly related. They are in effect the prism which breaks up the pure light of Jesus' remote epiphany into colors the reader can see. In John's narrative world the individuality of all the characters except Jesus is determined by their encounter with Jesus. The characters represent a continuum of responses to Jesus which exemplify misunderstandings the reader may share and responses one might make to the depiction of Jesus in the gospel.[16] The characters are, therefore, particular sorts of choosers.[17] Given the pervasive dualism of the Fourth Gospel, the choice is either/or. All situations are reduced to two clear-cut alternatives, and all the characters eventually make their choice. So must the reader. The evangelist, who stands entrenched within one perspective, uses all the powers at his disposal to coax the reader to his side.

---

[13] Harvey, *Character and the Novel*, p. 56.

[14] W. J. Harvey, *Character and the Novel*, pp. 58, 67. See also Scholes and Kellogg, *The Nature of Narrative*, p. 204. Wayne C. Booth, *The Rhetoric of Fiction*, p. 102, reduces the standing of the ficelle even further when, discussing Henry James, he defines ficelles as "characters whose main reason for existence is to give the reader in dramatic form the kind of help he needs to grasp the story." Booth's description of *The Portrait of a Lady* (p. 103) serves admirably well *mutatis mutandis* for the Gospel of John: "Thus we have the other main characters invented to reveal Isabel, and the ficelle invented to help reveal all of them. When we add such 'friends of the reader' to the explicit commentary—in the opening paragraph, for example, . . .—we find a large share of the book falling on the side of rhetoric consciously directed to the reader; almost nothing except Isabel's character is left on the side of 'subject.'"

[15] Harvey, *Character and the Novel*, p. 124.

[16] For a similar interpretation of John's characters see Raymond F. Collins, "The Representative Figures of the Fourth Gospel." I am also indebted to a seminar paper by David M. Hughes.

[17] Harvey, *Character and the Novel*, p. 144.

Characterization in the Gospel of John

Before turning to the individual characters in John, we must face the question of the legitimacy of treating the people described in a historical writing as characters. If the evangelist drew upon oral tradition which derived from those who knew the various people involved in the story and told of events which actually happened, is it not a blatant distortion to apply the canons of fictional literature to the study of these people? On the other side, does it not distort the concept "characterization" to apply it to the description of persons in historical or biographical literature?

These questions bristle with difficulties. No doubt there are various concepts of "characterization."[18] There is certainly a divergence of opinion as to how much of John can be considered "history" and how much "fiction." The differences, however, do not diminish the importance of our questions. We are presently interested in characterization as the art and techniques by which an author fashions a convincing portrait of a person within a more or less unified piece of writing. Even if one is disposed to see real, historical persons behind every character in John and actual events in every episode, the question of how the author chose to portray the person still arises. With what techniques or devices has he made a living person live on paper, and how is this "person" related to the rest of the narrative? In any description there is necessarily an element of selectivity. What principles or norms for selection are operative within John? How does what the author chooses to tell about some characters relate to what he chooses to tell about others? Even if the figure is "real" rather than "fictional," it has to pass through the mind of the author before it can be described. It is therefore, for our present purposes, immaterial whether the literary character has its origin in historical tradition, memory, or imagination. The writer has a distinct understanding of a person and his or her role in a significant sequence of events. How does he, sometimes with only a few words, communicate his understanding of the person to a reader and represent a convincing portrait?[19] We are presently interested in the relationships between author and text and text and reader rather than the origin of the characters or the relationship of historical persons to the author. So, for example, we are dealing with Jesus as he is portrayed

---

[18] See Rawdon Wilson, "The Bright Chimera," p. 730.

[19] Ian Watt, "Realism and the Novel Form," pp. 96–97, compares readers to a jury: "both must be satisfied as to the identities of the parties concerned. ..." The analogy is particularly appropriate for John, for the entire gospel can be seen as a trial narrative. See A. E. Harvey, *Jesus on Trial.*

in the story, not with the historical person. The writer's basic means of characterization are few but highly supple. Characters are fashioned by what the narrator says about them, particularly when introducing them, what they say, what they do, and how other characters react to them.[20] Each of these is important in the Gospel of John.

Apart from the Father and Jesus, whose characterization dominates the gospel, the other characters fall into a limited number of groups: the disciples; "the Jews," the Pharisees and those aligned with them; and the crowd and those minor characters caught between Jesus and those who oppose him. The minor characters, as we will see, have a disproportionately high representational value. They are vital to the fulfillment of the gospel's purposes.

JESUS AND THE FATHER

Jesus. We have already noted the centrality of Jesus in the gospel. There is hardly a scene in which he does not appear. Because virtually the whole gospel is devoted to what he says and and how others react to him, only the central features of his characterization can be selected for emphasis.

One measure of the enormity of Jesus in John is that he has some role in all five of the time periods identified in Chapter 3: the pre-historical past, the historical past, the narrative present, the historical future, and the eschatological future. As the divine *logos* he was always with God and was His agent in creation. In this respect the *logos* assumes the role which had been attributed to Wisdom in earlier literature.[21] The life of men, which has the potential of being received for eternity, derives from him (1:4). During the historical past, the history of Israel, he came into the world and enlightened those who had eyes to see him (1:9). Moses and the prophets wrote about him (1:45; 5:46), and Abraham saw his "day" (8:56). Isaiah, presumably in his heavenly vision (Isaiah 6), saw "his glory" (12:41). No one actually saw him, just as no one was able to see God (1:18; 6:46), but there is little doubt that for John the *logos* was the inspiration of the prophets and Jesus was the fulfillment to which they pointed. What he did fulfilled their hopes (12:38; 13:18; 15:25; 17:12; 19:24, 36). The gospel itself presents Jesus as the incarnation of the *logos* continuing the work of revelation, healing, and creation. It is entirely

---

[20] Abrams, *A Glossary of Literary Terms,* p. 21; Rhoads, "Narrative Criticism and the Gospel of Mark," p. 417; Robert Alter, *The Art of Biblical Narrative,* pp. 116–17.

[21] Charles H. Talbert, *What is a Gospel,* pp. 53–77.

appropriate that he has power over nature (i.e., walking on water), over the broken and imperfect bodies of men, and even over death. After all, he was the creator and source of life. No one had ever heard of such things being done (9:32). Fittingly, his act of breathing spirit into his disciples re-enacts the primordial image of the creation of man (cf. Gen. 2:7; John 20:22). The resurrection tacitly demonstrates that his self-manifestation was in fact the self-manifestation of God.[22] In spite of the blindness of most of Jesus' contemporaries, the reader should see that all that Jesus does and says points to his identity as the divine *logos*. During the author's present, the period of the church, Jesus is present and active through his words and above all through the Paraclete.[23] Much of what Jesus says, particularly in the farewell discourse, is intended for the disciples, or the church, in the story world's future. Finally, in the eschatological future, Jesus will be "the Son of Man" who raises the dead and pronounces judgment (5:21–29; 8:28). These activities are foreshadowed, and indeed have already begun, in Jesus' ministry. He raises Lazarus, and the judgment is determined by the world's response to Jesus (3:19). Not only does Jesus have roles in the past and future as *logos,* Son of God, or Son of Man, but there is a basic continuity which is not confined to individual periods. Each period serves as an interpretive context for every other period. No one period is large enough to reveal him adequately.

The introduction of Jesus, therefore, had to be handled carefully in order for the reader to be able to begin immediately to understand what he did. Jesus is introduced elaborately but somewhat indirectly. The prologue speaks of the *logos,* light, and life. Jesus' name is first mentioned along with the nominal title "Christ" in juxtaposition to Moses in 1:17. From the context, one is to infer that he is the one who was spoken of earlier. The next verse states that he is in the bosom of the Father and has made him known. By the end of the prologue the reader knows Jesus' origin and status and the primary significance of his life. The reader also knows the nature of his relationship to God (the Father), darkness, John the Baptist, the world, "his own," and Moses. John the Baptist, who has been identified as a man "sent from God," bears witness before opposition that Jesus is:

1.   the one coming after him who was before him (1:15, 27, 30);
2.   the lamb of God that takes away the sin of the world (1:29);
3.   the one on whom the Spirit descended (1:32–33);
4.   the son of God (1:34).

---

[22] Hans W. Frei, *The Eclipse of Biblical Narrative,* p. 315.

[23] See D. Moody Smith, "The Presentation of Jesus in the Fourth Gospel," p. 376.

The prologue and the divinely authorized testimony of John together provide the following "script" for Jesus: he will come to his own, authorize those who believe to become "children of God," give grace and truth, reveal God, and take away the sin of the world. The reader can expect that he will be rejected by his own, witnessed to by John, and believed by some. All of these expectations are later fulfilled, but the introduction to Jesus gives no real clues as to what he will do or how he will fulfill his commission. There is no reference to his "works" or his death. Jesus then appears for the first time in the narrative in 1:29, but does not speak until 1:38. There his first words are a question whose meaning can be extended to existential depths: "What are you seeking?" By the time Jesus appears it is clear that he bears and establishes all the religious norms and ideals but that he will be opposed by the religious authorities. The basis is thereby laid for a trenchant critique of the Jewish religious authorities.

What Jesus says about himself and his mission progressively defines his relationship to the Father and exposes the blindness of others. Jesus' dialogue gives the impression that he is always conscious of his dependence on the Father.[24] In an important character-defining statement Jesus says that his food is "that I may do the will of the one who sent me and that I may complete his work" (4:34). In the next chapter he employs a proverb: "the Son can do nothing of his own accord, but only what he sees the Father doing" (5:19). The works he does have been given to him by the Father that he should complete them (5:36), and they will not be finished until his death (19:30; cf. 17:4). One of the most complete statements of this will that guides Jesus is found in 6:40—"For this is the will of my Father, that every one who sees the Son and believes in him should have eternal life; and I will raise him up at the last day." It is to carry out this will, Jesus says, that he "came down from heaven" (6:38). His highest claim for himself is that he and the Father are one (10:30; cf. 10:36, 38). Unity with the Father colors Jesus' characterization throughout the gospel. He is omniscient, like the Father, and there is apparently nothing that the Father knows that Jesus does not know (in contrast to Mark 10:40; 13:32). Jesus knows who his betrayer is from the beginning (6:64) and speaks not only of his return to the Father but of his past in the history of Israel and his role on "the last day." He knows of his "hour" from the very beginning (2:4) and knows what is in the hearts of men (2:24; 1:47–48; 6:15). At times the evangelist takes extra pains to protect Jesus' omni-

---

[24] Cf. J. Ernest Davey, *The Jesus of St. John*, esp. pp. 77–78; J. A. T. Robinson, "The Use of the Fourth Gospel for Christology Today," p. 68: ". . . a man whose life was lived in *absolutely intimate dependence* (stressing all three words) upon God as his Father." See also C. K. Barrett, "'The Father is Greater than I' (Jo 14, 28)," pp. 144–59.

science, as in 6:6. Because he knows all things, Jesus never needs to ask for information and is never told anything he does not know. Because he is one with the Father, he never prays that the Father's will might be changed (cf. 12:27–28; Mark 14:36).[25] What Jesus does ask for in his prayer in chapter 17 is the fulfillment of the Father's will, the glorification of the Father, and security and unity with God for the disciples.[26] Likewise, when the Father speaks to Jesus it is not because Jesus needs confirmation but for the sake of the crowd (12:28–30; contrast the more private experiences of the heavenly voice in Mark). Jesus is supremely the Father's emissary fulfilling the Father's will.

Jesus' statements about himself not only employ the divine "I am" (8:24, 28, 58) but also press the gospel's images and themes into service. Each image is developed in various passages and related to Jesus. Each serves in one way or another to enrich the disclosure of Jesus' identity. Since these will be treated in detail in the next chapter, it is sufficient merely to list the predicates of Jesus' "I am" statements here: the bread of life (6:35, 48), the bread which came down from heaven (6:41), the living bread (6:51), the light of the world (8:12), the door of the sheep (10:7, 9), the good shepherd (10:11, 14), the resurrection and the life (11:25), the way, the truth, and the life (14:6), the vine (15:5). Just as there is glory to be seen in the flesh, so the mundane can point to a higher reality, which Jesus both embodies and reveals to those who will believe him.

Another group of statements shows that Jesus knows all along the outcome of his mission. He speaks not only of his return to the Father, but of the continuing struggle of belief against unbelief. "The world," often represented by "the Jews" or their leaders, will continue in darkness and unbelief. Those who believe will be persecuted (15:18–16:4). Peter will die a martyr's death (13:36; 21:19), but the community will continue under the leadership of the Paraclete. Jesus' words about himself, his relation to the Father, and his mission are therefore a defining feature of his characterization. His own summary or characterization of his public ministry, which has the appearance of a soliloquy, ends with, "What I say, therefore, I say as the Father has bidden me" (12:50).[27]

One of the most interesting aspects of the gospel's characterization of Jesus is the range of emotions and motives it ascribes to him. While Jesus is not entirely lacking in human emotions, his emotional responses are noticeably different and therefore convey a sense of his being distant or

---

[25] Raymond E. Brown, *The Community of the Beloved Disciple*, p. 115.

[26] On prayer in ancient literature see Scholes and Kellogg, *The Nature of Narrative*, pp. 200–01.

[27] On the formal characteristics of soliloquy see Chatman, *Story and Discourse*, pp. 178–79.

aloof. Whatever the precise connotation of his words to his mother during the wedding at Cana (2:2), there is a certain coldness about them. At the temple he acts out anger, but his actions are interpreted as zeal (2:17). The words used to describe Jesus' anger elsewhere (ὀργή, ὀργίζομαι, cf. Mark 3:5; 1:41) are not used of Jesus in John. The feeling of distance is strengthened by the comment that Jesus did not trust himself to those who did not have an adequate faith (2:24–25). His "dig" at Nicodemus (3:10) shows a touch of sarcasm along with freedom from social and religious conventions: "Are you a teacher of Israel, and yet you do not understand this?" This freedom, however, does not reflect on his piety, for he faithfully travels to Jerusalem for each of the major festivals. Travel may weary him (4:6), but water and food are for him primarily symbolic of higher realities (4:7, 32; 18:11; 19:28). Others come to him for bread (6:26, 30–31) and water (4:14; 7:37), but there is no statement of his compassion for the hungry multitude (cf. Matt. 14:14; Mark 6:34). In fact "compassion" (σπλαγχνίζομαι, σπλάγχνον) is not in John's vocabulary (cf. 1 John 3:17), although each of the other evangelists uses it to describe Jesus' actions on several occasions.

The gospel does not "humanize" Jesus by having him surrounded by children either (cf. Mark 10:13–16 par.). In fact, although touching and physical contact with Jesus are important in the synoptic gospels, there is none of this in John.[28] The only time the verb "to touch" (ἅπτεσθαι) is used is in 20:17—"Don't touch me!" Jesus exerts his authority in religious matters such as sabbath observance and the Law, and he shows disregard for established prejudices by engaging the Samaritan woman in conversation (compare the disciples' reaction—4:27). He perceptively challenges the lame man's desire to be well, and he tests Philip (6:6). Others, however, seem to have little or no influence on him, for repeatedly he denies their requests and even when he ultimately complies he moves at his own time and initiative (2:3ff.; 7:3ff.; 11:3ff.). While "manifesting" himself to the world, he shuns public appeal and political activity. Shrewdly, he always seems to know just when his opponents have reached the boiling point and when to withdraw (3:22; 6:15; 8:59; 10:39–40; 11:54; 13:36). On the other hand, he is capable of bold, public confrontations. His concern that others believe in him leads him on more than one occasion to find individuals who have been challenged by his opponents (5:14; 9:35).

There are more references to Jesus' emotions in John 11 than in any other chapter, and at this point they become particularly intense. Still, there is the difference. Jesus loves Martha, Mary, and Lazarus (11:3, 5, 36), but delays before responding to their call for help. He rejoices in

---

[28] André Feuillet, *Johannine Studies*, p. 24.

John, but only one time: he rejoices when Lazarus dies, because his death provides an opportunity for the disciples to believe (cf. 2:11; 6:64). When Jesus sees Mary and those accompanying her weeping he is deeply moved. The verbs in John 11:33 denote strong emotions, possibly but not necessarily anger. Jesus' emotion rises again when he approaches the tomb and when he considers his own death (11:38; 12:27 [quoting Ps. 6:3–4]; and 13:21). The pattern of these emotions suggests that it is the approach of his own death rather than death in general or Mary's lack of understanding which moves him so deeply. The verbs and contexts allow for various interpretations and shades of meaning. The point remains, however, that Jesus' emotion again in this instance is peculiar; it seems to arise from his foreknowledge of his own death. Only his weeping in 11:35 and his gratitude to God in 11:41 are entirely normal human reactions. The verb used in 12:44 to describe Jesus' speech is used in the synoptics for crying out, the cry of demoniacs, and the death cry of Jesus; but in John it appears to be used with a less intense sense. John the Baptist and Jesus "call out" as they preach and teach (1:15; 7:28, 37). The narrator tells us that Jesus loves the Beloved Disciple and "his own" as well as Mary, Martha, and Lazarus (13:1, 33, 34; 14:21; 15:9, 12; 17:23; 19:26; 20:2; 21:7, 20), but except for Jesus' defense of Mary (12:7–8), the footwashing, and the favored place for the Beloved Disciple at the table, there is little evidence of warmth in these relationships. There is a great deal of talk about love in John, but Jesus does not seem to be very loving. As Jesus enters his final hours (after Judas' departure), he seems to be entirely placid. The absence of any reference to his emotions in chapters 14–19 may be due to the shift to an external point of view that one finds here and to John's emphasis on Jesus' control over these events. At most one has evidence of acted out emotion: Jesus confronts his accusers boldly (18:6, 23), he does not defer to Pilate as to a superior, and he shows concern for his mother in his final moments. His thirst has high symbolic and thematic significance, but it is entirely appropriate. He does not return the warmth and affection of Mary Magdalene, but rather is moved by a higher commitment (20:16–17). Finally, his appearance to Thomas may have been motivated by concern for Thomas and the belief of others (20:26–29).

In John, therefore, Jesus is demonstrably less emotional than in the synoptic gospels, and one suspects that this aspect of his characterization fits with John's insistence that Jesus was the incarnation of the preexistent *logos*. He is "not of this world" (8:23; 17:14). His emotions tend to run on a rather flat plane from troubled to untroubled, and there are no real highs. If John's emphasis on Jesus' "logo-nature" requires or explains his failure to give a more convincing portrayal of Jesus' "human nature," then Ernst Käsemann's verdict that John shows Jesus as a god

"striding upon the earth" is not far from the truth, and later docetic interpretations of the gospel are not entirely ill-founded.[29]

Not only are Jesus' emotional responses peculiar, but his exchanges
with other characters often provoke rejection. Jesus seems to be congeni-
tally incapable of giving a straight answer.[30] When the Samaritan woman
asks how it is that he is asking her, a woman of Samaria, for a drink, Jesus
answers that if she knew the gift of God she would have asked him for a
drink (4:9–10). When the crowd asks why he came to Capernaum, he
says, "You seek me, not because you saw signs, but because you ate your
fill of the loaves" (6:26). He almost deliberately alienates the Jews who
ask how he can give his flesh by answering, "Unless you eat the flesh of the
Son of man and drink his blood, you have no life in you" (6:53). Even his
disciples find him so enigmatic (13:36–38) and confrontive (14:8–10) that
they are afraid to question him (4:27; 16:17–19). Jesus' non-answers
allow him to retain control while moving conversations to higher planes,
but it is not hard to understand why he provokes hostility.

John insists on the recognition of Jesus' divinity and his origin from
above. Rather than a narrative approximation of the later Chalcedonian
confession, this gospel provides a canonical balance which legitimizes the
later confessions. Still, there remains a "heart of darkness" in the character of Jesus in the sense that the "central mystery is never quite penetrated," never fully exposed.[31] Like most good plots and all good characters, John and its Jesus retain areas of shadow and mystery it will not
illuminate for the reader. That is part of its power and its fascination.

The Father. In 1975 Nils Dahl labeled the theme "God in the New
Testament" "The Neglected Factor in New Testament Theology."[32] Although a survey of Johannine literature shows that "God" has fared better
there than in New Testament theology as a whole, if only because of
interest in the Father-Son relationship,[33] Dahl's assessment still stands:

---

[29] *The Testament of Jesus According to John 17*, p. 73. Cf. Brown, *The Community
of the Beloved Disciple,* pp. 97–123, esp. p. 116, and R. Alan Culpepper, *The
Johannine School,* pp. 282–83. See also Robinson, "The Use of the Fourth
Gospel for Christology Today," pp. 65–67.

[30] A. D. Nuttall, *Overheard by God,* p. 131.

[31] Harvey, *Character and the Novel,* p. 71.

[32] "The Neglected Factor in New Testament Theology," pp. 5–8. See also John R.
Donahue, "A Neglected Factor."

[33] C. K. Barrett, "Christocentric or Theocentric," pp. 361–76; G. B. Caird, "The
Glory of God in the Fourth Gospel"; Edwin K. Lee, *The Religious Thought of
St. John,* pp. 32–55; Juan P. Miranda, *Der Vater, der mich gesandt hat;* G.
Schrenk, "*Patēr,*" pp. 996–1003; M. C. Tenney, "Topics from the Gospel of
John"; David A. Fennema, "Jesus and God According to John."

insufficient attention has been given to the theo-logy of the gospel *per se*.[34]

It is difficult to describe the characterization of God in the gospel because God never appears and the only words He speaks are "and I have glorified it, and I will glorify it again" (12:28). God is characterized not by what He says or does but by what Jesus, His fully authorized emissary, says about Him. Even to describe the situation in these terms, however, is to risk distortion, for John takes pains to have Jesus affirm that he who has seen him has seen the Father (14:9), that the works he does have been given to him by the Father (5:36), that his words are not his own but the Father's (12:50), and that he can do nothing of himself (5:19). It might be better, therefore, to say that God is characterized by Jesus and that having understood the gospel's characterization of Jesus one has grasped its characterization of God. Yet in spite of the gospel's emphasis on the unity of the two, they are separate, Father and son; and the Father, who is referred to 118 times in John, requires independent consideration.[35]

If Jesus is "aloof" or "distant," God is necessarily more so. His predominant "character"-istic is that he sent Jesus. He is referred to in various forms as "the one who sent" (ὁ πέμψας με πατήρ) twenty-three times, and seventeen times ἀποστέλλω is used of His sending Jesus.[36] "Sending" characterizes God's self-revelation. The Father "gives" or invests Jesus with Life (5:26), his works (5:36), what he should say (12:49; 14:10, 24, 31; 17:8), his name (17:11), and his glory (17:22, 24).[37] The implicit corollary is that the one who sent is in some sense distant from those who receive. John the Baptist (1:6) and Jesus (7:29; 9:16, 33; 16:27; 17:8), and all that he mediates, are "from God" (1:14; 5:44; 8:26, 40; 10:18; 15:15, 26; 17:7). The dualism between that which is from God and that which is not is thereby established, so being "from God" has more spiritual than spatial connotations. God is the reality beyond, the transcendent presence.

The references to God are less numerous and more static than the references to "the Father." "God" often appears in the genitive: "children of God" (1:12; 11:52), "the lamb of God" (1:29, 36), "the angels of God" (1:51), "the kingdom of God" (3:3), "the words of God" (3:36), "the gift of God" (4:10), "the love of God" (5:42), "the works of God" (6:28; 9:3), "the bread of God" (6:33), "the holy one of God" (6:69), "the glory of God"

---

[34] One measure of this inattention is the fact that there is no section on God in Robert Kysar's comprehensive review of contemporary Johannine scholarship (*The Fourth Evangelist and His Gospel*).

[35] Tenney, "Topics from the Gospel of John," p. 38, counts 118 references. Schrenk, "*Patēr*," p. 996, counts 115.

[36] Tenney, "Topics from the Gospel of John," p. 43, makes the interesting observation that the word *sent* occurs five times in each of the main confrontations with the Jews (chapters 5, 6, 7, and 8) and twice in 20:21.

[37] D. Bruce Woll, *Johannine Christianity in Conflict*, p. 50.

(11:40; 12:43), "the son of God" (10:36; 20:31). More direct are the statements "God is light" (3:21), "God is true" (3:33), "God is spirit" (4:24) and "the only (true) God" (5:44; 17:3). These statements further emphasize His distance or otherness. There are only a few verbs (apart from sending) which have God as their subject: God loved the world (3:16), set his seal on the Son of Man (6:27); spoke to Moses (9:29), and allegedly does not hear sinners (9:31). "The Father" (in semantic though not ontological contrast) is much more active: he loves the son (3:35; 5:20; 10:17; 15:9), seeks those who will worship him in spirit and truth (4:23), is still working (5:17), raises the dead (5:21), bears witness to Jesus (5:36, 37; 8:18), gives bread from heaven (6:32), gives followers to Jesus (6:37), draws them to him (6:44), has taught Jesus (8:28), glorifies him (8:54), knows him (10:15), sanctified and sent the word into the world (10:36), will honor believers (12:26), and has given a commandment (12:49) and all things into Jesus' hands (13:3). He will love those who love Jesus (14:21, 23), will send the Paraclete (14:26), and give to those who ask in Jesus' name (15:16; 16:23). He loves the disciples (16:27). The important statement "I am going to my Father and your Father" (20:17) drives home the point made repeatedly in the farewell discourse: by believing that Jesus is from God, the believer is able to know God as Father.

Jesus repeatedly challenges the Jews' contention that they know God (7:28–29; 8:19, 54–55; 15:21; 16:3; 17:25), saying that they do not know God because they do not know him, but he knows God (10:15). And, he who knows Jesus knows his Father and has eternal life (14:7; 17:3). In John, therefore, there is a conflict of concepts of God, a conflict of understandings of how God is known (preeminently through Jesus or preeminently through the Torah), and a resulting conflict in commitments and self-understandings. Jesus reveals a god who loves the world, including Samaritans and sinners (9:2–3, 34), and who values healing above strict observance of the sabbath (5:16–17). The heart of the conflict, however, is less a difference in the concept of God than difference in the locus of his ultimate self-revelation. Jesus' claims of preeminence over all prior revelation, claims which express the Christology of the church, are the point of contention.

No one has seen God, but Jesus has made Him known (1:18). While John stringently maintains God's transcendence, it also depicts God as a "Father" who loves and seeks a believing response in the world. All initiative remains with Him as He "gives" and "draws" believers, but believing, more precisely believing in Jesus as the revealer, is necessary. Those who believe become children of God in that they know God as Father, and He abides in them through the Paraclete. They will know the truth and have peace, joy, and eternal life. The effect of the revelation in

Jesus, therefore, is to enable others to share in his relationship to the Father. This is the experience the author seeks to pass on to readers of the gospel.

THE DISCIPLES

The role of the disciples in John has escaped the intense interest which has recently been turned on their role in Mark.[38] Collectively and individually the disciples are models or representatives with whom readers may identify. They are marked especially by their recognition of Jesus and belief in his claims. Yet, they are not exemplars of perfect faith, but of positive responses and typical misunderstandings.[39] At times they have a significant role in the development of the plot; they are above all those who become "children of God." They are also surrogates for the church and the reader in the farewell discourse, and often ask the questions that may naturally occur to the reader along the way. For this reason, it is significant that John uses the term "disciples" (seventy-eight times) much more frequently than "the twelve" (four times) or "the apostles" (never; cf. 13:16). "Disciples" more easily includes believing readers, though John stops short of presenting any command to "go and make disciples" (cf. Matt. 28:19).

The disciples enter the story when John the Baptist points two of his followers to Jesus (1:35ff.). The conversation is typically Johannine in that it yields to multiple meanings. Jesus turns and asks, "What are you looking for?"—a question with profound existential overtones. The two answer by addressing Jesus as "rabbi" and asking, "Where are you staying [or abiding]?" The eventual answer will be that he abides with them (14:23; 15:4–10), but Jesus answers, "come and you will see." In following Jesus they will see his glory, and in seeing him they will see the Father (2:11; 14:9). Philip is the only disciple Jesus explicitly calls (1:43; cf. 21:22). The other disciples who are named begin to follow Jesus because they have been told about him by another of the disciples. The pattern for the role of the disciples in bringing faith to others is therefore established

---

[38] See, however: R. Moreno Jiménez, "El discípulo de Jesucristo"; Anselm Schulz, *Nachfolgen und Nachahmen*, pp. 137–44, 161–76.

[39] Urban C. von Wahlde, "The Witnesses to Jesus in John 5:31–40 and Belief in the Fourth Gospel," pp. 399, 404, describes the disciples as "perfect models for the total response to the witness of the Father." Marinus de Jonge, *Jesus*, p. 15, offers a better analysis: ". . . the disciples, both in their acceptance and their misunderstandings of Jesus' words, are portrayed as models for future generations of believers."

at the very beginning. The disciples confer virtually all of the church's titles for Jesus upon him at the outset: Messiah or Christ (1:41), the one of whom Moses and the prophets wrote (1:45), the son of God (1:49), the king of Israel (1:49). In sharp contrast to the Gospel of Mark, where the disciples struggle without much success to discern who Jesus is, in John they know from the very beginning. The disciples do not have the benefit of the prologue's affirmation of Jesus' pre-existence, but other than that the disciples have a fair start with the reader; both know who Jesus is, both know what others in the story will learn only later. It is arguable that the disciples do not at this point understand all of the ramifications John attaches to these confessions, but neither does the reader. The reader and the disciples will move more or less together through the story, but of course the reader will be aided by the narrator.

The next crucial step is the faith of the disciples. By separating the affirmation that they beheld his glory and believed (2:11) from their coming to Jesus with high confessions, the evangelist leaves the implication that the two are in fact to be distinguished. The faith of the disciples is at first a faith based on signs (2:11). Their believing is based on seeing (1:36, 39, 46, 51). Others "believe in his name" because they see the signs, but Jesus does not entrust himself to them (2:23–24; cf. 1:12 and 2:11). What is the difference between these and the disciples? Both begin with a signs-faith, but the disciples have already shown a willingness to "follow" Jesus (1:37, 38, 40), and they remember what Jesus said (2:22). Faith which does not lead to following is therefore inadequate. "Abiding" is the test of discipleship (cf. 8:31).

The succeeding chapters show the disciples fulfilling the role of a rabbi's pupils. They spend time together (3:22). They address him as "rabbi" (1:38, 49; 4:31; 9:2; 11:8), and they go to buy food for him (4:8, 31). They also baptize (4:2—though this verse has the appearance of a gloss). Their awe of Jesus becomes apparent in that while they are amazed that he would speak to a woman they will not question him (4:27; cf. 16:19). Moreover, although they believe they still do not understand everything Jesus says (4:33). Like others in the story, they at times miss his true meaning by seizing the surface meaning of his metaphors. Did the disciples go to Jerusalem for the feast (chapter 5)? John's silence about the disciples throughout chapter 5 and the suggestion of Jesus' brothers in 7:3 imply that the disciples were not with Jesus everywhere he went or that only a part of this sizable group actually followed him around (3:26; 4:1; 6:66).

The crisis comes in John 6. First they witness the feeding of the multitude. Andrew calls attention to the boy with the bread and fish, but the disciples have no real part in feeding the crowd. They only collect the scraps. Jesus does not send them across the lake but comes to them in their distress. The crisis itself comes rather unexpectedly. The disciples started out with the grand confessions in chapter 1 and beheld Jesus' glory at Cana. Why do some of them defect? The stumbling block is not opposition from Jesus' opponents or demands that the disciples share in cross bearing. Jesus' words are the offense. The issue is the acceptability of the revealer, not the danger of persecution. The defection follows: (1) Jesus' first ἐγώ εἰμι (I am) sayings (6:20, 35, 41, 48, 51; cf. 4:26), (2) his implicit claim to superiority over Moses (esp. 6:32–35), and (3) the eucharistic language of the preceding discourse: "This is a hard saying [λόγος]; who can listen to it?" (6:60). Some misunderstand—it is hard to see how they could do otherwise—and defect from the group. Although they are disciples, they do not believe (6:64)! Those who remain with Jesus do so precisely because he has "the words of eternal life" (6:68). Abiding and abandoning are both responses to Jesus' words; the difference derives from the perception of the hearer. "The twelve" are mentioned for the first time in 6:67. There is no mention of their being appointed or commissioned (see, however, 6:70; 13:18; 15:16, 19). They are more nearly the remnant that survives this collapse of Jesus' following, and one of them will betray him. In this context, the next reference to the disciples may be tinged with some irony. The brothers challenge Jesus to go to Jerusalem so that his disciples can see his works. The previous episodes have made it clear, however, that while Jesus' works attract disciples his words drive them away. Most of the disciples were willing to accept Jesus as a worker of wonders but not as the *logos* of God, His authorized emissary, the revealer. This is the real test of the disciple: "If you continue in my word [λόγος], you are truly my disciples" (8:31).

John is again silent about the disciples throughout Jesus' most intense confrontation with "the Jews." The only mention of them in the four chapters following 7:3 is 9:2, where they show that their understanding of sin and retribution is the popular notion that affliction and misfortune are God's judgment upon a sinner. Here they are little more than a foil or contrast for Jesus' response to the blind man. Their time for confrontation with the Jews has not yet come (cf. 15:18ff.). It is again noteworthy that neither Jesus' conflict with the Jews nor the threat of persecution and death seems to discourage the disciples at all. The next reference to them shows that they are ready to go back to Judea with him even if it means dying with him (11:7–16). In this conversation they again misunderstand Jesus because they take his metaphor for death (i.e., "sleep") literally. This misunderstanding is part of a pattern. The disciples do not understand Jesus' words about his body as temple (2:21–22); they do not understand what sustains Jesus (4:32–33); they do not understand the relationship between sin and suffering (9:2); they do not understand the experience of death (11:11–15); and they do not understand the significance of the entry into Jerusalem (12:16). These things will only be clear to them later. In the meantime their lack of understanding does not pose any threat to their discipleship. (Here again there is a significant difference between John and Mark.) The narrator reported that they believed as early as 2:11, but they still need to believe (11:15). They have not yet grasped the meaning of the ζωὴ αἰώνιος (LIFE) Jesus gives to those who believe. When Jesus withdraws, the disciples go with him (11:54). They are again with him at the home of his friends in Bethany (12:4) and enter Jerusalem with him (12:16, 20ff.).

What has only been implied about the experience of the disciples becomes much clearer when Jesus washes their feet, though the disciples themselves will only understand it later (13:7). Jesus' assumption of the role of a servant exemplifies the attitude they should have toward one another (13:12–17): they will be set apart by their love for one another (13:34–35). Jesus' answer to Peter earlier (13:10) may again affirm the continuing nature of the disciples' dependence on Jesus—although they are clean (cf. 15:3), they still need to have their feet washed. Jesus still has to die for them, and some of them will need to die for him![40] The disciples will also need other upper room experiences. Such experiences will be possible through the Paraclete. In the farewell discourse Jesus speaks further about the ideal role of the disciples and their future experience, but this reflects John's concept of discipleship rather than his characterization of the disciples. What does emerge about the disciples from their questions (13:36; 14:5, 8, 22) is that they have grasped very little of what Jesus has revealed to them. They do not know where he is going (13:36;

---

[40] James D. G. Dunn's interpretation, "The Washing of the Disciples' Feet in John 13:1–20," is persuasive: "The footwashing thus stands as one of the long line of metaphors and pictures . . . Jesus in washing his disciples' feet is acting out what his death will accomplish for his disciples." Herold Weiss' thesis in "Foot Washing in the Johannine Community," ". . . that the Johannine community performed the act as preparation for martyrdom" (p. 320), has the strength of relating the practice to the Johannine community and the clear and present threat of martyrdom (16:2). The connection he draws between the disciples' mandate to bear fruit (15:8) and the requirement that the seed die before it can bear fruit (12:24–25) is plausible. Transference of the parable interpreting Jesus' death to the role of the disciples is problematic, however. Martyrdom is only one path of discipleship. Peter represents the type of disciple who will experience martyrdom, but the Beloved Disciple is no less loved because he will not be martyred. Weiss' suggestion that members of the community were looked upon either as servants (who may have stayed only temporarily) or friends (pp. 321–23) should be modified to take into account the ultimate designation of the disciples as "brothers" and children of God (see R. Alan Culpepper, "The Pivot of John's Prologue," pp. 26–31).

14:5). They do not know "the way" to the Father or that they have seen Him in Jesus (14:5–11). They have in fact scarcely gotten beyond a "signs faith" (14:11). They do not understand what Jesus says about the "little while" (16:17–18). Even at the end of the discourse, when the disciples think they have got it, they can only parrot proudly what Jesus has just said (cf. 16:27, 29). Their answer is scarcely more than Nicodemus' opening statement (3:2): "You are a teacher come from God." Jesus confirms that their faith is still imperfect with his skeptical query: "Do you now believe?" (16:31). They will each be scattered to their own homes (16:32). Only his death and resurrection, his glorification, will enable them to understand what he has revealed.

The disciples follow Jesus to his appointment with destiny. In the garden they do not abandon Jesus (cf. Mark 14:50). He offers to go with his powerless captors on the condition that the disciples be allowed to go free (18:8–9; cf. 6:67). Peter offers zealous if misguided resistance, but Jesus lays down his life for his friends. Peter follows Jesus at a distance. He would take on Malchus with a sword, but the servant girl and the hostile courtyard are too much for him. While Annas is concerned that Jesus' disciples may pose a threat, Peter is busy denying Jesus (18:19). Only the Beloved Disciple is mentioned at the cross (19:26–27). Joseph of Arimathea, a disciple in hiding, buries Jesus assisted by Nicodemus (19:38–39). The disciples, presumably, are hiding.

The last two chapters resolve the difficulties between Jesus and the disciples and confirm their standing as "children of God" and their future roles. The "race" between Peter and the Beloved Disciple and their responses to Jesus in the lake scene confirm Peter's leadership and pastoral roles and the Beloved Disciple's special relationship to Jesus, his discernment, and his reliability as a witness. The disciples are finally commissioned and inspired (literally) for their work as apostles (20:21–23). Jesus' work, taking away the sin of the world (i.e., unbelief; 16:8–9), will be continued by the disciples, but they are totally dependent upon the risen Lord. They are not even able to convince one of their own (Thomas). The mini-drama of Thomas' refusal to believe is resolved by another appearance, and his doubt is given representative value for all future skeptics (20:29).

From within the inner group of disciples, seven emerge as individuals in the course of the narrative. *Andrew* remains in the shadow of his more illustrious brother, which is true to the way the narrator introduces him: "Andrew, Simon Peter's brother" (1:40). He is given the honor of introducing his brother to Jesus with the confession for which Peter would be famous in other circles: "We have found the Messiah" (1:41; cf. Mark 8:29 par.). Andrew responds to each situation by introducing others to

Jesus: his brother (1:41), the boy (6:8), and the Greeks (12:22).[41] Like his more famous brother, though in a different way, he too is an appropriate model of the disciple that bears much fruit (15:8).

Andrew is otherwise paired with *Philip,* who is also from the village of Bethsaida (1:44; 6:7–8; 12:21–22). In this pair, Philip is the less perceptive (6:5–7; 12:21–22; 14:8). Although he begins well by bringing Nathanael to Jesus, he fails both his "bread" test and his "Greek" test. He does not understand that the Father is revealed in Jesus. Regardless of how limited his understanding is, however, he is still a disciple.

Next to Jesus, *Peter* is the most complex character. Peter's story traces his preparation for the twin tasks of shepherding and martyrdom. He is given the task of tending the sheep, and like the good shepherd he will have to lay down his life for the sheep (10:14–16; 21:15–19). At their first meeting Jesus already knows his name, "Simon," but says he should be called "Cephas" (i.e., "rock"; 1:42), but why? Is it because Jesus perceived his future potential for stable leadership (a future that is at best only alluded to in John) or because Jesus knows how fickle he will be? The Johannine equivalent to Peter's confession at Caesarea Philippi is his confession at the crisis, "Lord, to whom shall we go? You have the words of eternal life; and we have believed, and have come to know that you are the Holy One of God" (6:68–69). He has grasped the importance of Jesus' words, his glory, and the life his words give. Paradoxically, the words of life may also require death, and this Peter has not yet grasped. Because he has not understood that Jesus must give his life in service to "his own," he refuses to let Jesus wash his feet. Still misunderstanding, he then fails to see that he is clean (from Jesus' word?—15:3). The foot washing is probably related to the anointing of Jesus' feet for his burial (12:3, 7; 13:6–7).[42] Peter does not understand the connection or the meaning of the foot washing at the time, but he will later. He is not able to follow Jesus because he has not seen that "the Holy One of God" (6:69) must lay down his life. In this respect the Johannine characterization of Peter is strikingly similar to the synoptics (cf. Mark 8:29, 31–32 and par.). Ironically, he will make good his boast of following Jesus; the disciple who resists Jesus' dying will himself follow Jesus in martyrdom, but later (13:36–38). His misunderstanding leads him to take the sword in needless, violent defense of Jesus. In doing so Peter unfortunately represents a whole host of later would-be disciples. Significantly, what Peter denies in John is not that Jesus is Lord but that he is his disciple (18:17, 25, 27). Jesus is on his way to death and (at the time at least) Peter is no follower of his. Peter conse-

---

[41] Cf. Peter N. Peterson, *Andrew, Brother of Simon Peter.*

[42] Weiss, "Foot Washing in the Johannine Community," pp. 312–14.

quently does not share the Beloved Disciple's closeness to Jesus or his perceptiveness (20:8; 21:7). Although Jesus must be sure that the priorities of his love are right (21:15), Peter will have a leading role in the work of the disciples. This work is depicted alternately as harvesting (4:3), shepherding (10:1-16; 21:15-19), bearing fruit (15:1-8), and fishing (21:3-14). Symbolically, Peter is portrayed as pulling the untorn net full of fish (every kind of fish?) and given the task of tending the sheep even though it means following Jesus in martyrdom (21:11, 15-19). When Peter three times affirms his love for Jesus, he has finished his preparation. He has been humbled. The promise of his earlier misdirected and unenlightened zeal can now be realized. He is ready to "follow" Jesus.[43] The Beloved Disciple needs no such period of maturation. He and Peter each have their own roles.[44] Peter will be a μάρτυς (martyr); the Beloved Disciple will give true μαρτυρία (testimony).

The Beloved Disciple plays a distinctive role in John's gospel (13:23-25; 19:26-27, 35; 20:2-10; 21:7, 20-24. The references in 1:37ff. and 18:15 are debated.) He appears close to Jesus in the gospel's climactic scenes, and the evangelist carefully defines his relationship to Jesus, Peter, and the Johannine community. It is now generally agreed that the Beloved Disciple was a real historical person who has representative, paradigmatic, or symbolic significance in John. In this he is unlike the other Johannine characters only in that he is the ideal disciple, the paradigm of discipleship. He has no misunderstandings.

The first reference to the Beloved Disciple graphically defines his relationship to Jesus. He is loved by Jesus and reclines on Jesus' chest at the last supper. This detail indicates not only favored position and intimacy, it recalls Jesus' relationship to the Father in 1:18. Just as Jesus was "in the bosom" of the Father and is therefore able to make him known, so the Beloved Disciple is uniquely able to make Jesus known. Because he abides in Jesus' love, this disciple can share Jesus' knowledge of the Betrayer's identity. He alone of the disciples is mentioned at the foot of the cross, and it is to him that the mother of Jesus is given. Together, mother

---

[43] For an interpretation of "follow" in 21:19, 22 see Eduard Schweizer, *Lordship and Discipleship,* p. 83.

[44] The often observed juxtaposition of Peter with the Beloved Disciple has led some to see a polemic against the authority of Peter: G. F. Snyder, "John 13:16 and the Anti-Petrinism of the Johannine Tradition"; S. Agourides, "The Purpose of John 21," pp. 127-32. While it is true that Peter does not have the pre-eminence he enjoys in Matthew in particular, he remains an important representative of discipleship with his own misunderstandings and his own role to fulfill. If there is a polemic, it is against an enlarged view of his authority, one which would extend his authority over the Johannine community. Raymond E. Brown, et. al., *Peter in the New Testament,* pp. 129-47, finds little anti-Petrine polemic in John.

and son, they form the nucleus of the new family of faith. The other disciples are "brothers" and members of his family; all believers are the children of God.

The Beloved Disciple's relationship to Peter is defined by the scenes in which they appear together. At the last supper Peter cannot, or at least does not, ask Jesus who the betrayer is. He motions for the Beloved Disciple to do so, but he is not privileged to know the answer to his question. Peter denies Jesus three times; the Beloved Disciple follows Jesus to the cross. The Beloved Disciple gets to the empty tomb first. Peter enters first, but only the Beloved Disciple perceives and believes. At the lake the Beloved Disciple is again the first to perceive who the stranger is. Peter will no longer boast that he loves Jesus more than the other disciples, among whom is the Beloved Disciple. When Peter begins to question the future role of the Beloved Disciple he is told that it is no concern of his. He is to follow Jesus just as the Beloved Disciple was already doing. Although Peter would be honored as a martyr, the Beloved Disciple would also fulfill Jesus' will. The gospel's portrayal of these two seems intended to provide an answer to those who may have been pressing claims of authority derived from Peter over the Johannine community, which derived its authority from the Beloved Disciple's testimony. If there is an anti-Petrine polemic in John, it is defensive rather than offensive in tone. In the community's gospel it is clear that there is no basis for pressing Peter's superiority over the Beloved Disciple, but there is no denial of Peter's pastoral role either.

The conclusion of the gospel (21:24–25) finally makes it clear that the Beloved Disciple is the link with Jesus, the source and authority of the traditions contained in the gospel and affirmed by those who speak of themselves as "we." The conclusion renders the inclusion of 19:35 among the references to the Beloved Disciple probable. He is above all the one who has borne true witness. He has reminded the others of all that Jesus said and did, for there were many other things which could not be included in the gospel (20:30; 21:25). The similarity between Jesus' words regarding what the Paraclete would do after his death and the allusions to what the Beloved Disciple did after Jesus' death are suggestive. The Paraclete was to remain with the disciples (14:17), teach them everything (14:26), remind the disciples of all that Jesus had said (14:26), declare what he has heard (16:13), and glorify Jesus because he will "receive from me [Jesus] and declare to you" (16:14). From all indications this is exactly what the Beloved Disciple has done. He has come from the bosom of Jesus and has made him known to those who now affirm his testimony. He has taught, reminded, and borne a true witness. The words of Jesus in the gospel are the words that he has received from the Lord and written or caused to be written. The Beloved Disciple is not the Paraclete, of course, but he has embodied the Paraclete for others and shaped their understanding of the work of the Holy Spirit in their midst. The Beloved Disciple is therefore not only the authority and representative of the Johannine tradition vis-à-vis Peter, he is the epitome of the ideal disciple. In him belief, love, and faithful witness are joined. He abides in Jesus' love, and the Paraclete works through him.[45]

The other named disciples also have representative roles. *Nathanael* is the "true Israelite" (1:47), a representative of the true Israel.[46] Jesus is identified to him as the one of whom Moses and the prophets wrote and he is seated under a fig tree, a traditional place for the study of Torah.[47] It is important for the plot of the gospel that Nathanael comes to Jesus before any hostility develops (cf. John 5). In contrast to the Jews, he earns Jesus' acclamation by coming to him, overcoming his provincial skepticism about Jesus' "origin" from Nazareth, and confessing him "king of Israel" (1:45–49). He is in every respect the model Israelite, John's designation for the true or faithful Jew. In view of John's characterization of the Jews, Nathanael is a well-placed protest against any sweeping condemnation of Jewish people. In him there is "no guile"; he does not take offense at Jesus. He too will later have a role in the missionary work of the disciples (21:2).

Thomas is called $\Delta i\delta\nu\mu\sigma$ or "twin" (11:16; 21:2), though we are told nothing of his twin or how he came to have this name. He is the model of the disciple who understands Jesus' flesh but not his glory. Thomas is therefore the opposite of Peter, who saw Jesus' glory but could not accept his suffering.[48] Does the Fourth Gospel use Thomas as the character through which it addresses readers who, going a step beyond Mark, em-

---

[45] For further discussion of the Beloved Disciple see above, pp. 43–49, and Culpepper, *The Johannine School*, pp. 264–70. See also Raymond E. Brown, *The Gospel According to John*, vol. 2, pp. 1141–3; David J. Hawkin, "The Function of the Beloved Disciple Motif in the Johannine Redaction"; de Jonge, *Jesus*, pp. 211–13; Collins, "The Representative Figures of the Fourth Gospel," pp. 129–32.

[46] Richardson, *Israel in the Apostolic Church*, p. 188.

[47] The meaning of "under the fig tree" is still uncertain, though some connection with Israel and/or the Torah is widely accepted: Ferdinand Hahn, "Die Jüngerberufung Joh. 1, 35–51," pp. 187–88, lists the current alternative interpretations. J. R. Michaels, "Nathanael Under the Fig Tree," pp. 182–83, argues that Nathanael is a "representative of the 'true Israel,'" and cites Hos. 9:10; Gen. 27:35; 32:28. C. F. D. Moule, "A Note on 'Under the Fig Tree' in John 1. 48, 50," pp. 210–11, suggests that "the phrase 'under the fig tree' indicates something far more prosaic, namely, accurate knowledge of a person's whereabouts and movements" and cites Susanna and M. Sanhedrin v. 2. See also Severino Pancaro, *The Law in the Fourth Gospel*, pp. 288–304.

[48] Eva Krafft, "Die Personen des Johannesevangeliums," p. 27.

phasized Jesus' crucifixion but discounted the resurrection appearances? Thomas enters the story as the clear-eyed realist who knows that following Jesus back to Judea means risking death. He calls the others to go with Jesus even if it means dying with him (11:16), but Thomas does not understand that Jesus' death will be his exaltation. He does not understand where Jesus is going: "Lord, we do not know where you are going; how can we know the way?" (14:5). He cannot comprehend an appearance of the risen Christ: "Unless I see in his hands . . . I will not believe" (20:25). Realist more than doubter, Thomas stands in for all who, like Mary Magdalene, embrace the earthly Jesus but have yet to recognize the risen Christ.

Judas, in John, is subtly different from the synoptic Judas. He represents the humanization of the cosmic forces of evil.[49] His role is determined "from the beginning" (6:64). He is picked by the devil (13:2) and controlled by him (13:27). He is in fact "a devil" (6:70; cf. 13:18). Whereas Jesus and the Father will enter the disciples (14:20, 23), Satan enters Judas.[50] John introduces Judas as "the betrayer" (6:64; cf. 21:20). His name is given variously as Judas (13:29; 18:2, 3, 5), Judas the Iscariot (12:4), Judas, son of Simon the Iscariot (6:71; 13:26), and Judas, son of Simon, the Iscariot (13:2).[51] John is the only gospel to identify his father as Simon or to connect the designation "the Iscariot" with his father. This shift lessens the likelihood that "Iscariot" is derived from the *sicarii* and favors the interpretation that Judas is from the town of Kerioth in southern Judea, an interpretation which fits with John's impressive knowledge of Judean sites. If this interpretation is commended, then it also weakens any interpretation of Judas as a zealot or revolutionary. In fact John, typically, is unconcerned about any psychological or political motivations for Judas' actions. Judas does not betray Jesus for the money—the silver is not mentioned in John—though he was guilty of pilfering from the common purse (12:6). So, John strips Judas of psychologically plausible motivations. What matters to him is that Judas is the representative defector, and such people are of the devil (cf. 8:44; 1 John 3:8, 10). Judas is related to the children of the devil, who hate and kill, in much the same way as the Beloved Disciple is related to the children of God, who are marked by love (cf. 1 John 3:10). Fittingly, Judas shows no remorse in John (contrast Matt. 27:3–10); we can only understand that he has done exactly what he intended to do. John has no story of Judas' death; it is enough that he has gone out into the darkness. More than betrayer,

---

[49] Billings, "Judas Iscariot in the Fourth Gospel," pp. 156–57.
[50] Woll, *Johannine Christianity in Conflict,* p. 88.
[51] Brown, *John,* vol. 1, p. 298.

however, Judas represents *the disciple* who betrays Jesus, for John emphasizes that Judas was "one of the twelve" (6:71), one of his disciples (12:4; cf. 6:64, 70). He is introduced in the context of mass defection. John's characterization of Judas is given greater depth by his assertion that Judas was given to Jesus by the Father along with the other disciples (17:12; cf. 6:65). His loss, therefore, is Jesus' failure (17:12); however true a son of perdition Judas may have been, Jesus was not able to make him clean (13:11) or alter his course by the gesture of love (13:26).[52] Like later members of the Johannine community, Judas went out into the world and its darkness (13:30; 1 John 2:19; 4:1). He is a model of the many "antichrists" (who were also once within the community—1 John 2:18–19). Judas is the representative defector.

THE JEWS

Set in distinct contrast to the disciples, who behold Jesus' glory, is the other important group in the gospel, the Jews. Closely associated with them are the Pharisees and other representatives of Judaism, the chief priests, rulers, Levites, and their servants. Our concern, again, must be limited strictly to John's *characterization* of the Jews. It follows from this, incidentally, that I have not thought it necessary to use quotation marks for every reference to the Jews, since it should be clear that we are no more concerned with the "historical" Jews than with the historical Jesus.

The primary concern of recent scholarship on this topic has been to distinguish various groups designated by the term 'Ιουδαῖος in John. Severino Pancaro, for example, identifies five: "(1) the opponents of Jesus; (2) the 'common' people or 'crowd' (ὁ ὄχλος); (3) the Jewish people as opposed to the Gentiles; (4) the contemporaries of Jesus with their customs and practices; (5) Judeans."[53] In the most systematic study of the issue to date, Urban C. von Wahlde reduces the "neutral use" of 'Ιουδαῖος (Jew) in John to two categories: the Jews as a distinct religious/ political/cultural grouping, and the people of Judea or Jerusalem.[54] In con-

---

[52] See J. A. T. Robinson, *The Roots of a Radical*, pp. 139–43, who treats Judas as Jesus' failure, part of the shadow that has yet to be claimed.

[53] *The Law in the Fourth Gospel*, p. 293. A similar list of references is provided by Gregory Baum, *The Jews and the Gospel*, pp. 101, 274; Erich Grässer, "Die antijüdische Polemik im Johannesevangelium," p. 76; U. C. von Wahlde, "The Terms for Religious Authorities in the Fourth Gospel," p. 234; and R. J. Bratcher, "'The Jews' in the Gospel of John," pp. 401–9. See also Reginald Fuller, "'The Jews' in the Fourth Gospel," pp. 31–37; Wayne A. Meeks, "'Am I a Jew?'—Johannine Christianity and Judaism," Part I, pp. 180–83.

[54] "The Johannine 'Jews,'" p. 46.

trast, the "Johannine use" of the term has no nationalistic meaning since it distinguishes "Jews" from others of the same national, religious, cultural group and designates a group with a constant, unchanging hostility toward Jesus. In all but two instances (6:41, 52), von Wahlde concludes, these Jews are authorities rather than common people, and these two verses are the only occurrences of the hostile, Johannine use of the term for people outside of Judea. He therefore attributes these verses to a redactor rather than the evangelist.[55]

In many respects von Wahlde's work is sound and clarifying. The criteria he suggests to demonstrate that the "Johannine" Jews are almost always authorities are particularly helpful. Although it is obvious that "Jew" and "Jews" are used in various ways in John, the limitation of current analyses is that they lead to the conclusion that the reader of the gospel must always be asking whether the Jews in a given passage are the Jewish people in general, Judeans, or authorities hostile toward Jesus. If this is the case, the literary critic would need to analyze the characterization of each of these three groups. On the other hand, the amount of discussion generated by John's varied use of the designation shows that the gospel does not attempt to distinguish and separate these groups; all are called 'Ιουδαῖοι. They are one group in John. Nevertheless, recent analyses may help us to see that John offers a three (or more) sided characterization of this group. How is this characterization worked out? How does it develop? And, what is its effect on the experience of reading the gospel?

We have already noted that the Jews are closely associated with the response of unbelief, and therefore they are integrally related to the advancement of the plot. We have also seen that the gospel is episodic. When each of the episodes is examined, some of the diversity of John's references to the Jews is clarified; for development within each episode is apparent, and there is generally an escalation of hostility from one episode to another.

Only ten of the gospel's seventy references to the Jews occur in the first four chapters. Likewise there are only three references to the Pharisees (1:24; 3:1; 4:1) and no mention of the crowd in these chapters. The role of these chapters in establishing the narrator's perspective was discussed in the previous chapter. Because of this "primacy effect"—establishing the narrator's perspective as the reader's first impression of who Jesus is— there is virtually no opposition to Jesus prior to John 5. The Jews are first mentioned in 1:19. Jewish leaders in Jerusalem send Pharisees to question John, the man sent from God. The opposition between the Jews in

---

[55] "The Johannine 'Jews,'" p. 44.

Jerusalem on the one hand and God, represented first by John the Baptist and then by Jesus, on the other is implicit, but only implicit here. The Jews make their first appearance asking questions, and most of the time their speech is reported in the first ten chapters they are asking questions. Thereafter, they ask only a few questions. The questions, of course, challenge, generate confrontation, and eventually demonstrate that the Jews cannot accept the answers they are given.

The first episode in Jerusalem is introduced by a reference to the festival of the Jews (2:6). The Jews question Jesus in the temple after his dramatic demonstration there. The questions convey disbelief, but not hostility. Jesus does not trust himself to those who believe, and Nicodemus, a ruler of the Jews, cannot understand the answers he is given, but he is not hostile toward Jesus. The episode in Samaria distinguishes the Jews from the Samaritans and says that salvation comes from the Jews (4:22). Jesus himself has just been identified as a Jew (4:9). Elsewhere when a positive sense is intended, the evangelist normally uses the term "Israel" (1:31, 47, 49; 3:10; 12:13).

A second episode in Jerusalem (chapter 5) is again introduced with a reference to a festival of the Jews. In the healing of the man at the pool, the Jews appear opposite Jesus, and the man finally sides with them. The role of the Jews in the gospel is not established until 5:16, 18. In these verses they receive their "script" for the rest of the story: they will seek to kill Jesus because he violates the sabbath and commits blasphemy. The force of this characterization is obvious: the narrator is telling the reader what to expect from the Jews. The rest of the chapter is Jesus' discourse in response to this script. It begins to explore, from Jesus' perspective, why the Jews reject him. The plot line of the prologue has begun to unfold—Jesus comes to his own and his own people do not receive him (1:11).

John 6, likewise, opens with a reference to a festival of the Jews (6:4), but this time Jesus stays in Galilee. Again there is a repetition of the development of escalating hostility within the episode. The people are at first referred to as "the crowd" (6:2, 5, 22, 24). They think that Jesus is a prophet and want to make him their king (6:15), but when he eludes them and will not feed them again they grumble, and now they are referred to as Jews (6:41). The grumbling then escalates to quarreling (6:52). This is the first sign of division within their ranks, but they draw away many of Jesus' followers.

Another episode in Jerusalem (chapter 7) begins with the now expected reference to a festival of the Jews. This episode, however, begins at a higher level of intensity, since the aim of the Jews to kill Jesus is repeated at the outset (7:1). There is now some separation of the Jews from the crowd. Some of the crowd believe (7:12, 31, 40–41), and fear of the Jews is mentioned for the first time (7:13). The reasons for the response of unbelief, a matter to which we shall return, are explored in the central chapters of the gospel. The belief of part of the crowd in chapter 7 spreads to some of the Jews in the next chapter (8:31), but the reader was told earlier that Jesus would not give himself to those who believed in Jerusalem (2:23–24). They do not abide in his word (8:31), so they cannot be his disciples. After the most heated exchange in the gospel, the Jews take up stones against Jesus (8:57).

John 9 and 10 seem to form another episode. The reason for fear of the Jews is now explained: they had agreed to exclude from the synagogue any who confess that Jesus is the Christ (9:22), but we are also told again of division among the Jews (10:19). The nearness of the end is intimated by the Jews' question in 10:24, "How long?" Again the episode climaxes with an attempt to stone Jesus (10:31, 33), and he is forced to withdraw from Judea.

In John 11 and 12, which serve as the climax to Jesus' public ministry, the division within the Jews is heightened, and the sympathetic, receptive Jews in chapter 11 become the receptive, if unenlightened, crowd in chapter 12. Early in the episode (11:8), the attempts to stone Jesus are recalled. Many Jews, however, go out to Bethany to comfort Mary and Martha (11:19, 31, 33, 36), and many of these believe in Jesus as a result of the raising of Lazarus (11:45), but others report to the Pharisees. As a result of the council's decision to execute Jesus, he is unable to go about among the Jews, for many would report him. But many Jews believe in him (12:9, 11), and a receptive crowd *of Jews* hail his coming. By this point the opposition to Jesus has solidified, and the gospel has explored its reasons. Jesus has come to his own, and his own have not received him. But some have. The division within the Jews has meant that some of them have become part of the crowd, which is receptive but generally lacking in understanding. Others will arrest him and kill him. At the trial and crucifixion the hostile Jews press for his execution, but the crowd is never mentioned.

The episodes in the first half of the gospel generally reveal a pattern, a rising level of conflict and opposition within each episode and from one episode to the next. This repetition of the development of the conflict allows for its reasons and causes to be explored. It also accounts for some of the oscillation between the neutral and hostile senses of ᾽Ιουδαῖος in the gospel. The Jews, however, must be understood as a group. Some are receptive but the others do not accept Jesus' revelation.

Just as the other Johannine characters carry representative value, so do the Jews. One indication of their representational role is the way in which the designation "the Jews" sweeps away all class distinctions. As Robert Fortna has observed, "Gone are the rich and poor, sinners and righteous, Sadducees, Herodians, Zealots, scribes, elders, tax collectors, prostitutes. John's phrase gives the impression of a stereotype."[56] How far this is true is further indicated by Jesus' repeated references to the Torah as "their Law" (7:19; 8:17; 10:34; 15:25), though he was himself a Jew. And when speaking to the disciples, themselves Jews, he could say, "as I said to the Jews" (13:33). The hostile Jews represent the response of unbelief and rejection of Jesus' revelation. In contrast to those who are blessed at the end of the gospel, "those who have not seen and have believed" (20:29), the Jews "have seen and have not believed" (6:36). The Jews legalistically maintain their observance of the festivals but do not recognize the reality they celebrate. At the festivals they are more concerned to catch Jesus in some offense. Even when a blind man is healed they show no delight, only concern that the law of God's day may have been broken. At the last festival, Passover, instead of celebrating how God spared them and delivered them from a foreign oppressor, they seize Jesus and deliver him to the Romans for execution. Having now no king but Caesar, the world's king, they kill in order to defend their nation and their holy place.

The reasons for the Jews' response are explained not in terms of their "Jewishness" but in universally applicable characteristics: they have never heard or seen the Father (5:37), they do not want to come to Jesus so that they might have life (5:40), they do not have the love of God in themselves (5:42), and they do not receive Jesus (5:43) or seek the glory of God (5:44). An even more basic reason emerges later: they are from a different world order. They live on the wrong side of John's dualism: "You are from below, I am from above; you are of the world, I am not of this world" (8:23). Thereafter they are associated with all of the negative categories and images in the gospel: the world, sin, the devil, darkness, blindness, and death. In their unbelief the Jews are "symbols, types of the universal human condition."[57] By not having heard or seen the Father, they are Jesus' opposite; in their response to Jesus they are the opposite of the disciples. The pathos of their unbelief is that they are the religious people, some even the religious authorities, who have had all the advantages of the heritage of Israel.

Through the Jews, John explores the heart and soul of unbelief.[58] As the representatives of unbelief, their misunderstandings touch all the vital

---

[56] "Theological Use of Locale in the Fourth Gospel," p. 90; cf. Grässer, "Die antijüdische Polemik im Johannesevangelium," p. 77 n. 10.

[57] Fortna, "Theological Use of Locale in the Fourth Gospel," p. 93.

[58] The paragraph which follows is informed by John Painter, *John: Witness and Theologian*, pp. 71–76.

issues. Jesus' origin and destiny with the Father are vital to the narrator's point of view. The Jews misunderstand both, and the weakness of their position is exposed by the conflicting charges. Jesus cannot be the Messiah because his origin is known: He is the son of Joseph (6:42) and he comes from Galilee (7:41, 52). On the other hand, the origin of the Messiah will be unknown (9:29). Their understanding of his destiny is equally dull. They think he is going to the diaspora (7:35) or that he will kill himself (8:21–22). With no understanding of Jesus' whence or his whither they misunderstand his words (6:41, 52; 8:27), his works (2:18; 6:30; 9:24; 11:46–47), and the witnesses to him (5:30–40). Although they search the scriptures, they cannot understand them (5:39; 7:23; 10:34) or obey them (7:19, 51). Moses himself will accuse them (5:45–47). Repeatedly Jesus emphasizes that it is *their* law (7:19; 8:17; 10:34; 15:25). By their law he should die (19:7). Their misunderstandings can be traced further. They arise from misdirected love: they love darkness rather than light (3:19–21), and the glory of man rather than the glory of God (5:41–44; 12:43; cf. 7:18; 8:50, 54). Another kind of false love is the love of one's life (12:25). They are blind (9:40–41) because they will not see beyond the literal, the superficial, the flesh, the signs, the earthly. As a result they ask "how" (6:41, 52; 7:15; 8:33; 9:10, 16, 19, 26; 12:34), but they cannot accept the answers. The alternative is that Jesus must be a sinner (9:24), demon possessed (8:48, 52; 10:20), or a Samaritan (8:48). Ultimately unbelief leads to attempts to stone Jesus (8:59; 10:31) and the cries, "Crucify him! Crucify him!" (19:6, 15).

The burden of unbelief which the Jews are made to carry is relieved in two ways, however. First, John affirms that belief must be given (6:37, 39). Believers must be called or drawn (10:3; 6:44, 65). Otherwise they cannot believe.[59] Second, some of the Jews do believe (8:31; 11:45; cf. 7:31; 19:38). Jesus' words cause division among the Jews, the crowds, and even the Pharisees (7:43; 9:16; 10:19); so John allows hope that for some at least (i.e., those who are given) belief is possible. Because of an abominable history of misinterpretation, it must again be repeated that in spite of the historical factors which may have led the evangelist to choose the Jews to represent unbelief, they like all the other characters in the gospel are representatives. The Jews carry the burden of the unbelief of "the world" in John. In that respect at least they are not unlike "the lamb of God that takes away the sin of the world" (1:29; cf. 16:9).

Closely related to the Jews are the *Pharisees*, who are mentioned 19 times in John. The Pharisees emerge as the leaders of the Jews. The Jerusalem Jews who sent to interrogate John the Baptist were Pharisees

---

[59] Bultmann, *Theology of the New Testament*, vol. 2, p. 21.

(1:19, 24). From the very beginning, therefore, there is the hint that the Jewish authorities are rival "senders" (1:19, 24; 5:33; 7:32; 18:24). Apart from these references and 11:3, the Gospel of John depicts God as the one who sends. The Pharisees are those most concerned about alleged violations of the law. At first at least they are depicted as being at some distance from Jesus. Hence the sending and the hearing of reports (4:1; 7:32). Only when the first attempts are made to seize Jesus do they become active (7:32ff.). They have authority to send priests and Levites (1:19, 24), they are in close association with the rulers (3:1; 7:48; 12:42) and chief priests (7:32, 45; 11:47, 57; 18:3), and the officers report to them (7:32, 45-47; 18:3). In fact, the Pharisees seem to be the power behind each of these other groups.[60] They are distinguished from the crowd for whom they show some disdain (7:45-49), but following 9:17 they blend with the Jews (cf. 9:16, 18 and 9:40; 10:19). By this point the Jews have been provoked to take official action against Jesus. The Pharisees have therefore succeeded in their efforts. By means of this pattern of characterization, the evangelist lays the blame for much of the Jews' opposition to Jesus at the Pharisees' feet. If the unbelief of the world is represented by the Jews, then in similar fashion the hostility of the Jews toward Jesus is concentrated in the Pharisees.

The crowd is associated with the Jews, but their role is even more restricted than that of the Pharisees. They are mentioned eighteen times in chapters 6, 7, and 12, with only two further references in 5:13 and 11:42. This very concentration places them in the context of controversy over Jesus' signs. Although we expect references to the crowd in the passion narrative, there are none. The term there is "the Jews" again (twelve times in the plural in chapters 18-19, not counting the title "the King of the Jews"). The Jews and their priests, not the crowd, call for Jesus' death.

The crowd is introduced by the narrator as "following" Jesus in Galilee as a result of his signs of healing (6:2).[61] The reader recalls the healing of the lame man and the cure of the official's son. Never mind that one of these healings was in Jerusalem and the other at a distance so that only the father knew what had happened, the healings are meant to be illustrative. Others are assumed. The point is made that the crowds come in response to the signs (6:2, 24, 26, 28, 30, 34). There is no mention of teaching until Jesus arrives in the synagogue in Capernaum (6:52). Instead of teaching the crowd, Jesus feeds them. Later the point will be made that Jesus and his words are the real bread. The grumbling of the

---

[60] See J. Louis Martyn, *History and Theology in the Fourth Gospel*, pp. 84-89.
[61] See Jouette M. Bassler, "The Galileans."

Jews and the disciples in Capernaum in chapter 6 is easily transposed into a dispute (γογγυσμός) among the crowds in Jerusalem (7:12). Some say that he is a good man, others that he deceives the crowd and has a demon (7:20). Still, many believe (7:31). Both of these responses have exact parallels where the Jews are mentioned (8:48; 8:31). It is the belief of many in the crowd that spurs the Pharisees to action (7:32). Some of the crowd hail Jesus as truly a prophet (7:40), but again there is division and some want to seize him (7:44). The Pharisees disdain the crowd as ignorant of the Law (7:49). In contrast, it is for their sake that Jesus prays at Lazarus' tomb (11:42). In 12:9 the crowd is a crowd of 'Ιουδαῖος, and again they are drawn to Jesus by a sign (Lazarus; cf. 12:12, 17, 18). The crowd is perhaps best characterized by the final references to it. The scriptures have not been clear to them (12:34); they hear the voice of God and some say it thundered but others say they heard the voice of an angel (12:29). John's treatment of the crowd lacks the hostility of his characterization of the Jews. The crowd represents the struggle of those who are open to believing, but neither the scriptures nor the signs lead them to authentic faith. They are the world God loves (3:16).

THE MINOR CHARACTERS

The Gospel of John is distinctive in its treatment of the minor characters of the gospel story. Characters which do not appear in the other gospels have etched themselves indelibly in Christian tradition because of their roles in John: Nicodemus, the Samaritan woman, the lame man, the blind man, and Lazarus. Those characters which also appear in the synoptic gospels often share only their names with their synoptic counterparts. John the Baptist is a witness rather than a prophet calling for repentance. Jesus' mother and Mary and Martha appear in scenes which are distinctively Johannine. Pilate, who is perhaps most like his synoptic counterpart, is part of a carefully constructed sequence of seven scenes and is interpreted by his dialogues with Jesus, which are again unique to John. The roles of these characters invite further examination.

John the Baptist (1:6–8, 15, 19–36; 3:23–30 [or 36?]; 4:1; 5:33–36; 10:40–42). John the Baptist appears more frequently and has a more carefully qualified role than any of the other minor characters. He is never called a prophet and there is no reference to his dress or diet (contrast Mark 1:6; 6:15; 9:13). He explicitly denies that he is *the* prophet (1:21). From the outset he is introduced as a witness to Jesus, a man sent from God (1:6–8, 15). For the evangelist that is the sole significance of his work. His mission is stated in 1:7, and his subordinate role in relation to Jesus is underscored by the following verse. In its nominal and verbal forms, the word "witness" is used repeatedly to define John's role. He is a true witness, a witness comparable to scripture, the works, or even the Father. But he is the bridegroom's friend, not the bridegroom, the lamp and not the light. He is not the Christ and he does no signs. Once he has borne his witness, therefore, he directs his followers to Jesus (1:35–36, 40; 3:25ff.), so that he may decrease in significance while Jesus increases. There may be good historical reasons for this characterization.[62] If he has representational value in John it is as a model of what his followers should do. In contrast to both the individual disciples and most of the other minor characters, John the Baptist has no deficiencies in his faith. Like the Beloved Disciple he is a model witness who, presumably because it is "given" to him, perceives who Jesus is. He bears witness so that all may believe (1:7).

Jesus' mother (2:1–5, 12; 19:25–27). In contrast to John the Baptist, who is introduced by name and role, Jesus' mother appears unintroduced in her two scenes. Her role is scarcely defined, and she is not even named. The paucity of description has not hindered, and indeed probably has stimulated, a variety of symbolic interpretations. She has been seen as representing Judaism,[63] Jewish Christianity,[64] the new Eve, and the Church.[65] C. H. Dodd dismissed any symbolizing of the scene at the cross.[66] That some symbolism is intended is indicated, however, by the symbolic overtones of both of the scenes in which Jesus' mother appears. The wedding at Cana with its exhausted supply of wine, its water pots, and its new wine, and the cross with its seamless robe, thirst, water and blood, expiration, piercing, and unbroken bones have been the most frequently quarried sources of Johannine symbolism. In both, Jesus speaks to his mother as "woman." The former points ahead to Jesus' hour. Jesus' mother has, and apparently can have, no role until that time. Jesus asks his mother, "What have you to do with me? My hour has not yet come," and she has nothing more to do with him until his hour has come. Then she is given to the ideal disciple. These two have been called "the two great

[62] See Brown, *John*, vol. 1, pp. lxvii–lxx; Rudolf Schnackenburg, "Das vierte Evangelium und die Johannesjünger," pp. 21–38.

[63] Krafft, "Die Personen des Johannesevangeliums," pp. 18–19; R. H. Strachan, *The Fourth Gospel*, p. 319; E. F. Scott, *The Fourth Gospel*, pp. 74–75.

[64] Rudolf Bultmann, *The Gospel of John*, p. 673.

[65] Brown, *John*, vol. 1, p. 109; vol. 2, p. 926; Max Thurian, *Mary*, pp. 144–66; Feuillet, *Johannine Studies*, pp. 285–88; I. de la Potterie, "Das Wort Jesu," pp. 191–219.

[66] *The Interpretation of the Fourth Gospel*, p. 428 n. 2.

symbolic figures of the Fourth Gospel."[67] The impact of this scene has been tremendous. Here are the man and "woman," the ideal disciple and the mother he is called to receive, standing under the cross of the giver of life. There is the beginning of a new family for the children of God. The problem becomes acute, however, when one attempts to define more specifically what Jesus' mother represents. Perhaps in some sense the description, "the new Eve," is not inaccurate. Other figures, however (Mary and Martha or the Samaritan woman), have a stronger claim to representing the ideal of female discipleship in John. The interpretation of Jesus' mother as symbolic of Judaism or Jewish Christianity lacks solid warrants in the gospel. Jesus' mother is scarcely related to the elaborate images of Judaism or the controversies with the Jews. The interpretation of her as a symbol of the Church is more plausible, though appeals to Revelation 12 cannot carry much weight until the relation between the apocalypse and the gospel is established more clearly. Jesus' mother stands with the Beloved Disciple. Both of course were Jews, but they share more important affinities. John McHugh has argued that Jesus' mother is "the prototype and exemplar of faith."[68] He reasons that she is presented as believing even before Cana (that is, apart from signs) and occasioned the sign that led the disciples to believe. He translates 2:4 accordingly: "What is that to me and thee, woman?" Both the Beloved Disciple and Jesus' mother, moreover, were human instruments in bringing the revealer to the church. Jesus' mother bore him, and the Beloved Disciple was the authoritative bearer of the words of Jesus. As they stand together under the cross, therefore, Jesus gives each to the other and thereby cares for his own to the end (cf. 13:1). His ministry is then completed (19:28). His act of "filial piety" is much more than that; it constitutes the believing community which can now receive the Spirit (19:30; 20:22). The disciples can now be called his "brothers" (20:17). What Jesus does and says to his disciples in chapter 20 is based on the constitution of the new family of faith at the cross.[69] In this process both Jesus' mother and the Beloved Disciple are given secondary but highly significant roles.

Nicodemus (3:1–10; 7:50–52; 19:39–42). Nicodemus is a model of the subtlety the evangelist is capable of achieving in a severely limited charac-

---

[67] Brown, *The Community of the Beloved Disciple*, p. 196.

[68] *The Mother of Jesus in the New Testament*, p. 403. McHugh summarizes and responds to the positions of F.-M. Braun and A. Feuillet on pp. 361–87 and develops his own position on pp. 388–403.

[69] Cf. E. C. Hoskyns, *The Fourth Gospel*, p. 530; Raymond E. Brown, et al., *Mary in the New Testament*, pp. 216, 289; R. F. Collins, "Mary in the Fourth Gospel."

terization. Nicodemus appears in only seventeen verses, three scenes, and speaks only sixty-three words, yet he is both individual and representative, a foil and a character with conflicting inclinations with which the reader can identify. Nicodemus seems to represent the many Jews in Jerusalem who believed in Jesus because they saw the signs he was doing (2:23; cf. 3:2), but he quickly takes on a more individual profile. He is a Pharisee and a ruler of the Jews, an eminently respectable religious leader. His confession, moreover, is perceptive and entirely proper so far as it goes: "You are a teacher come from God." The reader has been told that Jesus has come from God, and the disciples have called him "Rabbi" (1:38). The alert reader, however, will not expect too much of him: Jesus refused to trust himself to those who believed the signs in Jerusalem (2:24), Nicodemus came to Jesus in darkness (3:2), and the Pharisees and Jews have already been critical of both John the Baptist (1:19, 24) and Jesus (2:18). Nicodemus quickly confirms his lack of understanding by missing the double meaning of ἄνωθεν ("again" and "from above") and assuming Jesus was speaking of birth in the most physical and literal sense. As with all of the Johannine misunderstandings, Nicodemus here serves as a foil which enables Jesus to explain his meaning while vaulting the reader to an elevated position of superiority over the character's limited understanding. Nicodemus says Jesus is "from God," but he has not grasped the full implications of the origin. When Nicodemus speaks again (3:9; cf. 3:4), he asks, "How?" The question reinforces his lack of understanding and allows for further explanation. Nicodemus appears to be a man ready to believe but incapable of doing so. Jesus does not fit his categories.[70] In the conversation, which is epitomized by the question "how can a man be born when he is old," there is the pathos of age meeting youth, established religion meeting an emerging pneumatic movement, tradition confronting freedom. The scene culminates in a critical judgment on Nicodemus. Any expectations the reader may have had of the authority and enlightenment of a Jewish leader are overturned. Nicodemus is a teacher of Israel, but he cannot understand even earthly things. Having temporarily fulfilled his role, he fades from the narrative.

When Nicodemus reappears in 7:50 and 19:39, he is reintroduced by allusion to the earlier scene. He concretizes and personalizes the division among the Jews which develops throughout chapter 7. He also brings to the surface the irony of the Pharisees' response to the crowd in 7:47–48—"Are you led astray, you also? Have any of the authorities or of the Pharisees believed in him?" Yet, Nicodemus is "one of them" (7:50) a

---

[70] Cf. F. J. Moloney, "From Cana to Cana (Jn. 2:1–4:54) and the Fourth Evangelist's Concept of Correct (and Incorrect) Faith," p. 831.

ruler and a Pharisee. He does not confess belief in Jesus, but asks for due
process under their Law. This ruler of the Jews, like Pilate, is attracted to
Jesus, reluctant to confess faith but desirous of protecting Jesus, and
rebuffed by the Jewish leaders. In the end he comes forward to bury Jesus
(19:39–42). He expresses his grief by bringing expensive spices, but finds
no life in Jesus' death.[71] His association with Joseph of Arimathea provides evidence for regarding Nicodemus as another of the "secret disciples" who feared the Jews (19:38). Nicodemus and Joseph of Arimathea
represent those who believe but refuse to confess lest they be put out of the
synagogue (12:42). He remains, therefore, "one of them," not one of the
children of God.[72] Like the scribe in Mark 12:28–34, Nicodemus is "not
far from the kingdom of God," but he remains outside.[73]

The Samaritan woman (4:4–42). In sharp juxtaposition, the next character to engage Jesus in dialogue lacks all of Nicodemus' advantages.[74] He
is a male teacher of Israel; she is a woman of Samaria. He has a noble
heritage; she has a shameful past. He has seen signs and knows Jesus is
"from God"; she meets Jesus as a complete stranger.

The encounter of the leading character with his future wife at a well is
a conventional biblical type-scene (e.g., Abraham, Isaac, Jacob, and
Moses). Allusions to the patriarch (4:5, 12) underline the scene's scriptural associations. The encounter takes place in a foreign land, the protagonist is expected to do or say something characteristic of his role in the story,
one or the other of them will draw water, and the maiden will rush home
and prepare for the man's coming to meet her father and eat with them. A
wedding will follow.[75] In John, however, conventional elements are
treated unconventionally; Jesus asks for water but apparently receives
none. Dialogue rather than action carries the scene. Living water, of
which Jesus is the source, rather than well water, to which the Samaritan
woman has access, becomes the central concern. And the woman is no
marriageable maiden; she has had five husbands. Still, Jesus goes to her
village, and she receives him as her Lord.

Typically, the conversation begins on a mundane level, the universal

---

[71] Krafft, "Die Personen des Johannesevangeliums," p. 20.

[72] Martyn, *History and Theology in the Fourth Gospel*, p. 87; de Jonge, *Jesus*, pp.
29–47; R. F. Collins, "Jesus' Conversation with Nicodemus," p. 1411, concur in
this judgment, but Brown, *The Community of the Beloved Disciple*, p. 72 n. 128,
disagrees. The point remains debatable.

[73] Julius Wellhausen, *Das Evangelium Johannis*, p. 16.

[74] Krafft, "Die Personen des Johannesevangeliums," p. 20.

[75] Alter, *The Art of Biblical Narrative*, pp. 51–58. See also the suggestive observations of J. H. Neyrey, "Jacob Traditions and the Interpretation of John 4:10–
26," pp. 419–37.

physical need for water, and moves step by step over the barriers with which she attempts to protect her inner self. As Ian Ramsey put it, "thirsty Jew" becomes "strange water purveyor," "prophet," "Messiah," and finally "I . . . speaking . . . to you."[76] As the light of understanding begins to break, the Samaritan woman shows herself at each stage ready to receive it: "Sir, give me this water" (4:15); "Sir, I perceive that you are a prophet" (4:19); "Come, see a man . . . the Christ?" (4:29). Gradually the social and religious barriers separating man from woman and Jew from Samaritan are crossed. Although the disciples are more surprised that Jesus is speaking to a woman than that he is speaking to a Samaritan (4:27), neither distinction matters to Jesus. The woman becomes a missionary to her people. She evokes, therefore, the mission to the Samaritans. As nearly as possible in the narrative context she is given an apostolic role: she calls others as Jesus called the disciples, "Come and see" (4:29; 1:39), and others believe "because of her word" (4:39, 42; 17:20).[77] She precedes the disciples, laboring where they are sent. They will enter into her work (4:38). True to her traditional name, therefore, the "Samaritan woman" is a model of the female disciple and possibly a model of Samaritan believers also.

The royal official (4:46–53). The βασιλικός, probably a Herodian official, is one of the overlooked characters of the gospel. As a respondent to a sign he has a place alongside the lame man and blind man. Jesus laments the necessity of "signs and wonders," but the sign leads the official to believe. Central Johannine themes are developed through his response. The Samaritans had believed because of Jesus' word (4:41). The official also shows a willingness to believe apart from signs (4:50). Belief in Jesus' assurance of healing then gives life. His son recovers, and the official and all his house believe (4:53). The official therefore exemplifies those who believe because of the signs but show themselves ready to believe the words of Jesus. Theirs is an authentic faith, and they will have the life it gives (cf. 20:30–31).

The lame man (5:2–16). "The lame man" may be a misnomer since the text says only that he had been sick for thirty-eight years, that he could not get into the pool before others when the waters stirred, and that his cure was manifested by his getting up and walking around. His affliction prevented him from walking, but we do not know that he was lame. His "title" therefore is merely a term of convenience. As another example of

---

[76] Ian T. Ramsey, *Religious Language,* p. 125.
[77] Brown, *The Community of the Beloved Disciple,* pp. 187–88.

response to Jesus' signs, this man forms a contrast to both the official and the blind man. The official requests a healing, believing it is possible; Jesus asks the lame man if he wants to be well. It is not even clear that the lame man wanted to be healed. Both the official and the blind man come to believe, but there is no evidence of belief in the lame man. He complains that he cannot get into the water, not knowing that Jesus has living water in himself. To what extent his "naïveté" or "dullness" is culpable may be debatable, but there is little with which to excuse him. The man does not even know who healed him, but he is ready to blame his violation of the sabbath on his benefactor. Jesus seeks him out to tell him to sin no more, but the man, who can hardly have been so dense that he did not know the Jews were seeking to charge Jesus with sabbath violation (see 5:10–12), immediately reports him to the Jews (5:15). Neither the narrator's explanation that there was a crowd there (5:13) nor the man's report that Jesus made him "whole" is sufficient to offset the impression that the lame man represents those whom even the signs cannot lead to authentic faith. Later Jesus explains: "Believe me that I am in the Father and the Father in me; or else believe me for the sake of the works themselves" (14:11). The lame man could not.

The brothers of Jesus (7:2–10). The brothers of Jesus receive rather severe treatment in John. They challenge Jesus to go up to Judea so that his disciples *too* can see the works he is doing. Are there "disciples" in Judea who are not with those who followed him in Galilee in the previous chapter? If so, they may have been those to whom Jesus would not entrust himself (2:23–25). The reference to Judea rather than Jerusalem in 7:3 is probably significant in the light of the narrator's statement in 7:1 that Jesus did not want to go to Judea because the Jews (Judeans?) were seeking to kill him. It may be argued that the brothers at least believe that he is capable of doing "works" or signs, like Jesus' mother, who came to Jesus at the wedding at Cana. Both requests are denied and then later acted upon. But whereas Jesus' mother is later shown in a positive light, the brothers are not. Their request is also remarkably similar to Satan's in the temptations in Matthew and Luke. In both instances Jesus is challenged to make a public display of his power in Jerusalem (cf. Matt. 4:6; Luke 4:9; and John 7:4; each temptation begins with "if you are" [or "do"]). The narrator explains that the brothers did not believe in Jesus (7:5), and Jesus adds that the brothers belong to the world. His statement that their time is *always* ready may mean either that their time is the world's time and will always be such or that the time for them to believe is already given and ready (7:6). The former, negative connotation is the more probable and fits better in the context. The brothers are of the world and will always belong to the world. They go up to Jerusalem, where Jesus will be rejected, and at once become a part of "the Jews" (7:10–11). Later Jesus' mother is given a new son, the Beloved Disciple (19:25–27), and Jesus' disciples become his "brothers" (20:17–18). Henceforth the mother, who may symbolize the church, will live with the Beloved Disciple, not in Jerusalem (19:27). The brothers, although venerated in other circles as leaders of the church in Jerusalem, remain a part of the world in John.[78]

The blind man (9:1–41). In seven memorable scenes, the rise of the blind man to spiritual insight and the progressive unmasking of the Pharisees' blindness are impressed upon the reader.[79] Like the royal official, the blind man is healed because he obeys Jesus' words. He goes and washes. More extensive parallels can be drawn to the healing of the lame man:

The lame man	*The blind man*
1. The man's history is described (38 years; 5:5).	1. The man's history is described (from birth; 9:1).
2. Jesus takes the initiative to heal (5:6).	2. Jesus takes the initiative to heal (9:6).
3. The pool (Bethesda) has healing powers for some.	3. The man washes in the pool (Siloam) and is healed (9:7).
4. Jesus heals on the sabbath (5:9).	4. Jesus heals on the sabbath (9:14).
5. The Jews accuse him of violating the sabbath (5:10).	5. The Pharisees charge that Jesus violated the sabbath (9:16).
6. The Jews ask who healed him (5:12).	6. The Pharisees ask how he was healed (9:15).
7. The man does not know where Jesus is or who he is (5:13).	7. The man does not know where Jesus is (9:12).
8. Jesus finds him (5:14) and invites belief.	8. Jesus finds him (9:35) and invites belief.
9. Jesus implies a relationship between sin and suffering (5:14).	9. Jesus rejects sin as the explanation for the man's suffering (9:3).
10. The man goes to the Jews (5:15).	10. The Jews cast the man out (9:34–35).

---

[78] Brown, *The Community of the Beloved Disciple,* pp. 187–88.

[79] For an outline of the seven scenes see above, p. 72 n. 27; Martyn, *History and Theology in the Fourth Gospel,* pp. 24–36.

| 11. Jesus must work as his Father is working (5:17). | 11. Jesus must do the works of the one who sent him (9:4). |

The story of the blind man is told in much more detail and the sequence of the features is not always the same, but cumulatively they demonstrate the extent to which the blind man serves as counterpart and contrast to the lame man. He resists the threats of the Pharisees and gradually comes to see Jesus as "the man" (9:11), "a prophet" (9:15), "from God" (9:33), "the son of man" (9:35–38). His progressive enlightenment is similar to the Samaritan woman's. By repeatedly affirming that the man only went to the pool and washed the mud Jesus had put on his eyes, the text preserves the mystery while once more pointing away from the significance of the question "how?" (9:10, 15, 19, 26). The questions "who" (9:17, 21) and "whence" (9:29–30) are more important. The blind man accepts Jesus as a healer and miracle worker from the beginning but needs to learn who Jesus is. The man is a model of those who come from signs to an authentic faith and are excluded from the synagogue.[80] They are cut off from family because they confess that Jesus is the Christ and do not fear the Jews (9:22–23). When they become a part of the flock, Jesus comes to them and leads them out (cf. ἐκβάλλω in 9:34, 35; 10:4). Both Jesus and Peter will lay down their lives for such as these.

Mary, Martha, and Lazarus (11:1–46; 12:1–11). The patterns of Christian discipleship are sketched in further detail in the figures of the family from Bethany. Each requires individual treatment, although Lazarus never speaks. Together, however, they carry forward the theme of Jesus as the bringer of Life. Like others before, Mary and Martha accept Jesus as a miracle worker and healer and call him to help their brother.[81] Their misunderstanding is that they do not see that Jesus himself is now the resurrection and the life for those who believe. Their misunderstanding lies in their failure to relinquish or modify the traditional futuristic eschatology for the Johannine realized eschatology. R. F. Collins has plausibly suggested that the misunderstanding is one that would have been shared by readers anxious about the delay of the Parousia and the death of family members (cf. 1 Thess. 4:13–18).[82] Rather than giving assurances about the future, the author shows how those expectations have

---

[80] The definitive interpretation of the significance of the blind man is Martyn, *History and Theology in the Fourth Gospel.*

[81] The awkward introduction of Lazarus in 11:1, 2, 5 may be a vestige of the linking of Lazarus to the better known sisters from Bethany (cf. Luke 10:38–42). Cf. Brown, *The Community of the Beloved Disciple,* p. 192 n. 341.

[82] "The Representative Figures of the Fourth Gospel," p. 46.

already been realized among Jesus' "friends." John returns to this theme again, especially in chapter 14.[83]

Instead of grafting dialogues onto a miracle story as in earlier chapters, the evangelist here delays the miracle and interprets it by means of preliminary conversations. Mary, Martha, and Lazarus are identified as those whom Jesus loved (11:3, 5). The only other individual in John of whom it is said that Jesus loved him is the Beloved Disciple. Lazarus is also a "friend" (11:11; cf. 15:13-15; 3:29). Since the raising of Lazarus is the final offense which sets in motion the plot to kill Jesus—and he was well aware that it would be (11:7, 8, 16)—Jesus actually lays down his life for a friend by returning to bring life to Lazarus (cf. 15:13). These references identify Lazarus as a disciple who is especially close to Jesus, one like the Beloved Disciple.[84] What Jesus does for Lazarus is meant to reflect the giving of resurrection life to every believer. As has often been observed, the eschatological expectations adduced earlier are transposed into present experience; one who is in the tomb hears Jesus' voice and comes out (5:28; 11:17, 43, 44).[85] His is not a resurrection like Jesus', however, for he is still bound by the grave clothes. Lazarus, therefore, represents the disciple to whom life has been given and challenges the reader to accept the realization of eschatological expectations in Jesus.[86]

The first conversation is with Martha (11:21-27). In it Martha moves from the affirmation of traditional eschatological expectations ("the last day") to the climactic confession, which is echoed in 20:30-31—"I believe that you are the Christ, the Son of God, he who is coming into the world" (11:27). This is the confession which in other traditions was made by Peter (cf. Matthew 16:16). Here it is made by a female disciple and tied securely to the Johannine affirmation of Jesus as the resurrection and the life (11:25). Of the two sisters, Martha is the one with discerning faith.

Mary is identified from the beginning as the one who anointed Jesus with nard and wiped his feet with her hair (11:2). When she comes to Jesus in 11:32 she is again, characteristically, at his feet, but this time grieving. She represents the response of devotion and uncalculating, ex-

---

[83] See Jürgen Becker, "Die Abschiedsreden Jesu im Johannesevangelium," pp. 222-28.

[84] The following scholars have proposed that Lazarus was the Beloved Disciple: R. Eisler, J. N. Sanders, F. V. Filson, and K. A. Eckhardt (see Hawkin, "The Function of the Beloved Disciple Motif in the Johannine Redaction," p. 136 n. 1). Although one can readily understand why Lazarus might have the place of honor at the last supper and why the brethren might think he would not die, it is not sufficiently clear that the gospel intends this identification.

[85] See Dodd, *The Interpretation of the Fourth Gospel*, p. 365.

[86] Cf. C. F. D. Moule, "The Meaning of 'Life' in the Gospel and Epistles of St. John," pp. 114-25; L. Paul Trudinger, "The Meaning of 'Life' in St. John."

travagant love, and in contrast to her sister never verbalizes her faith in Jesus.[87] She does not even understand the significance of her anointing of Jesus. Martha serves (12:2; cf. Luke 10:40); Mary fills the house with the fragrance of devotion.[88] Later, the disciples would have to learn that Jesus and the Father would come to abide with those who love him (14:23). In exaggeratedly simple terms, admittedly bordering on allegorization, Martha represents the ideal of discerning faith and service, Mary unlimited love and devotion, and Lazarus the hope of resurrection life. Together they are almost a Johannine characterization of the Pauline virtues—faith, hope, and love.

Pilate (18:29–19:16, 21–22, 31, 38). As in the other gospels, Pilate is coerced into authorizing Jesus' death. The dialogues, which have no parallel in the synoptics, develop and explore Pilate's role more thoroughly than the other gospels. Seven scenes which are alternatively outside and inside the praetorium artfully depict the trial.[89] Because the Jews refuse to defile themselves by entering the praetorium, Pilate is forced from the beginning to honor their demands by going out to meet them. His first response is an effort to avoid having to hear the case (18:31). His first words to Jesus take up the Jews' accusation and afford the evangelist a suitable theme for exploring both Jesus' kingship and the contrast between his and Pilate's authority: "Are you the King of the Jews?" (18:33). That question has been answered earlier in the narrative (1:49); the issue now is whether Pilate will recognize Jesus' kingship (18:34). Pilate's "curtain line" asks the important question "what is truth?" (18:38), but on his lips the words have a cynical ring. He does not wait for an answer. He has heard enough to decide the case and announces Jesus' innocence. From this point on, the issue is not Jesus' guilt or innocence but whether Pilate will defend Jesus against the Jews. His question to the Jews with its reference to Jesus as the "King of the Jews" only baits their hostility. They choose Barabbas. Failing to avoid the case or have Jesus released without pronouncing a verdict, Pilate attempts to mollify the Jews by having Jesus whipped. Normally this was part of the punishment (see Matt. 27:27–31 and Mark 15:16–20). After the scourging and mockery by the soldiers, Pilate again announces Jesus' innocence (19:4). If this is another ploy to secure Jesus' release, it too fails. The chief priests and their officers shout for Jesus' condemnation. At this point Pilate would

---

[87] T. E. Pollard, "The Raising of Lazarus (John xi)," pp. 440–41.

[88] Cf. Krafft, "Die Personen des Johannesevangeliums," p. 31.

[89] The identification of the seven scenes, now widely accepted, can be traced to Strachan, *The Fourth Gospel*, p. 310.

tolerate a lynching if only he could avoid responsibility for it (19:6). For the third time he maintains his judgment that Jesus is innocent. The real source of hostility against Jesus is then unmasked: Jesus claims to be the Son of God. This revelation only heightens Pilate's anxiety. The second of his dialogues with Jesus opens with the question "whence?" Origin and authority are closely related, and Jesus chooses to deal with the latter. As usual Jesus' words have more than one level of meaning, and Pilate is challenged to discern and accept the higher meanings. The extent to which Pilate is capable of understanding and accepting what Jesus says, or inclined to do so, may be debated, but just as he failed to secure a compromise by placating the Jews he also finds Jesus unwilling to offer him a middle road. Again he attempts to secure Jesus' release (19:12), but now he has nothing more with which to bargain. This time the Jews find his most exposed nerve, fear of a charge of infidelity to Caesar. The outcome is settled, but Pilate does not hand Jesus over until he has won from the Jews both a denial of their theocratic heritage and an oath of loyalty to Caesar: "We have no king but Caesar" (19:15). In a sense Pilate defeats both his antagonists. The Jews deny their religious loyalties, and Jesus is condemned; but it is a hollow victory. He has sought to avoid making a decision and has finally had to deny what he senses is truth and condemn one he knows to be innocent. The title, the permission to hasten death by having the legs broken, and the approval of a proper burial for Jesus can all be construed as Pilate's efforts to atone for his concession to the Jews. Pilate exercises worldly power and in the end stands with the world by his failure to stand with Jesus against it.[90] John does not play upon Pilate as a representative of either Rome or the state, however.[91] Like other characters caught between the Jews and Jesus (principally Nicodemus, the lame man, and the blind man), Pilate is a study in the impossibility of compromise, the inevitability of decision, and the consequences of each alternative. In the end, although he seems to glimpse the truth, a decision in Jesus' favor proves too costly for him. In this maneuver to force the reader to a decision regarding Jesus, the evangelist exposes the consequences of attempting to avoid a decision. Pilate represents the futility of attempted compromise. The reader who tries to temporize or escape through the gate of indecision will find Pilate as his companion along that path.

Mary Magdalene (19:25; 20:1–2, 11–18). One other issue remains to be dealt with through characterization: the difference in the believers' pre-

---

[90] See Bertil E. Gärtner, "The Pauline and Johannine Idea of 'To Know God' Against the Hellenistic Background," p. 225.
[91] Cf. Brown, *John*, vol. 2, pp. 863–64.

and post-Easter relationships to Jesus, or put more broadly, the relationship of the risen Lord to the earthly Jesus.

Mary appears as Jesus' devoted follower at the cross and again at the
tomb. Her understanding is limited entirely to her relationship to Jesus as
her earthly friend and teacher. Although she sees how he dies, discovers
the tomb empty, sees the angels, and even sees the risen Lord himself,
these experiences do not enlighten her. Witnessing each of the key moments of the passion story gives her no advantage or insight.[92] She can think
only that the body has been removed. She does not understand the significance of Jesus' glorification, his "whither."[93] When she recognizes Jesus
it is not through seeing the risen Lord, but through hearing his words.
Her intuition then is to hold on to him. Like Peter's double-edged misunderstanding in first preventing Jesus from washing his feet and then re-
questing that he wash him all over (13:6–10), Mary first does not recognize Jesus standing before her and then seeks to retain his presence by
holding on to him. Her misunderstanding is corrected by the explanation
that Jesus is going to his Father. Henceforth the relationship between
believer and Lord will be different, as close but less direct. The disciples
have become his "brothers"; they are now children of God. They will
abide in his word and he in them through the Paraclete as he had promised (14:23; 15:4, 7). Her experience of the change in relationship to Jesus
effected by his glorification provides a context for the Easter message "I
have seen the Lord" (20:18). Although there may have been some followers of Jesus who in the first months and years after his death needed to
learn the Magdalene lesson, there can hardly have been many among the
gospel's readers who still wanted to continue a human relationship to
Jesus. There may, however, have been some who did not understand
Jesus' death as glorification or the potential for relationship to the risen
Lord. They lived with the repeated lament, "They have taken away my
Lord" (20:2, 13, 15). Others perhaps invested so much in the historical
evidence of the empty tomb or the lists of appearances (cf. 1 Cor. 15:3–8)
that they did not realize that the words of Jesus were more important than
the historical data, and abiding in the risen Lord more important than
assent to historical witnesses. Neither the empty tomb nor the vision of
Jesus lifted the veil for Mary Magdalene, only the words of Jesus. Although she does not supply all of the answers, Mary Magdalene focuses
the issues in such a way that in the context of the rest of the gospel the
reader can understand Jesus' glorification, his "whither," his "ascension"
to the Father.

---

[92] Krafft, "Die Personen des Johannesevangeliums," pp. 31–32.
[93] Paul S. Minear, "'We Don't Know Where . . .' John 20:2."

Conclusion

What an odd collection of characters John brings together: a teacher of Israel who cannot understand elementary truths, a high priest who prophesies unknowingly while plotting to legalize a killing, a Samaritan woman who leaves her jug yet returns from the well with living water, a lame man who tells on his healer. The Wizard of Oz with its tin man in search of a heart, its lion looking for courage, and its little girl who just wants to go home is no more incongruous. Yet, each character's role contributes to the overall design and affective power of the gospel.

John's characterization is also peculiar in that it does not give the age or physical characteristics of any character. Only the barest outline of their past is ever related: the Samaritan woman had five husbands, the lame man had been afflicted for thirty-eight years, and the blind man had been blind from birth. Instead, the characters are individualized by their position in society and their interaction with Jesus. This means that they may easily become types. They are not so individualized that they have much of a "personality." On the other hand, their position in society and interactions with Jesus are verisimilar and realistic. They must be for the reader to accept them and, more importantly, accept the evangelist's characterization of Jesus.

The functions of the characters are primarily two: (1) to draw out various aspects of Jesus' character successively by providing a series of diverse individuals with whom Jesus can interact, and (2) to represent alternative responses to Jesus so that the reader can see their attendant misunderstandings and consequences. Because these functions are served through interaction with Jesus, the disciples do not interact with the Jews, and the minor characters seldom interact with each other. Jesus is at the center of all exchanges. Where one minor character does interact with another (Judas and Mary in 12:4-5; Peter and the servant girl in 18:17; John the Baptist and his disciples in 3:25-26; the Pharisees and the blind man in 9:15ff.; or the Greeks and Philip in 12:20-21)—and there are not many such exchanges—it generally serves as a witness to Jesus or as a foil for him. Judas' criticism of Mary is a foil for Jesus' praise of her. Peter's exchange with the servant girl is a foil for Jesus' response to the chief priest. The response of the blind man's parents serves as a contrast for their son's response to the Jews, which is simultaneously a response to Jesus. Like the grain in wood, the interactions between the characters in John tend to run in one direction, that is, in response to Jesus. Where this is not the case their interaction serves as a contrast or analogy which either defines Jesus' identity further or highlights the nature of a particular response to him.

This use of characterization allows one to observe analogies which create and break norms.[94] When several characters who are colorfully different from one another respond to Jesus in a similar manner, it creates a type of response. The consequences of their response, whether depicted through Jesus' words, dramatic action, or a comment from the narrator, serve as the author's (or implied author's) judgment on this response (i.e., an expression of his ideological point of view). Through characterization, therefore, various responses to Jesus, and indeed to the gospel itself, are held up for the reader's scrutiny while his or her judgment is gently swayed toward the evangelist's perspective.[95] Norms of acceptable responses to Jesus are established, while other norms are broken and rejected.[96] At the extremes one finds an apology for the Beloved Disciple's relationship to Jesus and a trenchant critique of the Jewish officials, who might be expected to establish the norms.

Between these extremes several other types of response to Jesus are represented which are identifiable by observing analogies between characters. The complete range is as follows. The first response is rejection, the rejection of the world hostile to Jesus. It is characterized primarily by the Jews, and the story explores its root causes: they are not called, not drawn, not given. They love darkness rather than light, the glory of men rather than the glory of God. They misunderstand the heritage of Israel, Moses and the prophets. They do not know God and consequently their final act is a denial of their heritage and an affirmation of the lordship of Caesar. The brothers of Jesus are not directly identified with the Jews, but they never move beyond their unbelief.

The second response is acceptance without open commitment. The characters who illustrate this response are the secret disciples: Joseph of Arimathea and Nicodemus. Pilate probably belongs, though somewhat uncomfortably, to this group. Joseph is explicitly identified as a secret believer. The other two both appear to be inclined to accept Jesus but refuse to make the concomitant sacrifices belief would require. Nicodemus would lose his standing among the Jews; Pilate would no longer be a friend of Caesar. The security of their positions prevents them from accepting Jesus, and the search for a compromise leads only to grief.

---

[94] Sternberg, *Expositional Modes*, p. 154.

[95] Frank Kermode, *The Genesis of Secrecy*, pp. 98–99, observes that narratives generate character, and the characters generate new narrative. To what extent John's narrative generated its characters or vice versa is an intriguing question, but one to which I would not venture an answer.

[96] See Wolfgang Iser, *The Act of Reading*, p. 100.

The third response is acceptance of Jesus as a worker of signs and wonders. Jesus does not trust himself to those who believe because of his signs in Jerusalem (2:23–25). Many of the disciples cease to follow Jesus when he calls them beyond this level of commitment (6:66), and the futility of recognizing Jesus merely as a healer is epitomized by the lame man, who betrays his healer. He makes so little progress toward faith, however, that he may illustrate no more than the attitude of the world toward Jesus, that is, rejection. These characters, even if they begin to recognize Jesus because of his signs, fall back into the second response, like the parents of the blind man, and ultimately remain part of the hostile world.

The fourth response is belief in Jesus' words. The Samaritan woman (without a sign) and the royal official and the blind man (for whom a sign is worked by their obedience to Jesus) each eventually find faith because they are ready to trust the words of Jesus. Both positive and negative consequences of their faith are portrayed: the official's household believes, the Samaritan woman brings faith to her village, and the blind man is cast out of the synagogue. For these, trust in the words of Jesus leads to authentic faith.

The fifth response is commitment in spite of misunderstandings. The disciples believe, they see Jesus' glory, yet most of them misunderstand in one way or another. Nathanael at first holds Jesus' origin against him, but in contrast to the Jews overcomes this obstacle. He is a true Israelite. Peter cannot accept Jesus' death, Thomas his resurrection and glorification. Philip does not understand Jesus' power to sustain life, his significance for the Greeks, or his revelation of the Father. Yet, he too is a disciple. Mary and Martha do not understand that the hope of resurrection and eternal life are already realized in Jesus. Mary Magdalene does not understand the resurrection or the relation of the risen Lord to his followers or to the empty tomb. In John's story, however, disciples and believers do not have to understand perfectly. As long as they follow the revealer, revelation is in progress.

The sixth response is paradigmatic discipleship. It blends with the top end of the previous response in that there is no further criticism of those who surmount misunderstandings. Peter will receive a pastoral role and martyrdom. Thomas and Martha offer climactic confessions. Mary Magdalene is allowed to report the resurrection she has misunderstood. Jesus' mother, though she enters the story out of season, is given (to) the Beloved Disciple. Others have no history of misunderstanding, if only because not all the characters are fully developed; for example, Lazarus and Mary. Mary loves. Lazarus lives. John the Baptist bears faithful witness, and Andrew brings others to Jesus. The paradigm of discipleship, however, is the Beloved Disciple, who abides in Jesus' love, believes, and bears a true witness. His name, or lack thereof, "the disciple whom Jesus loved," and his position in society, in the bosom of Jesus, quickly communicate that his is the ideal response. For the reader to respond in like manner must mean, at the least, accepting the truth of his testimony.

The seventh response is defection, and Judas is its infamous paradigm. He leaves the fellowship of Jesus and the disciples and goes out into the darkness. He is lost (17:12). The disciples who withdraw just as Judas is introduced (6:66) are also representative defectors. Peter too denies his discipleship but he illustrates further the potential for the restoration of defectors. His defection does not even bar him from a pastoral role. So, the final response (defection) leads back to the first response (rejection) but illustrates that the categories are fluid. A character can progress or regress from one to another. Such is life.

The interdependence of plot and characterization was noted at the beginning of Chapter 4. It is even clearer now. The affective power of the plot pushes the reader toward a response to Jesus. The characters, who illustrate a variety of responses, allow the reader to examine the alternatives. The shape of the narrative and the voice of the narrator lead the reader to identify or interact variously with each character. As Wolfgang Iser explains: "'identification' is not an end in itself, but a stratagem by means of which the author stimulates attitudes in the reader."[97] The reader is attracted to the paradigmatic disciples (response 6), sympathetic with those whose response is positive though less adequate (responses 2, 4, 5), and alienated from those who reject and defect (responses 1, 3, 7). As the narrative progresses it permits associative interaction, that is, readers may place themselves in the role of each character successively while searching for the response they will choose. Through the construction of the gospel as narrative, therefore, the evangelist leads the reader toward his own ideological point of view, the response he deems preferable. The characters give the narrative much of its richness and power: they make the plot live.

---

[97] *The Implied Reader*, p. 291.

Chapter Six

IMPLICIT COMMENTARY

Pontius Pilate contracted his brows, and his hand rose
to his forehead in the attitude of one who probes the
deeps of memory. Then after a silence of some
seconds—"Jesus?" he murmured, "Jesus—of Nazareth? I cannot call him to mind."

Anatole France
"The Procurator of Judea"

In reading any irony worth bothering about, we read
life itself, and we work on our relations to others as we
deal with it. We read character and value, we refer to
our deepest convictions.

Wayne Booth
A Rhetoric of Irony

The wide use of irony in John's Gospel may indeed
bear witness to a particular body of people who have
lived long enough together with a shared faith, a shared
practice, and a shared Beloved Disciple that a subtle
manner of discourse is also shared. This gospel is their
shared story. They know when to wink and when to
weep. And they tell the story as they do that others
might also know.

Paul D. Duke

"In a symbol," wrote Thomas Carlyle in his handbook
for symbolists, *Sartor Resartus*, "there is both concealment and revelation." But if everything were revealed,
then nothing would be symbolized; and if everything
were concealed then too nothing would be symbolized.
Thus a symbol is a sort of excluded middle between
what we know and what we do not know—or better, as
Carlyle put it, a meeting point between the finite and
the infinite.

Harry Levin
Contexts of Criticism

The impact of the gospel's characterization is only one aspect of the "silent" communication between author and reader. In conversation such communication proceeds through the meaningful pause, the knowing glance, the frown, the wink, and the "body language" as well as through the implications of a carefully chosen word or a surprising turn of phrase. In John, the reader finds that the evangelist says a great deal without actually saying it. Having drawn readers to his side by means of the prologue, the evangelist trusts them to pick up the overtones of his language, the irony of conversations and events, the implications of the misunderstandings into which various characters blunder, and the symbolism of the places, things, and abstractions which serve as more than stage props for his story. D. C. Muecke has written that the art of saying something without really saying it "is an art that gets its effects from below the surface, and this gives it a quality that resembles the depth and resonance of great art triumphantly saying much more than it seems to be saying."[1] The continuous implicit communication within the Fourth Gospel is a major source of both its power and its mystery. What seems clear and simple on the surface is never so simple for the perceptive reader because of the opacity and complexity of the gospel's sub-surface signals. Various textual features, principally the misunderstandings, irony, and symbolism, constantly lead the reader to view the story from a higher vantage point and share the judgments which the "whispering wizard" conveys by means of various nods, winks, and gestures. It is the discovery of sub-surface signals which had previously escaped the reader's notice that allows the gospel to be read again and again with pleasure and profit. Traffic on the gospel's subterranean frequencies is so heavy that even the perceptive reader is never sure he or she has received all the signals the text is sending. The goal of this chapter is to explore some of the ways the gospel maintains its "silent" communication with the reader and to analyze the messages that are sent on these frequencies. Even if it were possible to collect and analyze all of the gospel's misunderstandings, ironies, and symbols—and fortunately it is not—to do so would be more an act of vandalism which would deprive the reader of the pleasure of fresh discoveries

---

[1] *The Compass of Irony*, p. 5.

than a contribution to his or her appreciation of the gospel. My intention, therefore, is to indicate the ways in which the evangelist uses these means to communicate with the reader and suggest the principal themes of this communication and its effects upon one's reading experience.

MISUNDERSTANDING

One of the distinctive features of the Gospel of John is the frequency with which its secondary characters misunderstand Jesus. These misunderstandings may be characterized in general terms by the following elements: (1) Jesus makes a statement which is ambiguous, metaphorical, or contains a double-entendre; (2) his dialogue partner responds either in terms of the literal meaning of Jesus' statement or by a question or protest which shows that he or she has missed the higher meaning of Jesus' words; (3) in most instances an explanation is then offered by Jesus or (less frequently) the narrator. The misunderstandings, therefore, provide an opportunity to explain the meaning of Jesus' words and develop significant themes further. They are more, however, and their effect on the reader is greater than if the meaning had merely been stated plainly from the beginning.

Rudolf Bultmann contended that Johannine misunderstandings do not arise from a word having two meanings and the respondent choosing the wrong one but from "concepts and statements, which at first sight refer to earthly matters, but properly refer to divine matters. The misunderstanding comes when someone sees the right meaning of the word but mistakenly imagines that its meaning is exhausted by reference to earthly matters. . . ."[2] Bultmann cited similar passages in the Shepherd of Hermas and the Hermetic literature,[3] and C. H. Dodd agreed that the closest parallels to John's dialogue form are to be found in this literature:

It is clear, then, that the same formative principle is at work in the Fourth Gospel and in the Hermetic dialogues, however different the content may be. The evangelist, it seems, has moulded his material in forms based upon current Hellenistic models of philosophical and religious teaching, instead of following the forms, of Jewish origin, represented in the Synoptic Gospels. The typical Johannine dialogue must

---

[2] *The Gospel of John,* p. 135 n. 1.
[3] *The Gospel of John,* p. 127 n. 1. The parallels he cites are "C. Herm. 13; Hermas vis. IV 1.4f.; sim. IX 9.2; cp. Reitzenstein, Poimandres 246."

be accepted as an original literary creation owing, so far as form is
concerned, little or nothing to the primitive Christian tradition.[4]

In John, however, misunderstanding is developed and integrated into the
gospel more artistically than in any comparable revelatory discourses.
The parallels adduced are not really of comparable quality. Bultmann's
definition seizes upon what is most distinctively Johannine, the use of the
earthly to illuminate the divine, but it is too restrictive and excludes misunderstandings which fit the pattern in other respects. For example, commenting on John 11:11, Bultmann writes "the disciples misunderstand
the statement in a quite gross manner (v. 12), as the Evangelist's addition
in v. 13 explains."[5] In a footnote, however, he claims "this is no 'Johannine' misunderstanding . . . for it has nothing to do with the confusion of
the heavenly and earthly. Rather a primitive artificial device of the source
lies behind this (cp. Mark 5:39)."[6] The evangelist may well have taken
over the suggestion of a misunderstanding here from source materials, but
the point remains that the imposition of criteria concerning content arbitrarily excludes some of the misunderstandings from consideration.

Herbert Leroy has produced the most extensive study to date of misunderstandings in John, and it remains the best compendium of information on the subject. Through form-critical analysis he defines the Johannine misunderstandings as concealed riddles. There are only eleven such
passages, all in John 2–8.[7] Bultmann, he contends, was mistaken; all of
the misunderstandings arise from a concept with a twofold meaning
("einem doppeldeutigen Begriff") which usually belongs to the peculiar
vocabulary ("Sondersprache") of the Johannine community.[8] Readers
within the Johannine community understood the special meaning of these
terms, but to outsiders their special meaning was impenetrable. The ordinary meaning left them baffled.[9] The misunderstandings, therefore, can
be traced to the material used in the preaching and catechetical teaching of
the community and demonstrate that the Jews did not and could not
understand Jesus or receive his revelation.[10] Leroy significantly advanced
the study of the Johannine misunderstandings and placed future studies

---

[4] *Historical Tradition in the Fourth Gospel*, p. 321.

[5] *John*, pp. 399–400.

[6] *John*, p. 399 n. 6.

[7] *Rätsel und Missverständnis*, pp. 1, 6. The eleven passages are 2:19–22; 3:3–5;
4:10–15; 4:31–34; 6:32–35, 41f.; 6:51–53; 7:33–36; 8:21–22; 8:31–33; 8:51–53;
and 8:56–58.

[8] *Rätsel und Missverständnis*, pp. 46, 157–60.

[9] *Rätsel und Missverständnis*, pp. 146, 167.

[10] *Rätsel und Missverständnis*, pp. 183–93.

in his debt. The major weakness of his work is that his effort to isolate a textual form, all examples of which fit a single characterizaton, led him to impose too rigid a definition on his subject matter. He discusses briefly but dismisses John 11:11–15; 12:32–34; 11:23–26; 13:27–29; and 13:7–11 because they do not follow the normative form on which his definition of the misunderstandings as concealed riddles is based.[11]

François Vouga criticizes Leroy's limitation of the misunderstandings to the eleven which fit his definition, maintaining—properly, I think—that John does not use misunderstanding as a "technique" which is applied in the same manner in every instance. John's method is supple and variable. The misunderstandings arise from his concept of revelation: inevitably those who did not accept Jesus misunderstood him. Vouga expands the list of misunderstandings to include the following passages grouped according to the dialogue partners: the Jews (2:19–22; 3:3–5; 7:33–36; 8:21–22; 8:31–36; 8:56–58), the crowd (6:32–35; 12:28–29), the disciples (4:31–34; 11:15–16; 13:36–38; 14:4–6; 14:8–9), Martha (11:23–25), and Mary (20:15–16). The list is not intended to be exhaustive, however; most of chapter 8 is one long misunderstanding, as are Jesus' conversations with Pilate.[12]

C. K. Barrett and John Painter both trace the misunderstandings to a historical root: "They represent in miniature the total reaction of Judaism to Christ; the Jews perceived only what was superficially visible in Jesus and naturally rejected the absurd suggestion that he should be the Son of God; if they had penetrated beneath the surface they would have seen its truth."[13] Painter returns repeatedly to the significance of the misunderstandings and summarizes his findings as follows: "The misunderstanding motif is historically based, dramatically developed and has a pedagogical purpose in the structure of the Gospel. John wrote to remove inadequate attitudes to Jesus which would not be able to stand the test of Jewish persecution."[14]

This brief survey of the study of Johannine misunderstandings reveals

---

[11] *Rätsel und Missverständnis*, pp. 6–7. Cf. Raymond E. Brown's review in *Biblica* 51, pp. 152–54. D. A. Carson, "Understanding Misunderstandings in the Fourth Gospel," offers a devastating critique of Leroy's identification of misunderstanding as an identifiable form. Carson also attempts to show that the misunderstandings in John must be traced to Jesus' ministry. Although Carson clearly demonstrates that misunderstanding plays a broader role in John than is explored here, I think he dismisses misunderstanding as a literary device by demanding an artificially high degree of formal uniformity and consistency. John allows a great deal of variety in all of the literary elements of his gospel.

[12] *Le cadre historique et l'intention théologique de Jean*, pp. 32–33, 36.

[13] Barrett, *The Gospel According to St. John*, p. 200.

[14] *John*, p. 82.

that attempts to limit the category on the basis of strict criteria of content (Bultmann) or form (Leroy) have excluded passages which ought to be considered. Whether the misunderstandings are described as a "motif," "technique," or "device" is probably of little consequence as long as their frequency, variability, and effects are recognized.[15] Our central concern— the function of the misunderstandings and their effect upon the reader— has not been explored fully by earlier studies.

The first misunderstanding (2:19–21) occurs after the cleansing of the temple. The Jews ask for a sign and Jesus responds "Destroy this temple, and in three days I will raise it up." The misunderstanding turns on the metaphorical use of "temple" in reference to the body of Jesus, a usage which was known in the church (cf. Mark 14:58; 15:29; Heb. 9:11) but would not have been clear to an outsider. The Jews miss Jesus' metaphor and respond in terms of the impossibility of rebuilding the temple, which had been under construction for forty-six years, in such a short time. The impossibility of rebuilding the temple in three days should compel the Jews to find an alternate interpretation of Jesus' statement. In order that the reader may not be caught along with the Jews as a victim of Jesus' metaphor, the narrator intervenes (v. 21) to supply the meaning, that is, the "tenor," of John's metaphor. That meaning is clearly dependent upon the post-Easter perspective of the narrator. The first misunderstanding, therefore, is resolved for the reader and points ahead to the resurrection of Jesus, an event which is here alluded to for the first time.

In the second misunderstanding Jesus tells Nicodemus "unless one is born anew [$ἄνωθεν$, = 'again' / 'from above'], he cannot see the kingdom of God" (3:3). Nicodemus takes the wrong meaning of the term ("again") and understands birth in a literal, physical sense. This time there is no protective intervention by the narrator and no resolution. Instead, Jesus moves on to restate the matter in other terms: unless one is "born of water and Spirit . . ." (3:5). The character of the misunderstanding as a misinterpretation of an "earthly" metaphor with a "heavenly" meaning is implied by a later response: "If I have told you earthly things and you do not believe, how can you believe if I tell you heavenly things?" (3:12). Nicodemus apparently never understands what it means to be born from above.

The Samaritan woman stumbles over a similar metaphor (4:10–15). Jesus offers her "living water," which might also mean fresh "flowing water" instead of well water, but the woman responds in terms of the depth of the well and Jesus' lack of a vessel with which to draw water. Then she asks for the water just so that she would not have to come to the

---

[15] Cf. David W. Wead, *The Literary Devices in John's Gospel*, pp. 69–70.

well each day. The conversation moves on, and the metaphor, which is not explained, is dropped until later in the narrative (7:38). Whether the woman ever understands its meaning is unimportant; the metaphor has been placed before the reader, who knows to look beyond its literal meaning. Further clues will be given later.[16]

When the disciples return from the village they urge Jesus to eat (4:31–34). Jesus responds: "I have food to eat of which you do not know." The disciples suppose that someone has brought him something, so Jesus explains, "My food is to do the will of him who sent me, and to accomplish his work." The metaphor "food" ($\beta\rho\hat{\omega}\sigma\iota\varsigma$) was apparently not a common one—it does not appear elsewhere in the New Testament—and the reader would have had no clues to its meaning. Once the metaphor is introduced through this misunderstanding, however, it can be taken up and developed further in a later chapter (6:27, 55).

The next misunderstanding is the counterpart of the metaphor of living water. The crowds who were fed the day before challenge Jesus to give them a sign, like Moses who fed their fathers on bread from heaven (6:31). Jesus answers, using their quotation from scripture, but moves from "it was not Moses who gave you the bread from heaven" to "my Father gives you the true bread from heaven." The crowd misses the subtle transition and asks to have this bread always. The analogy of previous misunderstandings provides a firm basis for assuming that their request is for a perpetual supply of bread such as they had eaten the previous day (cf. 4:15). They are thinking of the material because they understand only the literal meaning of Jesus' words. Jesus again resolves the misunderstanding, though he still speaks in metaphors: "I am the bread of life: he who comes to me shall not hunger, and he who believes in me shall never thirst" (6:35). The last clause recalls the earlier misunderstanding over living water.

As the metaphor of bread is extended in the ensuing discourse, Jesus eventually says, "and the bread I shall give for the life of the world is my flesh" (6:51). Here the misunderstanding is less explicit, but the Jews quarrel over the meaning of this statement, and Jesus speaks further about the importance of eating his flesh and drinking his blood. The crass, physical interpretation which troubled the Jews is rejected, but while a

---

[16] Cf. Bultmann, *John*, p. 181: "The point of the misunderstanding is to bring home the fact that the water which men call 'living' is not really 'living water' at all. The use of ὕδωρ ζῶν to refer to the revelation is based on the peculiar type of 'dualism' which we find in John, according to which all earthly goods are apparent, false, goods, and natural life is only inauthentic life. Only what is given by divine revelation can be said to have the character of the real, the genuine, the ἀληθινόν."

eucharistic interpretation is suggested it is not stated. The giving of his flesh is clearly, on one level at least, a reference to his death.

In 7:33–36 and 8:21–22 Jesus tells the Jews that he is going to the one who sent him. They will seek him, but they will not find him because they are unable to come where he is. The statement is clear enough for the reader because of earlier references to "the one who sent me" (4:34; 5:23, 24, 30, 37; 6:38, 39, 44; 7:16, 18, 28). In the first instance, the Jews speculate that Jesus will go to the Diaspora to teach the Greeks, which is probably intended as a veiled statement of truth. In the second passage they wonder whether perhaps he will kill himself. The meaning is sufficiently clear for the reader, so no explanation is provided. Jesus will go to the Diaspora but not as the Jews think, and he will lay down his life, but *they* will kill him. In place of a superfluous explanation, the Jews repeat Jesus' words in both passages to drive home the irony of their conjectures. Because they have not accepted Jesus they cannot understand his death and exaltation, but the reader sees what they cannot see.

To "the Jews who had believed in him" Jesus promises that if they abide in his word they will truly be his disciples; they will know the truth and the truth will make them free (8:31–32). Their reply shows that not only can they not abide in his word, they cannot even understand it. The misunderstanding here turns on the meaning of "free." Taking it in a political sense, and turning a blind eye to certain eras of their national history, the Jews respond, "We are descendants of Abraham, and have never been in bondage to any one." They then repeat Jesus' promise skeptically. Jesus answers with an appeal to the difference in status between the son and the servant in a household; the son has authority to grant freedom. In this misunderstanding the Jews again mistake Jesus' meaning because their understanding is limited to worldly matters while Jesus is speaking of the freedom which is a gift of God to those who believe in the son. Their appeal to the security of their status as the "seed of Abraham" shows further that they do not know "the truth" or the meaning of "real" freedom (cf. 8:36). The resolution of this misunderstanding is left for the reader to work out on the basis of clues provided elsewhere in the gospel.

In 8:51 Jesus promises, "If any one keeps my word, he will never see death." The Jews assume Jesus is speaking of physical death and charge that he is mad. They repeat the offensive statement asking how it can be so, thereby underscoring their lack of understanding. Ironically, they suggest the truth—Jesus is greater than Abraham and the prophets. The reader already knows, however, that Jesus has said that anyone who hears his word and believes has already passed from death into life (5:24).

The next misunderstanding develops further the superiority of Jesus over Abraham. Jesus claims, "Your father Abraham rejoiced that he was to see my day; he saw it and was glad" (8:56). The Jews misunderstand the technical meanings of both "see" and "my day" and stumble over the chronological impossibility of Jesus' claim. He is not even fifty years old! In the Johannine idiom, however, "seeing" means more than physical sight; it means perception. The meaning of "my day" is more difficult, but probably it means that Abraham was privileged to see proleptically the revelation which would come through Jesus. Such an interpretation fits with the later reference to Isaiah's having seen Jesus' glory (12:41; cf. Isa. 6:1ff.), but there is no event in the story of Abraham's life comparable to the vision of Isaiah. If a particular event must be proposed, the birth of Isaac, the promised child of the covenant, is the most probable.[17] The ensuing affirmation of Jesus' pre-existence ("Before Abraham was, I am"; 8:58) allows the reader to interpret the earlier claim as a reference to Abraham's having caught a glimpse of the era of fulfillment in the activity of God in his own time. "Day" is not used in exactly this sense elsewhere in John (cf. "in that day" 14:20; 16:23, 26), so a very precise resolution of the misunderstanding is not given to the reader.[18]

The next clear example of misunderstanding is in John 11:11–15. Jesus announces that Lazarus has fallen asleep and that he is going to wake him. The metaphor here preserves the drama of what will happen when Jesus returns to Bethany. The disciples take Jesus' words literally. The narrator explains the metaphor, presumably because for some readers at least an explanation was necessary. Then Jesus speaks plainly: "Lazarus is dead." This misunderstanding is excluded from the catena of "Johannine" misunderstandings by Bultmann and Leroy because it does not turn on the acceptance of an earthly meaning of a metaphor for a higher truth.[19] In all other respects it fits the form of the other misunderstandings, and it might be argued that the metaphor of "sleep" does point to a truth about death which the implied author has taken pains to communicate throughout the episode. One might think that the metaphor is too common to qualify as part of the distinctive idiom of the gospel, but the narrator's explanation indicates otherwise.

In the conversation with Martha which follows shortly (11:23–25), Jesus promises her, "Your brother will rise again." Martha assumes Jesus is talking about the expected resurrection "at the last day," but

---

[17] Cf. Raymond E. Brown, *The Gospel According to John,* vol. 1, p. 360.

[18] See Leroy, *Rätsel und Missverständnis,* pp. 84–85.

[19] For Bultmann's judgment that "this is no 'Johannine' misunderstanding" see *John,* pp. 399–400, and my discussion on p. 153. See also Leroy, *Rätsel und Missverständnis,* pp. 6–7. For a different position, see Vouga, Barrett, and Brown.

Jesus responds, "I am the resurrection and the life; he who believes in me, though he dies, yet shall he live. . . ." This time the misunderstanding turns on the premise that the hopes for the future are fulfilled in Jesus rather than on a metaphor or double-entendre. The misunderstanding arises directly from the unusual Johannine christological use of "resurrection" and is directly related to the gospel's distinctive Christology and realized eschatology.

The misunderstanding in John 12:32–34 differs from the others because it is based on the understanding of one meaning of a term which has two peculiar meanings in John. Jesus claims that if he is "lifted up" he will draw all men to himself. One would assume that the meaning of this claim would entirely escape the crowd. The narrator explains that Jesus was indicating the manner of his death, for a major concern of the gospel is to interpret Jesus' death as glorification rather than humiliation. Surprisingly, the crowd responds, "We have heard from the law that the Christ remains for ever. How can you say that *the Son of man must be lifted up?* Who is this Son of man?" The introduction of the term "Son of man" is unexpected. The last occurrence of the term was in Jesus' answer to Philip in 12:23, but it is used in both of the earlier references to Jesus' being "lifted up":

> . . . so *must the Son of man* be *lifted up,* . . . (3:14)
> When you have *lifted up the Son of man.* . . . (8:28)

The conversation with the crowd, therefore, assumes information given to the reader, who should recall these earlier sayings. The crowd was not present when Jesus spoke on these earlier occasions. Nevertheless, the crowd understands that being lifted up means that Jesus, the Christ and the Son of man, will be exalted (glorified). They apparently do not understand that this exaltation will coincide with his death on the cross, and it is precisely this point that the implied author is intent on conveying to the reader.

Peter's misunderstanding in 13:36–38 again concerns Jesus' death. In answer to Peter's question, "Lord, where are you going?" Jesus responds with a variation of what he had said to the Jews earlier: "Where I am going you cannot follow me now; but you shall follow afterward." With great irony, Peter asks why he cannot follow Jesus: "I will lay down my life for you." That of course is precisely what Jesus is talking about, but Peter does not realize it and in fact is not as ready to lay down his life as he thinks.

Thomas is the next victim. Again the theme is Jesus' "whither": "And you know the way I am going" (14:14). Thomas protests: "Lord, we do not know where you are going; how can we know the way?" Even after all of the previous pronouncements which dealt with this theme neither Thomas nor, presumably, any of the other disciples understands Jesus' meaning except perhaps the Beloved Disciple, who never misunderstands. Jesus explains by offering another metaphorical statement: "I am the way, and the truth, and the life; no one comes to the Father, but by me."

Philip challenges Jesus' answer with some impatience: "Lord, show us the Father, and we shall be satisfied." He has failed to understand Jesus' answer to Thomas, and a great deal of Jesus' earlier discourse as well. Jesus responds rather pointedly: "Have I been with you so long, and yet you do not know me, Philip?"

The last misunderstanding which conforms to the pattern of those discussed above occurs in 16:16–19. Jesus says, rather mysteriously, "A little while, and you will see me no more; again a little while, and you will see me." The reader can hardly be surprised that the disciples repeat the statement (relating it to the thematic pronouncement: "I go to the Father") and say, "We do not know what he means." Jesus explains, not too clearly, by using the metaphor of a woman in childbirth.

All of the misunderstandings arise from an ambiguous statement, metaphor, or double-entendre in Jesus' conversations. His dialogue partner responds with a question, scoff, challenge, request, or mystification which demonstrates that he or she has not grasped the intended meaning. At times Jesus explains, in other instances the narrator comments or the conversation moves on with the implicit assumption that the reader can resolve the misunderstanding.

Several other passages involve misunderstandings in one way or another but depart from this pattern sufficiently to warrant being treated as variations of it. Bultmann observed that Jesus' signs as well as his words could be misunderstood,[20] which shows that the misunderstandings discussed above are deeply rooted in John's concept of the world's reception of the revealer. If there is a misunderstanding in 7:42, it does not arise from a misinterpretation of an ambiguous saying.[21] In 9:39–41 the Pharisees overhear Jesus and, catching his implication quite accurately, ask "We are not blind too, are we?" (9:40, NASB). Jesus responds, relating the metaphor of blindness and sight to remaining in sin. The crowd is divided over the voice from heaven (12:28–29). Some say it thundered; others say they heard the voice of an angel. But there is no debate over the meaning of what was said. Peter does not understand the meaning of the footwashing (13:7–11), but it is a symbolic act rather than an ambiguous saying that gives rise to the misunderstanding and ensuing conversation.

---

[20] *John*, p. 218.
[21] Cf. Wayne A. Meeks, "Galilee and Judea in the Fourth Gospel," pp. 161–63.

In 13:21–29 Jesus makes an explicit, unambiguous statement about his betrayer, which is followed by an act which is not understood by any except (apparently) the Beloved Disciple. The disciples do not know who Jesus is talking about, but they understand that one of them will betray him. Judas (not Iscariot) asks Jesus to explain how he will show himself to them but not to the world (14:21–23), but this is not quite the same as misunderstanding or misinterpreting what he meant. Similarly, Pilate does not understand the nature of Jesus' kingship (18:33–38) or his authority (19:9–11), but does not jump to a lower or earthly meaning of Jesus' answers. The reader, however, recognizes the misunderstandings in these conversations. Mary's mistaken assumption that Jesus is the gardener (20:15–16) may be an "acted out" misunderstanding,[22] but Mary does not misunderstand an ambiguous or metaphorical statement. At the end of the gospel the narrator explains that what Jesus said about the Beloved Disciple had been misunderstood by "the brethren." They had misunderstood the meaning of $\mu\acute{\epsilon}\nu\epsilon\iota\nu$ (remain/abide) and assumed that Jesus meant that the Beloved Disciple would not die before the Lord returned. This passage suggests that at least some of the Johannine misunderstandings are presented to correct misinterpretations current at the time the gospel was written.

Before pursuing the function of the misunderstandings further, it may be helpful to tabulate the results of our survey. Eighteen passages follow a common pattern and several others contain variations of this pattern and may be considered as related passages.

Misunderstandings in John

Passage	Ambiguity	Partner	Theme	Explanation
2:19–21	"this temple"	the Jews	death and resurrection	by narrator
3:3–5	"born anew"	Nicodemus	how one becomes one of the children of God	restatement in other terms
4:10–15	"living water"	the Samaritan woman	the revelation or spirit which comes from Jesus	deferred (cf. 7:38)
4:31–34	"food"	the disciples	Jesus' relation to the Father	by Jesus
6:32–35	"the bread from heaven"	the crowd	Jesus' origin, identity, and mission	by Jesus

---

[22] Cf. Brown, *John*, vol. 2, p. 1009; Barrett, *John*, p. 564.

6:51–53	"my flesh"	the Jews	Jesus' death	by Jesus
7:33–36	"I go . . . where I am you cannot come"	the Jews	Jesus' glorification	no explanation
8:21–22	"I go away . . ."	the Jews	Jesus' glorification	no explanation
8:31–35	"make you free"	the Jews	the freedom conferred by Jesus to those who receive him	implied by contrast of "son" and "servant"
8:51–53	"death"	the Jews	eternal life	no explanation
8:56–58	"to see my day"	the Jews	Jesus as the fulfillment of God's redemptive activity (?)	no explanation
11:11–15	"sleep"	the disciples	death and eternal life	by the narrator then by Jesus
11:23–25	"your brother will rise again"	Martha	Jesus as the source of resurrection and eternal life	by Jesus
12:32–34	"lifted up"	the crowd	Jesus' death and glorification	no explanation
13:36–38	"I am going"	Peter	Jesus' glorification	no explanation
14:4–6	"Where I am going"	Thomas	Jesus' glorification	metaphorical explanation by Jesus
14:7–9	"you . . . have seen him"	Philip	Jesus' revelation of the Father	by Jesus
16:16–19	"a little while . . ."	the disciples	Jesus' death and return to the disciples	metaphorical explanation by Jesus

This tabulation shows the distribution of the misunderstandings, their relation to characterization and significant themes, and the variations regarding the explanation or resolution of the misunderstandings.

At times the reader gets the impression that the identity of the interlocutor is irrelevant or arbitrary. The author just needs someone to misunderstand so that the metaphorical character of Jesus' words can be emphasized or explained. Upon closer examination, however, there is a clear correlation between the misunderstandings and characterization.

The densest concentration of misunderstandings occurs in the debate with the Jews in chapters 7–8. Since the Jews represent complete lack of understanding of Jesus from the Johannine point of view, it is not surprising that they are the victims of misunderstanding in seven out of the eighteen passages we have selected. They repeatedly fail to comprehend (cf. 1:5) his death and resurrection (2:19–21; 6:51–53; 7:33–36; 8:21–22). The death of the Messiah (cf. 1:41; 4:25) is highlighted by the misunderstandings as the affirmation most scandalous to the Jews. Neither do they understand the freedom (8:31–35) or eternal life Jesus offers (8:51–53), or his "day" (8:56–58). Jesus, the heavenly revealer, is totally incomprehensible to those whose understanding is bound to the earthly. In this respect, Nicodemus is the paradigm of the Jews' inability to grasp the meaning of Jesus' metaphorical discourses and symbolic actions. The Samaritan woman, an example of one who comes step by step to accept Jesus, at first does not understand that Jesus is the bearer and source of "living water" (4:10–15). The crowd struggles to understand Jesus' origin and identity as "the bread from heaven" (6:32–35). Like the Jews they do not understand his death (12:32–34). Martha represents the follower of Jesus who has yet to grasp that all her expectations and hopes are fulfilled in him (11:23–25). The disciples as a group, who stand in the place of all who attempt to follow Jesus, must first understand that it is his fulfillment of the Father's will which gives him life (4:31–34), then that death, which is but like sleep, cannot take them from his love (11:11–15), and finally that although Jesus would die he would re-establish his presence with them in "a little while" (16:16–19). The misunderstandings of the interlocutors in the farewell discourse are consistent with the characterizations of the three disciples: Peter does not understand Jesus' need to die (13:36–38), Thomas cannot understand Jesus' exaltation and glorification (14:4–6), and Philip does not understand Jesus' revelation of the Father (14:7–9). Although the selection of the interlocutors may seem to be arbitrary, the correlation of the themes of the various misunderstandings with the gospel's characterizations shows that the misunderstandings sharpen the characterizations and enhance the representative value of each of these characters.[23]

Correlation of the themes of the misunderstandings with the study of the narrator's point of view reveals that the themes selected for emphasis or explication by this form of discourse generally arise from the narrator's ideological and temporal point of view. The theme that appears most frequently in the misunderstandings is Jesus' death / resurrection / glorification (eight times: 2:19–21; 6:51–53; 7:33–36; 8:21–22; 12:32–34; 13:36–38; 14:4–6; 16:16–19). The meaning of this event lies at the heart of the narrator's ideological point of view, and his interpretation of it reflects his temporal position.[24] Most of the other misunderstandings de-

---

[23] See Chapter 5, "Characters," esp. pp. 145–48.

[24] Cf. Wayne A. Meeks, "The Man from Heaven in Johannine Sectarianism," esp.

velop another of the gospel's primary concerns, that is, the identity and nature of the children of God: their "birth" (3:3–5), their "bread" (6:32–35; 6:51–53; cf. 4:31–34) and "water" (4:10–15), their "freedom" (8:31–35), their passage through death (8:51–53; 11:11–15; 11:23–25), their vision of the Father (14:7–9), and Jesus' continuing presence with them (16:16–19; cf. 12:32–34; 14:4–6). The readers who resolve the gospel's misunderstandings, as they must for a successful reading of the gospel, find themselves drawn again toward a fuller comprehension of the narrator's ideological point of view.

The effect of the misunderstandings upon one's reading experience is a dimension of the subject which has not received due notice in past studies. Their most obvious function is to enforce a marked distinction between "insiders" and "outsiders," between those who understand Jesus and those who do not. Explanations of the misunderstandings draw the reader farther into the circle of "insiders." Many of the misunderstandings, in fact, seem calculated to do just this, since it is hard to believe that anyone even upon first reading of the gospel would think Jesus was actually going to give the Samaritan woman a drink of fresh water from a hidden source, that Jesus was telling the disciples that someone else had brought him food, that Jesus was announcing his plans to go to the Diaspora, or that Lazarus was merely taking a restful nap. The misunderstandings, therefore, lead readers to feel a judgmental distance between themselves as "insiders" who understand the elusive implication of Jesus' revelatory discourses and those who have rejected Jesus. The "outsiders," one is led to believe, must be exceedingly dense or willfully and perversely blind to the truth to have missed it. The distance between the believers and the world, exemplified by the Jews in the gospel, is therefore maintained and even exaggerated. The reader is divorced in the course of reading the gospel from that which is characterized by the Jews. The question of whether "outsiders" or non-believers could have understood the idiom of the gospel will be dealt with in Chapter 7.

A further effect of the misunderstandings is to remove any doubt or misperception about key points in John's theology. The transition from "outside" (the world) to "inside" (believers or the children of God) cannot be seen as a superficial matter after attention has been drawn to the overtones of Jesus' pronouncement "you must be born ἄνωθεν [= 'again,' or 'from above']." Nor can the believing reader go on with an unchecked dread of death after the twin misunderstandings of the Jews in 8:51–53 and the disciples in 11:11–15, or feel that the fulfillment of hopes for eschatological deliverance and final communion with God must be deferred

p. 64; Painter, *John*, pp. 11–12.

to the future after Jesus' conversation with Martha. Like the report concerning the Beloved Disciple (21:23), some of the words of Jesus may have needed clarification for the gospel's intended readers.[25]

The most significant function of the misunderstandings, however, is to teach readers how to read the gospel. The misunderstandings call attention to the gospel's metaphors, double-entendres, and plurisignations. They also guide the reader by interpreting some of these and ruling out the literal, material, worldly, or general meanings of such references. Readers are therefore oriented to the level on which the gospel's language is to be understood and warned that failure to understand identifies them with the characterization of the Jews and the others who cannot interpret the gospel's language correctly. Those who fail to understand Jesus' $\pi\alpha\rho\omicron\iota\mu\iota\alpha\iota$ (riddles; 10:6; 16:25, 29) will eventually be "scattered" (16:31–32). The *dramatis personae* do not offer a model of how one is to understand.[26] They serve rather as representatives of the consequences of failure to do so. Jesus' responses to them guide the reader around some of the gospel's characteristic metaphors. As a result, when the reader encounters similar references with double or multiple meanings his or her pleasure and perception will be enhanced by this lesson in how to "see" and "perceive" their meanings: for example, comprehend / overcome (1:5), wind / spirit (3:8), "do you want to be well / whole?" (5:6), "show yourself to the world" (7:4), "I am not 'going up' to [at?] this feast, for my time has not yet fully come" (7:8), "living water" (7:38); "night" (9:4; 11:10; 13:30; 21:3), [Judas] "used to take [lit. 'lift'] what was put into the money box" (12:6), "die for" (11:50), "to the end" (13:1), "wash" (13:8), "follow" (13:36), "king" (19:14ff.), "it is finished" (19:30), "gave up [lit. 'handed over'] the spirit" (19:30).[27] In this respect, the misunderstandings are related to the use of irony in the gospel. Not only do some of the misunderstandings involve irony (e.g., 7:33–36; 8:21–22), but they point the reader to the detection of the multiple meanings on which irony is based.

IRONY

The "silent" communication between author and reader assumes its most intriguing form in the ironies of the gospel. The implied author smiles,

---

[25] Painter, *John*, p. 9.

[26] Dodd, *Historical Tradition in the Fourth Gospel*, p. 318.

[27] See Oscar Cullmann, "Der johanneische Gebrauch doppeldeutiger Ausdrücke als Schlüssel zum Verständnis des vierten Evangeliums," pp. 360–72; David W. Wead, "The Johannine Double Meaning," pp. 106–20; Barrett, *John*, p. 208; Brown, *John*, vol. 1, p. 308.

winks, and raises his eyebrows as the story is told. The reader who sees as
well as hears understands that the narrator means more than he says and
that the characters do not understand what is happening or what they are
saying. The fourth evangelist has been characterized repeatedly as a master of irony: C. H. Dodd describes John 9 as "rich in the tragic irony of
which the evangelist is master," and Wayne Meeks refers to him as "that
unknown master of irony and drama."[28] It is surprising, therefore, that
there has not been a monograph or a definitive article on the subject of
irony in the Fourth Gospel. George W. MacRae and David Wead made a
good beginning upon which later work can build;[29] Henri Clavier and
Jakob Jónsson, however, linked irony too closely with ridicule and comic
effect and did not explore the use of irony in calling the reader to share the
narrator's point of view.[30] The best treatment of John's irony is a recent
dissertation by Paul D. Duke.[31] Commentators have spotted most of the
gospel's ironies, but do not offer a systematic treatment of their themes,
techniques, and effects. The attention focused on irony in recent years by
D. C. Muecke and Wayne Booth calls for a fresh examination of Johannine irony.[32]

To say simply that irony "consists in saying one thing and intending the
opposite" or that it is "the disparity between the meaning conveyed and
the literal meaning of the words" does not adequately distinguish irony
from metaphor, symbol, or mockery.[33] Muecke astutely diagnosed the
problem inherent in such simple definitions: "The principal obstacle in
the way of a simple definition of irony is the fact that irony is not a simple
phenomenon."[34]

The analytical studies by Muecke and Booth define the essential components of irony. Muecke summarized his analysis as follows:

> We have now presented, as basic features for all irony, (i) a contrast of
> appearance and reality, (ii) a confident unawareness (pretended in the
> ironist, real in the victim of the irony) that the appearance is only an

---

[28] Dodd, *The Interpretation of the Fourth Gospel,* p. 357; Meeks, "The Divine
Agent and His Counterfeit in Philo and the Fourth Gospel," p. 59.

[29] MacRae, "Theology and Irony in the Fourth Gospel," pp. 83–96; Wead, *The
Literary Devices in John's Gospel,* pp. 47–68, and "Johannine Irony as a Key to
the Author-Audience Relationship in John's Gospel."

[30] Clavier, "L'ironie dans le quatrième évangile," pp. 261–76; Jónsson, *Humor and
Irony in the New Testament.*

[31] "Irony in the Fourth Gospel."

[32] Muecke, *The Compass of Irony,* and *Irony;* Booth, *A Rhetoric of Irony.*

[33] The definitions appear in G. B. Caird, *The Language and Imagery of the Bible,*
p. 134; and Wead, *The Literary Devices in John's Gospel,* p. 47. Both writers
understand irony better than these statements convey.

[34] *Irony,* p. 7.

appearance, and (iii) the comic effect of this unawareness of a contrasting appearance and reality.[35]

To these three he adds a fourth, the element of detachment. Both Muecke and Booth describe irony as a "two-story" phenomenon.[36] Below is the appearance or apparent meaning. Above there is a meaning, perspective, or belief that is contradictory, incongruous, or incompatible with the lower level. The victim, where there is one, is unaware of the higher level or blindly hostile to it. The reader is invited by the irony to leap to the higher level and share the perspective of the implied author. With this invitation "to come and live at a higher and firmer location" there is also "a strong sense of rejecting a whole structure of meanings, a kind of world that the author himself obviously rejects."[37] In order to make the leap from one level to the other, the reader must take four steps: (1) reject the literal meaning, (2) recognize alternative interpretations, (3) decide about the author's knowledge or beliefs, and (4) choose a new meaning which is in harmony with the (implied) author's position.[38] We may then decide "whether the reconstructed building is indeed a good place to dwell in" and whether the author was justified in requiring us to make the leap.[39] Inherent in this model is the implied superiority of both the reconstructed meaning and the perspective which supports it, and "a potential downward look on those who dwell in error." Booth continues: "The metaphor suggests thus a choice between two large structures of beliefs each so tightly associated that to reject or accept any one of them may well entail rejecting or accepting a whole way of life."[40]

Everyone familiar with the Gospel of John will be struck by the correspondence between the components of irony as analyzed by Muecke and Booth and the ways it is employed by the fourth evangelist. The gospel assumes a profound dualism which is depicted in spatial terms. There are earthly matters ($\tau\grave{\alpha}$ $\dot{\epsilon}\pi\acute{\iota}\gamma\epsilon\iota\alpha$) and heavenly matters ($\tau\grave{\alpha}$ $\dot{\epsilon}\pi\sigma\nu\rho\acute{\alpha}\nu\iota\alpha$ 3:12). Jesus is from above ($\mathring{\alpha}\nu\omega$); his opponents are from below ($\kappa\acute{\alpha}\tau\omega$; 8:23) or from the earth (3:31). The higher plane is associated with truth and the lower with falsehood, deception, and error. As we will see later, the imagery and symbolism of the gospel emphasize this duality of spirit and flesh, light and darkness. The lower level is the plane of appearances; the higher level the perception of right judgment. Jesus exhorts: "Do not

[35] *Irony*, p. 35; cf. Muecke, *The Compass of Irony*, pp. 19–20.
[36] Muecke, *The Compass of Irony*, p. 19; Booth, *A Rhetoric of Irony*, pp. 36–39.
[37] Booth, *A Rhetoric of Irony*, p. 36.
[38] *A Rhetoric of Irony*, pp. 10–12.
[39] *A Rhetoric of Irony*, p. 39.
[40] *A Rhetoric of Irony*, p. 37.

judge by appearances, but judge with right judgment" (7:24). A strikingly similar line by Haakon Chevalier is quoted by Muecke: "The basic feature of every irony is a contrast between a reality and an appearance."[41] The foils for Jesus' revelation of that which is from above are naively or blindly unaware of the higher plane, but the reader is invited to the "upper room" where he or she can share in the fellowship of the implied author who winks or scowls whenever the reader might miss an intended meaning or mistake appearance for reality.

The irony of the Fourth Gospel is always stable and usually covert. In covert irony meaning is hidden rather than explained, but when the meanings of stable ironies are reconstructed by the perceptive reader "they are firm as a rock."[42] John's ironies are also corrective; one perspective contradicts, exposes, and invalidates the other.[43] The norms of the implied author are ostensibly drawn from Jesus and revealed by him. The prologue, as we have seen, serves the crucial function of elevating the reader to the implied author's Apollonian vantage point before the spectacle begins. Prologues serving just such a purpose were developed by the tragic poets (especially Sophocles) and employed in New Comedy as well: "The omniscient prologue was almost indispensable in plays which exploited dramatic irony based on hidden identities."[44] The revelation of Jesus' identity at the outset provides firm footing for the reader's reconstruction of hidden meanings and reception of suppressed signals behind the backs or "over the heads" of the characters.

The possible approaches to the use of irony in the Fourth Gospel are as varied as those uses and their components. Irony may be classified according to various types. Muecke begins with the basic distinction between verbal irony, in which the ironist speaks ironically, and situational irony, in which the irony arises from some disparity or incongruity: incongruity between expectations and events (irony of events), the observer's knowledge of what the victim has yet to find out (dramatic irony), a character's "self-betrayal," or dilemmas and paradoxes (irony of dilemma).[45] One may also distinguish the objects (topics or themes) of the gospel's irony, the techniques by which the evangelist constructs his ironies, the profile of the implied author which emerges from them, the victims, the contexts, the functions, and the effects of its irony. Each is worthy of further study.

---

[41] *The Ironic Temper*, p. 42, quoted by Muecke, *Irony*, p. 30.

[42] Booth, *A Rhetoric of Irony*, p. 235.

[43] Muecke, *The Compass of Irony*, p. 23.

[44] Philip W. Harsh, *A Handbook of Classical Drama*, p. 316; cf. A. R. Thompson, *The Dry Mock*, p. 91; J. A. K. Thomson, *Irony*, p. 37; Wead, *The Literary Devices in John's Gospel*, pp. 47–51.

[45] Muecke, *The Compass of Irony*, pp. 42, 99–115.

We shall consider first the themes or objects of John's irony, then the techniques of the implied author, the victims of John's irony, and finally its effects upon the reader.

The Rejection of Jesus. The foundational irony of the gospel is that the Jews rejected the Messiah they eagerly expected: John states the incongruity simply at the outset: "He came to his own home, and his own people received him not" (1:11). Ironic development of various aspects of the theme of Jesus' rejection by his own permeates the narrative. The Jews should recognize Jesus because Moses and the prophets bore witness to him (1:45). Yet they search the scriptures looking for eternal life, and reject the one to whom the scriptures testify (5:39–40). They claim to follow Moses (5:45–47; 9:28), but fail to recognize the one about whom he wrote, even when he feeds them in the wilderness (6:30–31). Their rejection of Jesus is consequently a tragic and treasonous denial of their heritage, their scriptures, their prophets (e.g., Isaiah; 12:41), and their patriarchs (Abraham; 8:52–53). The theme culminates with a bitter irony. The final rejection of Jesus is simultaneously a denial of their allegiance to God and their theocratic heritage: "Crucify him . . . We have no king but Caesar" (19:15). The implied author does not wink or smile. Is that grim satisfaction or tears in his eyes?

The responsibility and culpability of the leaders of the Jews is repeatedly driven home with sharp thrusts from the sword of irony. A teacher of Israel cannot understand even earthly things (3:10). Some of the rulers of the people believe but hide their faith (7:26, 48, 50–51; 12:42). The Jews will therefore pay a high price for their rejection of Jesus. The twin passages concerning the temple (2:18–20; 11:48) imply that its destruction was a direct consequence of Jesus' death. The implication of his challenge, "Destroy this temple . . ." (2:18), is, for those who can grasp it, that in destroying Jesus they will also destroy their temple; but Jesus is the fulfillment of all that the temple represented. He is the ultimate sacrifice and the final meeting place of heaven and earth (cf. 1:51), God and man. Ironically, it was a misguided devotion to the temple which led the leaders of the people to agree to sacrifice Jesus: "If we let him go on thus, every one will believe in him, and the Romans will come and destroy both our holy place and our nation" (11:48). Barrett calls this verse "a striking example of Johannine irony" and explains:[46]

---

[46] *John,* p. 405. G. H. C. Macgregor, *The Gospel of John,* p. 256, quotes Dodd's observation: "In the irony of events Caiaphas used his high-priestly office to lead forward that one sacrifice which was for ever to take away sin and so make all further priestly office superfluous."

The Jews did not leave Jesus alone, but crucified him; and the consequences were precisely that which they desired to avoid. When this
gospel was written, throughout the world men were coming to Jesus by
faith (12:32, πάντας ἑλκύσω) and the Romans had destroyed the
temple and subjugated the Jews.

There is no mirth in the irony that they lost their national life and their
temple by trying to protect it (cf. 12:25).

The Origin of Jesus. The debate between Jesus and his opponents often
returns to the theme of his origin. The Jews are unaware of his real origin
and hold his apparent home against him. When Nathanael asks, "Can
anything good come out of Nazareth?" (1:46) the implied author smiles
wryly, but it is difficult to tell just what is behind that smile. It is obvious
that Nathanael is confidently ignorant of the ramifications of his question
and wrong in his assumption about the insignificant Galilean village he
maligns by innuendo. Jesus of Nazareth would be the source of more good
than Nathanael could imagine, and the question of Jesus' origin had
depths he could not yet fathom. But does the implied author, who is
notoriously inscrutable on this point, intend more? Jesus' Galilean home
is again the point of controversy in 7:52. The Pharisees rebuke the teacher
of Israel saying "search [the scriptures] and you will see that no prophet is
to rise from Galilee." Entering into the irony of the challenge, Ray Summers comments: "Their specialty was law, not history! Several Old Testament prophets had come from Galilee. Ever hear of Nahum or Jonah?"[47]
A few verses earlier (7:41–43) the crowd had presumed that the Christ
could not come from Galilee because the scriptures said he was to come
from the seed of David, from Bethlehem. Again the implied author's smile
is inscrutable. Does he smile because he knows the tradition that Jesus
was in fact born in Bethlehem and was a descendant of David? If so, this is
one of the few instances where his irony depends on information which is
never given to the reader (cf. 7:52; 11:48).[48] Because one of the author's
favorite devices is to allow Jesus' opponents to speak the truth unawares,
the balance is in favor of the assumption that the author and his intended
readers knew the tradition of Jesus' birth in Bethlehem. But the irony is
not a simple one; it has a deeper level. Whether Jesus is from Galilee or
Bethlehem is, as Barrett has said, "a trivial matter in comparison with the
questions whether he is ἐκ τῶν ἄνω or ἐκ τῶν κάτω (8:23), whether he is

---

[47] *Behold the Lamb,* p. 114.
[48] For this point I am indebted to an unpublished paper by Paul D. Duke.

or is not from God."[49] This is Jesus' real origin (cf. 1:1-2), but the Jews do not see it. Nicodemus says "we know that you are a teacher come from God" (3:2), but they do not understand either his teaching or that he is the son of God. They assume Joseph was his father (6:42) and imply that there was something improper about his birth (8:41). Again the implied author smiles inscrutably, maddening commentators, but the pattern of his smiles is beginning to give him away. He has heard more about Jesus' birth than he ever says, and assumes his readers have too.[50] His "silent" communication conveys more than his "verbal" communication. The final ironic twist to the Jews' ignorance of Jesus' origin is that they demand that the origin of the Christ will be unknown (7:27-29). They reject Jesus because they assume they know his origin. But they do not know the place of his birth much less his divine Father, and in the end they are forced to reveal that this basis for their rejection is groundless: "We do not know where he comes from" (9:29). Had they known, they would have known Jesus and his Father (8:19).

Jesus' identity. Although it lies at the core of most of the ironic passages in the gospel, the identity of Jesus and the various ways it is manifested and announced are frequently the specific object of irony. The reader knows that Jesus speaks of living water figuratively and can enjoy the Samaritan woman's blunders and evasions. The irony of events by which Jesus asks for water as he is dying (19:29; cf. 7:38), however, strikes with more horror than humor. While the Samaritan woman reasons that Jesus must be the Christ because he has told her all that she has done, Jesus is leading the disciples to understand his role in far greater terms (4:29-38).[51]

When Jesus is called simply "a man" the implied author winks at the reader. The sick man at the pool of Bethesda complains that he has no man to help him (5:7); in fact he has Jesus. Hard on the heels of this healing the narrator explains that the Jews were seeking to kill Jesus because he made himself equal to God (5:18). The officers sent to arrest Jesus return explaining their failure to do so: "No man ever spoke like this man" (7:46; see also 4:29; 9:16; 10:33; 11:47, 50; 18:17, 29). This motif reaches its climax at the trial, when Pilate says to the crowd: "Behold the

---

[49] *John,* p. 330.

[50] Barrett, *John,* p. 330, and Brown, *John,* vol. 2, p. 330, agree. The point is disputed by Bultmann, *John,* pp. 305-6 n. 6, and Meeks, "Galilee and Judea in the Fourth Gospel," pp. 161-63. See also Dodd, *The Interpretation of the Fourth Gospel,* pp. 90-91.

[51] Cf. Dodd, *The Interpretation of the Fourth Gospel,* p. 315.

man" (19:5).[52] All they beheld was a man, but others beheld his glory (1:14). A further irony is perhaps intended: Jesus was not just a man, he was the Son of Man.

When the crowds ask Jesus for a sign and suggest the giving of bread from heaven, they do not realize that not only has Jesus just given them precisely the sign they are asking for but that, in the evangelist's metaphorical system at least, he is himself the bread from heaven (6:30–31). When the Samaritan woman asks mockingly whether Jesus is greater than their father Jacob (4:12) and the Jews ask whether Jesus is greater than Abraham (8:53), the readers are sure that they know the right answer while the characters are implying the wrong one.

Not only is Jesus greater than the patriarchs, he is the king of the Jews. The trial before Pilate spins this irony into a fine and intricate tapestry. Pilate does not understand Jesus' kingship or his authority and finally condemns him when the Jews cry out that he will not be a friend of Caesar if he releases a man who makes himself a king (18:33; 19:12). But Jesus has the greater authority (19:11), and the evangelist presents the trial so that the reader can hardly miss the implication that it is Pilate rather than Jesus who is on trial. Pilate faces Jesus and asks, "What is truth?" (18:38). The reader has heard Jesus say "I am . . . the truth" (14:6), but Pilate does not wait for the answer. When he offers to release Barabbas, the Jews betray their lack of concern for justice by choosing a man who was guilty of the charge of which Jesus is innocent (18:39–40). The narrator underlines the irony: "Now Barabbas was a robber." The contrast between appearance and reality culminates when Pilate hauls before the crowd the beaten and abused prisoner, dressed as king, and says, "Behold the man" (19:5). Who would recognize such a king? Only when the Jews offer their confession of self-betrayal and apostasy, "We have no king but Caesar," in reply to the taunt, "behold your King," does Pilate hand Jesus over to be crucified. When Pilate writes the charge, "The King of the Jews," to be placed on Jesus' cross, the chief priests request that it be changed. This is not a weakening of the irony of the mockery in Mark but a more deft handling of the irony of Jesus' death as the king of the Jews.[53] Pilate's verdict is intended as a mockery of the Jews. In characteristic Johannine irony it is also his half-believed testimony which simultaneously betrays Pilate's duplicity in condemning an innocent man and proclaims Jesus' kingship to all the world in Hebrew, Latin, and Greek, the languages of religion, government, and culture (cf. 12:32).

---

[52] See Brown, *John,* vol. 2., p. 876, and Dodd, *The Interpretation of the Fourth Gospel,* p. 437, for discussion of alternative interpretations.

[53] Booth, *A Rhetoric of Irony,* p. 28 n. 21.

Jesus' ministry. Dramatic irony is used to highlight the symbolic story with which Jesus' ministry is introduced. In the first sign, Jesus, who will establish grace and truth in place of Law, changes water to wine. The reader is told that the water turned wine was drawn by the servants, but the chief steward is innocently unaware of its source. Our superior vantage point allows us to know that "the good wine" was not saved to the last, but there is a danger that the reader may be caught unaware of a yet higher plateau of meaning. The story is more than it appears to be; in it the disciples behold Jesus' glory. It is a "third day" view of Jesus' ministry.[54] In all that is to follow, Jesus will replace the water of the Jewish institutions, festivals, and Law with the wine of the Spirit and truth. In this sense, the good wine has been held back "until now," and Jesus can be likened to the bridegroom (3:29). The ways of God are different from the ways of "man" ($\check{\alpha}\nu\theta\rho\omega\pi\sigma\varsigma$ 2:10)! Jesus' ministry will be veiled so that only those to whom it is given to do so may rise to the plateau from which its true meaning can be seen.

The challenge of Jesus' brothers for him to show himself to the world is another example of John's ironic treatment of Jesus' ministry (7:3–4). His disciples had seen the works that he was doing and many of them had left him as a result, so there was little hope that the doing of signs was going to change the world! Dodd has suggested further ironies here.[55] On the lowest level the brothers challenge a "rustic prophet" from the provinces to "appeal to the great public of the metropolis." Above that the reader knows that the brothers are unconsciously appealing to the Messiah to show himself to Israel, and beyond that for the incarnate *logos* to reveal himself to the world. In 12:19 it is the Pharisees who utter a truth they are unaware of: "The world has gone after him." Again the evangelist smiles as he writes.

Jesus' death. The ironies spun from Jesus' death at the hands of those to whom he had come to bring life are more bitter. Jesus knows all along what is coming, as does the informed reader. The Jews quarrel over the enigma of Jesus' giving his flesh for the life of the world (6:51–52), but the reader who knows the end of the story before it is told knows what he means. When the Jews ask scornfully, "You have a demon! Who is seeking to kill you?" (7:20) the reader again knows the answer. Jesus is not just paranoid, nor is he suicidal. The Jews think he may mean that he will kill himself (8:22), but the reader knows otherwise. The partial truth

[54] Dodd, *The Interpretation of the Fourth Gospel,* pp. 297–300.
[55] *The Interpretation of the Fourth Gospel,* p. 351.

voiced by the Jews on this occasion is disclosed later: Jesus will voluntarily lay down his life (10:17–18; 15:13; 18:11).

So thoroughly ironical is the evangelist's view of Jesus' death that each step along the *via dolorosa* discloses fresh ironies. The betrayer is an object of the evangelist's tearful ironizing. Judas protests the waste of precious ointment at the proleptic anointment of Jesus for his burial, yet Judas bears a heavy share of responsibility for that burial. His pretense is concern for the poor, but he was pilfering from the common purse (12:4–6). Then, by an irony of events, the other disciples think Judas has gone out to "give something to the poor" when he slips off into the night to betray Jesus (13:29). From another vantage point one can see that he gave more to the poor than they realized.

When Judas meets them again he leads an armed band carrying torches to arrest the light of the world. Yet, armed they are powerless before Jesus (18:3–11). Having been arrested by those less powerful than he, Jesus is tried by those with less authority than himself. The religious leaders utter blasphemy and the civil authorities pervert justice. Jesus is tried on false charges, but the charges are ironically true. He was equal to God (5:18), and he was the king of the Jews (19:19–22). With subtle but deft irony the accused judges his accusers. Moreover, Jesus' death brought about the destruction of all that the conspirators sought to protect, the temple and the nation (2:18–20; 11:48). By seeking to save they lost, whereas by losing Jesus saved (cf. 12:25). The accusers are guilty, and the condemned is innocent. But through the perversion of justice (Law), grace and truth are established more powerfully. Life triumphs through death; that is both the fundamental irony of the evangelist's faith and the foundational irony of Christianity.

That Jesus' glorification and wider ministry should begin with his execution is an incongruity one would not expect the evangelist to let pass unnoticed. Jesus' "whither" is so important to the implied author's theological point of view that it is underscored by irony as well as misunderstanding. When the Jews conjecture that Jesus is going to the Diaspora to teach the Greeks (7:33–36), the reader knows that truth has again conscripted the tongues of unenlightened spokesmen. But the hour of the cross stands between this prophecy spoken unawares and its fulfillment (cf. 12:20–23). The call of the Greeks signals that the hour has arrived for the Son of Man to be glorified.

Discipleship. Most of the ironic passages which fall into this category concern Peter. When asked if they would leave Jesus also, Peter speaks for the twelve, "Lord, to whom shall we go?" (6:68). It is an irony of events, whether intended or not, that Peter is later the one who denies

Jesus so outspokenly. On that last night Peter resists Jesus' warning that he would not be able to follow him at that time (13:36–38). Irony makes the truth more bearable. Peter, speaking like an ἀλαζών or braggart, a familiar character to ancient audiences, boasts that he would lay down his life for Jesus. The intended readers probably knew that Peter eventually had the chance to make good his boast (cf. 21:18–19), but that night he denied Jesus. In fact, he denies Jesus at precisely the moment when Jesus is being interrogated about his disciples (18:19). The reader can see what the chief priest cannot: in their present condition the disciples pose no threat to anyone.

The evangelist's power and craft as an ironist are fully displayed in the delightful figures woven into the carpet of chapter 9. The blind man is the typical εἴρων, dissimulating and repeatedly professing his ignorance (9:12, 25). The Pharisees unknowingly play the role of the ἀλαζών, confidently claiming to know the truth about Jesus (9:16, 24, 29–30) and resisting instruction from the blind man (9:34). A variety of types of irony are adduced for the reader's enjoyment. The Pharisees falsely assume that Jesus cannot be from God because he does not keep the sabbath according to their requirements (9:16). Others expose the fallacy of their reasoning; the sign itself points to an alternative interpretation (9:16). Their attempts to evade their dilemma fail: the man who sees is positively identified as the blind beggar and the son born blind. When the Pharisees call the man for a second time their incongruous exhortation betrays their position: "Give God praise; we know that this man is a sinner" (9:24). Sarcasm drips from his reply to their next question: "You do not want to become his disciples too, do you?" (9:27, NASB). They proudly maintain that they are disciples of Moses, but the reader knows better (cf. 9:28; 5:45–46). In the next verse they damningly betray their ignorance: ". . . we do not know where he comes from " (9:29). The dull blade of sarcasm makes the next cut: "Why, this is a marvel! You do not know where he comes from, and yet he opened my eyes" (9:30). Their assumption that the man's blindness was the result of sin runs counter to Jesus' answer to the disciples at the beginning of the episode (cf. 9:34 and 9:3), so the reader again perceives the error of their reasoning. When the blind man asks who the Son of Man is, Jesus' claim to the title is cleverly underlined by his answer: "You have *seen* him" (9:37).[56] The blind man receives more than his sight, though. In the end Jesus adds the ironic twist that it is the Pharisees who are really blind, though they see, and therefore cannot be forgiven. Jesus characterizes his mission with a proverbial statement: "For

---

[56] Summers, *Behold the Lamb,* p. 125.

judgment I came into this world, that those who do not see may see, and that those who see may become blind" (9:39; cf. Isa. 6:9–10). Incredulously, the Pharisees ask, "we are not blind too, are we?" (NASB). If the readers do not see, they are willfully blind also.

Each of the passages in which irony can be detected has its own individuality, its own subtleties. Many of them involve words which have two or more meanings, one on the lips of the speaker and one or more understood only by the reader and the implied author. Most of them can also be broadly classified as dramatic irony since they depend upon the reader's knowledge of the character's ignorance (e.g., 2:9–11; 4:10ff.; 5:7; 6:30–31). More specific rubrics are therefore needed if one is to appreciate the variety and range of the evangelist's techniques for constructing ironies.[57] Because ironies are inevitably more subtle and complex than the rubrics under which they can be fitted, some of the passages fit under more than one. In spite of the difficulties of classification, appreciation for the evangelist's craft may be increased by recognition of the range of ironies he employs.

As examples of dramatic irony, in which the reader smugly enjoys knowing what the character has yet to discover, one can cite the chief steward's exercise in wine tasting (2:9–11), the Samaritan woman's conversation with Jesus about living water (4:10ff.), and the crowd's request for bread from heaven (6:30–31). The most common device employed by the evangelist, however, is the unanswered question, often based on a false assumption, in which the character suggests or prophesies the truth without knowing it:

1:46	Can anything good come out of Nazareth?
4:12	You are not greater than our father, Jacob, are you? (NASB)
6:42	Is not this Jesus, the son of Joseph, whose father and mother we know?
6:52	How can this man give us his flesh to eat?
7:20	Who is seeking to kill you?
7:26	Can it be that the authorities really know that this is the Christ?
7:35	Where does this man intend to go that we shall not find him? Does he intend to go to the Dispersion among the Greeks and teach the Greeks?
7:42	Has not the scripture said that the Christ is descended from David, and comes from Bethlehem, the village where David was?
7:48	No one of the rulers or Pharisees has believed in him, has he? (NASB)
8:22	Will he kill himself, since he says, "Where I am going, you cannot come"?
8:53	Are you greater than our father Abraham, who died?
9:40	Are we also blind?
18:38	What is truth?

---

[57] See Muecke, *The Compass of Irony,* pp. 64–82. Paul. D. Duke suggested some of the following techniques of Johannine irony.

For each of these questions the character assumes an answer the reader knows to be wrong, so we can congratulate ourselves on having such a superior grasp of the true state of affairs and the divine revelation they are mediating. By suggesting the truth in some of these questions, the interlocutors simultaneously expose the error of their assumptions.

Elsewhere the interlocutors reason falsely or confidently assert a falsehood or lower view of things (7:27–29; 7:52; 9:16; 13:37–38; 16:30–32). On other occasions the characters naively make statements which convey meanings they do not suspect:

5:7	Sir, I have no man . . .
7:4	If you do these things, show yourself to the world.
11:50	You do not understand that it is expedient for you that one man should die for the people, and that the whole nation should not perish.
12:19	Look, the whole world has gone after him.
19:14	Behold your King!

Each naively spoken truth spurs the reader on to detect yet other truths half hidden in the dialogue of John's characters. On other occasions, the slanders inflicted on Jesus expose the ignorance of the slanderers (8:19, 41; 9:24, 29). False charges are ironically true in John's world (5:18; 19:7, 19–22). Higher and lower views, appearances and realities, are juxtaposed (4:29–38; 18:17–19), and Jesus' opponents betray themselves in their attempts to expose Jesus (9:29; 19:15). The contrast of reality and appearances may be underlined (19:5) or the irony may develop from the symbolism of the scene (18:3–11). At times the narrator or Jesus states the incongruity baldly (1:11; 5:39–40, 45–46; 10:32). Elsewhere the mocking question (3:10) and sarcasm (9:27, 30) strike with unexpected force. The evangelist's construction and interpretation of events either suggests irony (2:18–20; 18:28) or leaves the irony of events for the reader to discover (6:66–68; 7:3; 12:4–6; 13:29; 18:39–40; 19:7, 28). Those who search for eternal life cannot accept it (5:39–40). Those who ask for a sign of bread from heaven have already received the sign but cannot accept the true bread (6:30–31). Those who seek to protect the temple and nation bring destructive judgment upon it (2:18–20; 11:48), and the mourner looking for Jesus' body cannot recognize him (20:14–15). In a world in which people get what they want to avoid, lose what they want to protect, and cannot find what they are looking for, it is understandable that the Christ would not be recognized by those who were looking for him. John's narrative world is therefore an ironic one, one which lends plausibility and verisimilitude to the ironic story he has to tell.

Although irony does not always require a victim, John's irony usually has three participants: the ironist, the victim, and the observer or reader.

The ironist may be either Jesus or the evangelist, but since we have argued that the gospel is not concerned with the *ipsissima verba* of the historical Jesus, we take it that the evangelist is the author of the gospel's ironies regardless of which character presents them to the reader. In fact, the gospel's ironies seldom come through Jesus, as they do in 3:10; 9:37; 10:32. More often, Jesus underlines the irony given voice by the interlocutor (e.g., 9:41; 13:18; 16:31–32). By his use of irony the evangelist paints a profile of himself as a person with a keen sense of incongruity, humor, and pathos.[58] Since his irony is generally specific as well as stable, Muecke's comment on this brand of irony is revealing: "It is characteristic of, though by no means confined to, a society with a more or less 'closed ideology,' that is a society whose values are more or less established, whose members, as a body, are 'assured of certain certainties.'"[59] This assurance of "certain certainties," which the evangelist no doubt shared with the readers whom he expected to see and enjoy his ironies, makes the author vulnerable to irony from a vantage point yet higher than his own.[60] Yet, it is the evangelist's unshakable faith that his position is that higher than which there is no other, in a word God's perspective, that makes him completely oblivious to this possibility. His is a "womb with a view"—the bosom of the Father (1:18; 13:25; 21:20).[61] Since it never enters the gospel, explorations of the possibility of the evangelist's being the unsuspecting victim of a higher irony can be left without further discussion, but it is appropriate to consider how a reader sympathetic with the perspective of the Jews would read the gospel's ironies.

The Jews and those associated with them (the Pharisees, Nicodemus, Caiaphas, and so forth) are the most frequent victims of John's irony. Their inability to comprehend Jesus' glory sets up most of the irony, since the reader is able to see both their blindness and Jesus' glory through the eyes of the evangelist. Muecke has commented that a victim of irony does not need to be willfully blind, though he may be. He need only be confidently unaware that things are not what he supposes them to be: "Other things being equal, the greater the victim's blindness, the more striking the irony."[62] As representatives of the world's unbelief, the blindness of the Jews in John could hardly be greater. They of all people, and especially their teachers, Pharisees, and priests, should have recognized the Messiah. The irony of their blindness is therefore all the more penetrating. Although they do not recognize who Jesus is, there is willfulness in

---

[58] See Booth, *A Rhetoric of Irony*, p. 120.
[59] Muecke, *The Compass of Irony*, p. 120.
[60] Cf. Muecke, *The Compass of Irony*, p. 31; and his *Irony*, p. 31.
[61] The phrase is Cyril Connolly's, quoted by Muecke, *The Compass of Irony*, p. 242.
[62] Muecke, *Irony*, pp. 28–29.

their blindness. They love darkness rather than light (3:19), they seek the glory of man rather than the glory of God (5:44), and in fact they see but reject what they see (9:39–41). As a result, they do not recognize the higher plane of their own words.

Most of the other characters find themselves, if only briefly, the victims of the evangelist's irony. Nathanael (1:46), the chief steward (2:9–11), Nicodemus (3:2, 10), the Samaritan woman (4:10, 12, 29–38), the lame man (5:7), the crowd (6:30–31; 7:26, 42), Peter (6:66-68; 13:37–38; 18:19), the Jerusalemites (7:27–29), the officers (7:46), Thomas (11:16), the disciples (16:30–32), Pilate (18:33–19:22), and Mary (20:14–15) each come in for their turn. In line with the general response of each character to Jesus, the sting of the irony is sharper, deeper, and more lasting with some than with others. The pervasiveness with which irony touches virtually all of the characters, however, underscores the fact that all are to a greater or lesser degree incapable of perceiving the revelation in Jesus. The glory of the one from heaven eludes all who are from "this world" even when they have "beheld" that glory. Only those who are given (6:37), drawn (6:44), or called (6:70; 10:3) can comprehend the glory; only those who are drawn or called to the side of the implied author, that is, only the readers, can grasp the irony of it all. Only from his vantage point, his point of view, is the higher plane accessible to the readers who will share his ironic view of the world and its redeemer.

It is possible, even probable one suspects, that many readers will not see or share in many of the gospel's ironies. In a sense, therefore, they become further victims through their blindness or unawareness of higher planes. The discovery of new ironies to which one had previously been unaware does not engender in the reader a feeling of having been victimized, however, but a greater appreciation for the implied author and his work and a stronger sense of communion with him. The work therefore gains from repeated readings, since it depends more on dramatic irony than mystery for its effect.[63] Never is the reader the victim of irony. On the contrary, inclusion is the strongest effect of John's irony. Even one who otherwise would not be inclined to share his point of view will find himself or herself walking with the implied author when they begin to mount from one plane of understanding to another, when apparent meanings are set aside and intended overtones are caught, when a wink or a smile creates a bond of secret communication.[64] As readers share more and more common ground with the implied author, they simultaneously feel the duality of

---

[63] Booth, *A Rhetoric of Irony*, p. 285.

[64] Booth, *A Rhetoric of Irony*, pp. 13, 28–29, esp. p. 28: "And every irony inevitably builds a community of believers even as it excludes."

their position as observers over against the victimized characters.[65] Intimacy with the implied author is created at the expense of distance from those of "this world," especially the Jews. The shock of incongruity which the reader often feels in reading John drives a wedge between the reader and the values and appearances of the unbelieving world. John's irony is calculated, therefore, primarily to include readers among the circle of believers committed to the evangelist's theology. The implied author's irony is not designed, like that of Socrates, to extract the truth, but to expose it and to include the observer in the circle of those who have recognized it. The irony is set up by the implied author, but the reliable narrator is never its victim either. The gospel's purposes could not be achieved if the reader did not trust him implicitly. The gospel's use of irony therefore sweetens and spices the fellowship between reader and narrator. The implied commentary conveyed through the gospel's misunderstandings and ironies creates an intimacy which has a purpose, namely the creation of a relationship which is shared only by those who are committed at the deepest levels to the same life-transforming beliefs. Whether the implied commentary is directed primarily at those who do not share those beliefs or at those who are not as deeply committed to them will be a central concern of the next chapter. In the hands of others irony becomes a sword, but in the hands of our author it is more like a net in which readers are caught and drawn to the evangelist's theology and faith (cf. John 21).

Reverting to the earlier metaphor of buildings and rooms, one can say that reading the gospel is an exercise in journeying by faith, living in tents as meanings are set up and then taken down so that we can travel on in the company of our reliable narrator and the master ironist, the implied author. When we reach his destination we find that it is a secure one, a city in which rooms with a view, a shared one, have been prepared for us, and some say it is a "city which has foundations, whose builder and maker is God" (Heb. 11:10).[66]

SYMBOLISM

The intellectual dance of the author and reader and the communion of the upper and lower spheres of reality and meaning become more intimate through the symbols which they share. The misunderstandings are a

---

[65] Muecke, *The Compass of Irony,* p. 218.

[66] Paul D. Duke, in an unpublished paper, wrote: ". . . in this gospel's house are many rooms—with a view. We are invited to abide there by irony as by faith."

dramatic portrayal of the plight of those whose understanding is limited to the mundane. The ironies of the story, like the misunderstandings but more subtly, invite the reader to share the implied author's higher vantage point. From it the blindness of the characters around Jesus and the half-hidden truths which fill their conversations may be clearly seen. The symbols employed by the implied author and his central character open even richer and more stimulating views into the order and mystery of the world above. Consequently, they are often the ladder on which readers, like the angels of Jacob's dream, may ascend and descend while moving to and from the heaven opened by the story (cf. 1:51). The symbols, like the images, metaphors, motifs, and themes to which they are related, often carry the principal burden of the narrative and provide implicit commentary and directional signals for the reader. Macgregor put the matter baldly: "No understanding of the Gospel is possible without an appreciation of the part played by symbolism."[67] Before such an appreciation is possible, however, symbolism must be distinguished from metaphor, signs, and motifs.

A great deal has been written recently on the nature and uses of metaphor.[68] For our purposes Friedman's simple definitive statement is sufficient: "The basic definition of *metaphor* is that it is a device which speaks of one thing (tenor) in terms which are appropriate to another (vehicle), with the vehicle serving as the source of traits to be transferred to the tenor."[69] When Jesus says, "I am the bread of life" (6:35) in the context of a discourse on the true bread, the reader is given both the tenor ("I") and the vehicle ("the bread of life"). Our task is to infer the relationship between the tenor and the vehicle and in doing so to understand those features of the identity of Jesus which led the author to use the metaphor. When the reader has inferred the relationship, that is, that Jesus confers and sustains the true life just as bread sustains physical life,[70] or that Jesus' body is symbolized by bread and that symbol is institutionalized in the eucharist, new insight is born and the reader has shared in a communicative process which draws together the maker and the appreciator of the metaphor. Ted Cohen has identified three aspects of this process: "1) the speaker issues a kind of concealed invitation, 2) the hearer expends a

---

[67] *John,* p. xxv.

[68] See the Autumn 1974 issue of *New Literary History* and the Autumn 1978 issue of *Critical Inquiry,* both of which are devoted to metaphor, and Philip E. Wheelwright, *Metaphor and Reality,* esp. pp. 70–91. Paul Ricoeur, *Interpretation Theory,* pp. 45–69, offers helpful observations on the relation of metaphor to symbol. George Lakoff and Mark Johnson, *Metaphors We Live By,* came to my attention after this chapter was written.

[69] *Form and Meaning in Fiction,* p. 289.

[70] John Painter, "Johannine Symbols," p. 33.

special effort to accept the invitation, and 3) this transaction constitutes the acknowledgment of a community."[71] Even if the maker of the metaphor is the evangelist rather than Jesus, by placing the metaphor in the dialogue as the words of Jesus the evangelist succeeds in large measure in transferring the reader's sense of identification from himself to Jesus, again achieving his larger purpose.

Signs, in a literary rather than Johannine sense, are important to us primarily so that John's symbols can be distinguished from them. Unlike symbols, signs more or less arbitrarily stand for or point to something other than themselves.[72] There is no intrinsic connection between a sign and the thing or person to which it points. The meaning of the sign must be learned, and whereas a symbol may point to many things, to be effective, a sign can point to only one. Symbols or metaphors can be used as signs, however, by a group of people who share the same expressions of a common ideology or theology. In such cases, the work of inferring the meaning of the metaphor or symbol is taken for granted. The use of metaphors or symbols as signs diminishes their revelatory power, however, and gives the language of a community an "in-group" value and meaning which can be discerned by outsiders only by recovering the original metaphorical or symbolic functions of the community's language and deciphering it in the light of their common history and ideology.

The etymology of the word "symbol" suggests its function. Σύμβολον is from συμβάλλω, which means to "put together." By nature, and in John consistently, a symbol is "a connecting link between two different spheres."[73] Whereas the tenor and the vehicle are given in a metaphor and the reader must discern the relationship, a symbol presents the vehicle. The relationship may be stated, implied by the context, or assumed from the shared background or culture of writer and reader. The reader's task is to discern the tenor or meaning of the symbol.[74] Unlike a sign, a symbol is not arbitrary but bears some inherent analogical relationship to that which it symbolizes. The reader understands that the symbol means or expresses something more or something else than its plain or superficial meaning. Again in contrast to signs, what symbols convey cannot be stated apart from the symbol; tenor and vehicle cannot be reduced to a one-to-one relationship. Both usually reserve a "surplus of meaning" or "seman-

---

[71] "Metaphor and the Cultivation of Intimacy," p. 8.

[72] Thomas Fawcett, *The Symbolic Language of Religion*, pp. 13–24, 28. C. S. Peirce made a major contribution to the theory of signs by defining them as an icon, an index, or a symbol. See Justus Buchler, ed., *The Philosophy of Peirce*, p. 102.

[73] Harry Levin, *Contexts of Criticism*, p. 200.

[74] Friedman, *Form and Meaning in Fiction*, p. 291.

tic energy" from past associations so that a given symbol may evoke different aspects of the same tenor or different tenors, and various symbols may be used to convey different features of the same tenor.[75] Symbols therefore often span the gap between knowledge, or sensible reality, and mystery. They call for explanation and simultaneously resist it. As William Tindall put it, "Though definite in itself and generally containing a sign that may be identified, the symbol carries something indeterminate, and, however we try, there is a residual mystery that escapes our intellects."[76] Or, as Harry Levin, drawing from Thomas Carlyle, wrote: "Thus a symbol is a sort of excluded middle between what we know and what we do not know—or better, as Carlyle put it, a meeting point between the finite and the infinite."[77] As a result, the more skillful and perceptive the reader the more deeply he or she will enter into the message and the mystery of a symbolic narrative.

Motifs may also have a symbolic function. William Freedman, who has contributed significantly to the definition of motifs, distinguishes a motif from a symbol in two ways: (1) while a symbol may occur singly, a motif "is necessarily recurrent and its effect cumulative," and (2) while a symbol is something described, a motif, "although it may appear as something described, perhaps even more often forms part of the description."[78] Five factors "determine the efficacy of a motif": (1) the frequency with which it occurs, (2) the avoidability or unlikelihood of its uses or appearance in certain contexts, (3) the significance of the contexts in which it occurs, (4) the consistency or coherence of all instances of the motif, and (5) the appropriateness of the motif to what it symbolizes.[79] A motif, according to Freedman, is therefore

> a recurrent theme, character, or verbal pattern, but it may also be a family or cluster of literal or figurative references to a given class of concepts or objects. . . . It is generally symbolic—that is, it can be seen to carry a meaning beyond the literal one immediately apparent; it represents on the verbal level something characteristic of the structure of the work, the events, the characters, the emotional effects or the moral cognitive content. It is presented both as an object of description and, more often, as part of the narrator's imagery and descriptive vocabulary.[80]

---

[75] See Wheelwright's definition of a tensive symbol, *Metaphor and Reality*, p. 94.
[76] "Excellent Dumb Discourse," p. 342.
[77] *Contexts of Criticism*, p. 197.
[78] "The Literary Motif," p. 124.
[79] "The Literary Motif," pp. 126–27.
[80] "The Literary Motif," pp. 127–28.

Like misunderstandings, ironies, metaphors, and symbols, motifs involve
the reader more deeply in the work by weaving consistency and continuity
while inviting the reader to discern patterns, implications, and levels of
meaning which lie below the surface of the literary work.

The types and functions of symbols and motifs are ultimately as varied
as the creative power of the artist allows. Before turning to the types of
functions found in John, it will be helpful to set a few rudimentary categories in place. The meaning of symbols may be entirely created by the
author and conveyed by context, "symbols of ancestral vitality" lifted from
earlier sources, archetypal symbols whose context is virtually universal, or
"symbols of cultural range" drawn from the social and historical context of
the author and his intended readers.[81] Wheelwright states that the special
enrichment of "symbols of ancestral vitality" which are borrowed from
earlier writings comes from "the merging of certain past meanings with
such new meanings as are indicated by the context into which the symbol
is freshly introduced."[82] "Symbols of cultural range," which have "a significant life for members of a community," generally express a view of the
world, society, and life (*Weltanschauung* and *Lebensanschauung*).[83] Symbols exhibit both flexibility and constancy,[84] and may therefore be adapted
to fit changing situations or views of one's situation. The Fourth Gospel's
adaptation of symbols drawn from Judaism suggests that established symbols are being given new meaning in order that they might retain their
viability and provide continuity in a context of profound crisis and change.
Jonathan Z. Smith has provocatively argued that "social change is preeminently symbol or symbolic change. . . . To change stance is to totally
alter one's symbols and to inhabit a different world."[85] The "symbolic
dialect" of John may therefore provide clues to its social and historical
context and the kind of change to which it calls the reader.[86]

Symbols are susceptible to as many classifications as irony. They may
be grouped according to the nature of the vehicle or image: material,
animal, personal, or numerological. The potential limits and effects of
each on the reader may then be assessed. Alternatively, and more prof-
itably, symbols may be classified according to their function within the
literary work: allegorical, transcending ("when a series of symbols are

---

[81] See Wheelwright, *Metaphor and Reality,* pp. 99–110.

[82] *Metaphor and Reality,* p. 105.

[83] *Metaphor and Reality,* p. 108, and Susanne K. Langer, *Philosophy in a New Key,* p. 287.

[84] Fawcett, *The Symbolic Language of Religion,* p. 29.

[85] "The Influence of Symbols Upon Social Change," p. 471.

[86] "Symbolic dialect" is Erich Fromm's phrase, quoted by Fawcett, *The Symbolic Language of Religion,* p. 29.

recognized as mutually related, as helping to explain each other, . . . we find suggested a shifting complex of significances each transcending individually the literal action of the story"), and orienting ("At times it is recognized that a single instance of symbolism reflects or gives rise to a series of possible extensions of meaning in elements of the action which do not in themselves suggest symbolic implications").[87] The relative value or importance of a work's symbols may be suggested by such classifications as "core and guide symbols," and co- and subordinated symbols.[88] Whatever categories one chooses, a clearer understanding of John's symbols emerges from observation of how the symbols cluster and interrelate.

Building on previous work, research on Johannine symbolism has shown renewed vigor in the past few years. The most seminal earlier work is that of C. H. Dodd. Writing in his magisterial work on the Fourth Gospel (1953), Dodd reflects the solid insights of earlier work and contributes his own perceptive observations.[89] The discourses appended to various narratives show that they are to be understood symbolically. John's symbols are drawn from everyday life, but derive their significance from the rich associations they have acquired in the Old Testament and apocalyptic literature. In John these symbols are "almost absorbed into the thing signified."[90] As the recurrence of ἀληθινός with an image suggests, the writer means the true or eternal reality symbolized by his image when he speaks of the true bread, the true vine, and so on. There is an integral relationship between the symbol and the reality it presents regardless of where the symbol occurs, in discourse, allegory, or historical event. The events themselves, the Johannine σημεῖα, are symbolic acts. The whole gospel, "narrative and discourse, [is] bound together by an intricate network of symbolism" and depicts "a world in which phenomena—things and events—are a living and moving image of the eternal, and not a veil of illusion to hide it, a world in which the Word is made flesh."[91]

Subsequently, Juan Leal described the following types of symbols in John: (1) allegorical symbolism, (2) nominal symbolism, (3) biblical symbolism, (4) symbolism in action, and (5) historical symbolism.[92] A decade later David Wead called for caution in efforts to find symbolism in the Fourth Gospel.[93]

---

[87] Wendell V. Harris, "Mapping Fiction's 'Forest of Symbols,'" pp. 141–42.
[88] Walter Hinderer, "Theory, Conception, and Interpretation of the Symbol," p. 98.
[89] *The Interpretation of the Fourth Gospel*, pp. 133–43.
[90] Dodd, *The Interpretation of the Fourth Gospel*, p. 137.
[91] Dodd, *The Interpretation of the Fourth Gospel*, p. 143.
[92] "El simbolismo histórico del iv evangelio," pp. 329–48.
[93] *The Literary Devices in John's Gospel*, pp. 26–28.

In the same year (1970), Günter Stemberger published the most substantial treatment of Johannine symbolism to date. In an impressive introduction he distinguishes symbol from sign, notes the dynamic quality of
symbol and its capacity for elucidating mystery, and contends that "the
ethic of John is essentially symbolic."[94] The first part of the book treats the
symbolism of ethical dualism, the second part the symbolism of struggle
for victory, and the conclusion notes the way in which the dualistic pairs of
images denote the same realities, offer the same ethical choice, and point
to Christ as the center, the personal center of John's ethic. This focus on
the moral categories of the gospel's symbolism and the attendant reduction
in the richness of its function within the narrative have been criticized by
Wayne Meeks.

In 1966 Meeks proposed that the geographical framework of John
functions symbolically.[95] Galilee and Samaria have a prominent role as
"positive symbols for the Christian movement," the places of acceptance in
contrast to Jerusalem, the place of rejection.[96] This symbolism is also
related to the history of the Johannine community. Six years later, Meeks
contributed a substantial essay toward the interpretation of the gospel's
metaphorical system.[97] Noting that even after Stemberger's volume "we
have not yet learned to let the symbolic language of Johannine literature
speak in its own way," and that "we have as yet no adequate monograph
on the Johannine symbolism as such," Meeks explores John's symbolic
language by focusing on the important motif of ascending and descending.
He locates the gospel's symbolism in the context of the conflicts of the
community of its origin with Judaism: "I shall argue that one function of
the 'symbolic universe' communicated in this remarkable body of literature was to make sense of all these aspects of the group's history."[98] That
history also "motivated" the reaction expressed in the gospel's symbolism.
Consequently, the whole gospel has "a self referring quality" and depends
on "a closed system of metaphors" which is virtually impenetrable and
incomprehensible to readers who do not share its perspective.[99] The
gospel itself, in fact, "functions for its readers in precisely the same way
that the epiphany of its hero functions within its narrative and
dialogues."[100] Either the reader, like the dialogue partners, stays with it
long enough to penetrate its metaphors and accept what is offered, or he or

---

[94] *La symbolique du bien et du mal selon saint Jean*, p. 21.
[95] "Galilee and Judea in the Fourth Gospel," pp. 159–69.
[96] "Galilee and Judea in the Fourth Gospel," pp. 165, 169.
[97] "The Man from Heaven in Johannine Sectarianism," pp. 44–72.
[98] "The Man from Heaven in Johannine Sectarianism," pp. 47, 49–50.
[99] "The Man from Heaven in Johannine Sectarianism," pp. 68–69.
[100] "The Man from Heaven in Johannine Sectarianism," p. 69.

she will reject the whole thing in anger. Although Meeks may have exaggerated the obscurity of the gospel's metaphors for readers who are not privy to the Johannine community's perspective and language, he has done a valuable service in taking the system as a whole, analyzing central metaphors, and relating it to both the gospel's social setting and its Christology.

The relationship of the gospel's symbolism to its historical accuracy and its sacramentalism have been tandem subjects of continuing interest. Oscar Cullmann argued that the juxtaposition of history and symbolism is misleading.[101] Both are present in John, and the historical points symbolically to realities which transcend history. Utilizing more recent studies on the definition and function of symbolism, Sandra M. Schneiders advanced these points anew in 1977.[102] She distinguishes symbol from sign and allegory, defining it as "1) a sensible reality 2) which renders present to and 3) involves a person subjectively in 4) a transforming experience 5) of the mystery of the Transcendent."[103] With this definition she is able to treat Jesus himself, his words, his works, and the community of believers as symbols. One may wish to take slight exception to her definition. While symbols may involve the observer or reader in a transforming experience of the mystery of the transcendent, not all symbols are so powerful and not all evoke the transcendent. Likewise, such an expansive concept of symbolism needs to be supplemented by further discussion of the types and functions of the symbols found in John. There is a significant difference between Jesus himself, his works, the images of water and bread, and the stone jars as symbols.

Xavier Léon-Dufour returned to the relationship between history and symbol in his presidential address to the Society for New Testament Studies at its meeting in Toronto in August 1980. Citing as a standard definition of a symbol "that which represents something else in virtue of an analogical relationship," Léon-Dufour contended that the symbolic operation should be understood as putting together the surface and deeper realities rather than as evacuating the surface of the text simply to reach the deeper reality.[104] Recognizing Jesus as the Son of God is "a symbolic operation which, by means of faith, connects the past and present, Jesus

---

[101] "Der johanneische Gebrauch doppeldeutiger Ausdrücke als Schlüssel zum Verständnis des vierten Evangeliums," esp. p. 361. See also his *Early Christian Worship.*

[102] "History and Symbolism in the Fourth Gospel," pp. 371–76.

[103] "Symbolism and the Sacramental Principle in the Fourth Gospel," p. 223.

[104] "Towards a Symbolic Reading of the Fourth Gospel," pp. 440–41. The definition is taken from Lalande, *Vocabulaire technique et critique de la philosophie,* p. 1058.

and the Son of God."[105] Past and present, symbol and reality symbolized, must therefore be held together for a satisfactory reading of the gospel as a symbolic narrative.

Perhaps the most significant article to date on John's symbolism is the one by John Painter.[106] Developing insights laid down in his earlier book, Painter uses John 9, "a parable or narrative symbol," as the central text for his study. John's symbols are regularly drawn from those applied to the Law by Judaism and interpreted Christologically. They were "focal points" of the conflict with Judaism.[107] Because everything was created by the *logos* and bears an organic relationship to him, "the world is a *store-house* of symbols which can *become* vehicles of the revelation."[108] The "I am" statements "present Jesus in terms of a number of *evocative symbols*."[109] These are not specifically sacramental since they transcend the sacraments and draw from elements of creation which can become symbols pointing to Jesus and the life he offers and sustains. John's "rein-terpretation of the sacraments in terms of his own use of symbols could [therefore] be considered anti-sacramental."[110] The symbols point to Jesus, who is himself a symbolic revelation of God. They are intended to function as vehicles of revelation or sight since all, like the blind man, are born blind, but they also judge those who mistake the symbol for that which it symbolizes or refuse to see that it points beyond itself. Painter has opened a promising path toward understanding John's symbolism even if one prefers to say that John is not anti-sacramental but shows how the sacraments should be understood symbolically along with other elements of the created order. The sacraments, therefore, are made to forfeit the exclusive position they enjoyed in other Christian communities while their symbolic function in presenting the mystery of the revelation is enhanced.

These studies have defined the nature and functions of John's symbols by distinguishing them from signs (in the non-Johannine sense), allegory, and de-historicizing interpretation. They have also shown that symbols must be related to the gospel's whole metaphorical system and the social setting in which it was composed. What is needed is a treatment of John's symbolism that: (1) is based on adequate definitions, (2) is sensitive to movement and development in the gospel, (3) relates the metaphors, sym-

---

[105] "Towards a Symbolic Reading of the Fourth Gospel," p. 442.
[106] "Johannine Symbols," pp. 26–41.
[107] See Painter, *John*, pp. 20–21, 48, 139.
[108] "Johannine Symbols," p. 32 (Painter's italics).
[109] "Johannine Symbols," p. 31 (Painter's italics).
[110] Painter, "Johannine Symbols," p. 32. R. Wade Paschal, Jr., "Sacramental Symbolism and Physical Imagery in the Gospel of John," pp. 151–76, rejects both
anti-sacramental and hyper-sacramental interpretations of John's symbolism.

bols, and motifs to one another, and (4) analyzes their function within the gospel as a literary whole. My present aim must necessarily be more modest; only the outline of such a study can be sketched.

Some initial progress may be possible by separating personal from impersonal symbols. It has been observed that Jesus himself is the principal symbol of the Fourth Gospel,[111] for he partakes of the being of God and reveals Him in this world. He is the "vehicle" of revelation. "Father" and "Son" are likewise symbolic metaphors in Johannine language. The Spirit is "Paraclete," and believers are "children of God." The representative functions of Jesus and the characters of the gospel have already been discussed, if not adequately treated as part of the gospel's symbolism, so we may turn to the impersonal symbols. These have the function of pointing to and interpreting the personal symbols, which are capable of more fully disclosing the personal dimensions of the revelation with which John is concerned.[112] The impersonal symbols in turn may be separated into two categories, if the line between them can be drawn more or less arbitrarily: core symbols and peripheral symbols.[113] The core symbols are those whose centrality is demonstrated by their higher frequency of recurrence and their appearance in more important contexts. The three core symbols of the gospel are light, water, and bread. Each of these points to Jesus' revelatory role and carries a heavy thematic load. To these are related several coordinate symbols, metaphors, and concepts in different passages: darkness, life, wine, flesh. Subordinate symbols can also be gathered around each. For example, among the subordinate symbols for light are lamps, fires, torches, lanterns, day (and night), morning, seeing, and healing the blind.

Often, concrete objects evoke images which are themselves symbols of abstract ideas. The result is "a peculiar mixture of abstraction and imagery."[114] Concrete objects in the visible world evoke the core symbols or presiding metaphors which point to the nature of the invisible reality. The core symbols are not static, fixed, or defined. They are rather what Edward K. Brown has called "expanding symbols."[115] His comments are suggestive for interpreting John's core symbols. As opposed to the fixed symbol, which can only serve by repetition,

---

[111] Schneiders, "History and Symbolism in the Fourth Gospel," p. 373; Edward Malatesta, "Blood and Water from the Pierced Side of Christ (Jn 19, 34)," p. 165.

[112] Schneiders, "Symbolism and the Sacramental Principle in the Fourth Gospel," p. 226.

[113] Hinderer, "Theory, Conception, and Interpretation of the Symbol," p. 108.

[114] Hinderer, "Theory, Conception, and Interpretation of the Symbol," p. 121. Hinderer uses the phrase in reference to Barlach's *Die Sündflut*.

[115] *Rhythm in the Novel*, pp. 55–59.

... the expanding symbol is repetition balanced by variation, and that variation is in progressively deepening disclosure. By the slow uneven way in which it accretes meaning from the succession of contexts in which it occurs; by the mysterious life of its own it takes on and supports; by the part of its meaning that even on the last page of the novel it appears still to withhold—the expanding symbol responds to the impulses of the novelist who is aware that he cannot give us the core of his meaning, but strains to reveal now this aspect of it, now that aspect, in a sequence of sudden flashes.[116]

The expanding symbol is, consequently, especially serviceable for the writer who wants to direct the reader to something behind or beyond the story. It is particularly suited for impelling the reader toward two beliefs:

First, that beyond the verge of what he can express, there is an area which can be glimpsed, never surveyed. Second, that this area has an order of its own which we should care greatly to know—it is neither a chaos, nor something irrelevant to the clearly expressed story, persons, and settings that fill the foreground. The glimpses that are all the novelist can give us of this area do not suffice for our understanding how it is that this order is important to us. The use of the expanding symbol is an expression of belief in things hoped for, an index if not an evidence of things not seen. It does not say what these things are like: It sings of their existence.[117]

The evangelist may be more convinced than the novelist that he knows what these things are like, but his core symbols still "sing of their existence" and provide continuity for diverse scenes and themes while inviting the reader to look beyond "the verge"—and believe.

Light. Philip Wheelwright observes that "of all archetypal symbols there is probably none more widespread and more immediately understandable than *light,* as symbolizing certain mental and spiritual qualities."[118] Because it is commonly associated with intellectual clarity as well as lordship and divinity, it is eminently suitable as a symbol for the Johannine revealer. From the beginning, the gospel "sings" of the existence of light. The prologue links *logos,* life, and light so powerfully that the cluster dominates the symbolic system of the entire narrative. The *logos* incarnate in Jesus is "the life [that] was the light of men" (1:4), and where

---

[116] *Rhythm in the Novel,* pp. 56–57.
[117] *Rhythm in the Novel,* pp. 58–59.
[118] *Metaphor and Reality,* p. 116.

there is light there is life and the perception of Life. The conflict of light
and darkness evokes a universal and primordial response. The symbols
are used universally in religious discourse and had deep roots both in Hellenism and in Judaism, where light was a common symbol for the Law.[119]
John asserts from the beginning that the *logos* is and always was the
exclusive source of light for men. The darkness has not overcome it (1:5).
John the Baptist was not the light but bore witness to it (1:8), for "the true
light" which enlightens every person was coming into the world (1:9).

The next time the symbol appears its significance is expanded to make
explicit the connection between witness and judgment: "And this is the
judgment: that the light has come into the world [cf. 1:9], and men loved
darkness rather than the light" (3:19). Eschatological expectations are
thereby collapsed into present realities and the basis for the acceptance
and rejection of Jesus is explored. Those who reject Jesus do so because
their works are evil and the light exposes their inherent bent toward evil;
they love the darkness (3:20). The one who does the truth, on the other
hand, comes to the light with the result that it discloses that his works are
of God (3:21). These verses increase the symbol's power. Light is not only
the revelation of the *logos;* it reveals the nature of all who come in contact
with it, and the judgment upon each person is determined by his or her
response to it. Light shines in darkness. It reveals. It also exposes.

Qualities inherent in the symbol are pressed into the service of the
gospel's dualism, eschatology, soteriology, and ethics. John the Baptist
was not the light but a burning and shining lamp (5:35). The Jews
rejoiced in his light for a while, but they would not accept the true light.
The subordinate image of the lamp symbolizes the role of the Baptist and
the superiority of Jesus. In the next reference to light, Jesus announces
that he is the light of which the prologue spoke: "I am the light of the
world" (8:12; 1:9). The identification of the symbol with Jesus is complete. It can now be used to depict his work as the giver of "the light of life"
(8:12; 9:5; 1:4). In the following chapter Jesus gives sight to the man born
blind. In Johannine thought all are born blind, and sight is always given.
Here blindness and sight, seeing and believing, are used to expand further
the symbolic value of light and to provide an index to the value of various
characters. The blind man moves from the natural condition of his past to
sight upon encounter with Jesus, response to his words, and a washing in
water. Sight becomes insight into the identity of Jesus, a willingness to
believe, and finally faith. Simultaneously, the Pharisees move from phys-

---

[119] See Dodd, *The Interpretation of the Fourth Gospel,* pp. 201–5; Stemberger, *La
symbolique du bien et du mal selon saint Jean,* pp. 25–49; and Painter, "Johannine Symbols."

ical sight with its attendant implication of understanding, to ignorance (which is exposed by irony), rejection of Jesus and the man who has accepted him, and finally the sentence of blindness. Sin is shown to reside not in the blindness of the one who has not been confronted by the light but in the blindness of those who have seen the light and rejected it. They have chosen to live in darkness because they love it (cf. 3:19), perhaps because in the darkness they can retain their power, but they recognize their blindness, and their sin "remains" (9:40–41). No more powerful account of the healing, exposing, and judging qualities of light could be given.

John 9 also confirms the symbolic use of day and night as subordinate symbols which evoke the core symbols, light and darkness (cf. 9:4–5; 11:9–10). Retrospectively, or upon re-reading, "night" functions as an index to the character of Nicodemus (3:2), the Jews (9:4; 11:10), and Judas (13:30). The reader, now thoroughly conversant with the symbol and its adjunctive images, can be admonished to walk in the light (12:35–36). Isaiah's seeing (12:41; cf. 8:56) and the quotation from Isaiah (12:40) acquire new meaning. The reader can also be expected to sense that torches and lanterns (18:3) are a pathetic substitute for the light of the world, and a charcoal fire (18:18) is a miserable alternative on a cold dark night and a painful reminder in the bright light of a new day (21:9). It is appropriate that Mary Magdalene goes to the empty tomb in darkness (20:1) and that the disciples find fishing at night to be futile but enclose an astonishing catch when it is early morning (21:4). The symbol has by the latter half of the gospel expanded to the point of explosion so that the mere suggestions of its presence evoke the heavy thematic and theological load it acquired in its earlier, more explicit development. By the last chapter most of the narrative's meaning is suggested by symbols the reader is expected to understand, but the symbols are so powerful, some so loaded with earlier associations and some so ambiguous through lack of earlier development that the reader senses implications and overtones which cannot be defined with certainty but which continue to excite imagination, expose mystery, and evoke response.

Water. The image of water appears surprisingly frequently and with the most varied associations of any of John's symbols.[120] There are conversations about water, water pots, rivers, wells, springs, the sea, pools, basins, thirst, and drink. Context and discourse provide clues to the symbolic value of water in the various passages, but in general, while water is

---

[120] See further the rewarding treatment by Birger Olsson, *Structure and Meaning in the Fourth Gospel*, esp. pp. 212–18.

a dominant motif and expanding core symbol, it is less unified and more variable than either light or bread.

Early in the gospel, water is associated with baptism and cleansing. John the Baptist announces: "I baptize with water," but there is another who will baptize with Holy Spirit (1:26, 31, 33). Water as a means of washing or external cleansing points to the inner cleansing which occurs when one accepts John's witness. But it is given temporary or secondary status by the promise of cleansing by the Spirit. The changing of water to wine in the next chapter symbolizes the fulfillment of John's prophetic announcement. The stone containers, which the narrator explicitly says were used for purification by the Jews (2:6), are filled. The *crux interpretationis* in this passage is whether the servants then drew from the filled containers (which is suggested by 2:9—"the water now become wine") or from the well (which is perhaps suggested by the verb ἀντλέω, which is used for drawing water from a well in 4:7, 15). What can be said is that the scene fits the recurring theme of the fulfillment of Jewish expectations and the replacement of Jewish festivals and institutions. Even if the water become wine was drawn from the vessels (ὑδρίαι), as seems probable, the vessels themselves are no longer of any value and can be left behind like the Samaritan woman's vessel (ὑδρίαν 4:28). Jesus is the source and giver of good wine and living water. The connection between the wedding scene and the Baptist's witness is further suggested by his use of the metaphor of the bridegroom and the friend of the bridegroom in 3:29. Wine, of course, is not used like water for cleansing, but evokes a rich set of associations from its use in the Old Testament, apocalyptic literature, and Hellenism. The wedding of the Messiah and his people, the eschatological banquet, the messianic age, and the bounty of God's blessing on Israel lie close at hand. The reference to the third day (2:1) means that eucharistic overtones must also be considered. In the changing of water to wine cleansing gives way to joy and celebration.

When water is mentioned in the third chapter it is still juxtaposed with Spirit and set in the context of the new birth of the children of God and initiation into the new life. The meaning of "water and spirit" in 3:5 is another well-known crux. The emphasis of this phrase is not that baptism is necessary but that any baptism which does not involve cleansing by the Spirit is defective. This interpretation accords well with the secondary position given to baptism by water (alone) in chapter 1, the replacement in chapter 2, and the distinction between that which is born of flesh and that which is born of Spirit in the following verse (3:6). Baptism remains in a somewhat equivocal position, however; Jesus baptizes alongside John (3:22–23, 26; 4:1), but the narrator then insists, rather unconvincingly, that Jesus himself did not baptize (4:2). Although baptism seems to remain the normative practice for those entering the new life, the fourth evangelist qualifies its importance by tying it to the wider symbolic value of water, belief, and the work of the Spirit.

In John 4, well water is contrasted with "living" or flowing water, spring water; and living water is a symbol for the new life or the Spirit of which Jesus is the giver and source. Living water sustains the new life, for once having drunk of it one is never thirsty again. Better than a fountain of youth, it is a fountain of eternal life. In this discourse, the symbolic image functions as a catalyst for change or an impetus to insight. The Samaritan woman, and ultimately the reader, is enticed and challenged by the core symbol to perceive something about Jesus which will impart understanding of the mystery Jesus himself represents and reveals. Perception, however, is organically linked with faith in the revealer of the mystery. The change in the woman is symbolized by the vessel she leaves behind (4:28). She will no longer need it.

In John 5 water, this time in the pool of Bethesda, becomes an ineffective means of healing. By mistakenly believing that the water itself has healing power, the sick man has spent thirty-eight years futilely competing for its therapeutic effect. The scene dramatically shows that Jesus is the source of the healing that was thought to reside in water and exposes the man's ignorance. Although healed, he remains crippled by his failure to grasp the identity of the healing agent and unable to enter the realm of mystery to which he points.

By this point the expansion of this symbolic image is virtually complete. At least there is no further need for intensive treatment. The power of the symbol can be evoked by more indirect references. It is uncertain whether the disciples' crossing of the sea and Jesus' walking on it should be related to the water motif or explained primarily in terms of its re-enactment of the exodus experience. Allusion to the exodus is almost certainly intended, but the scene also portrays dramatically Jesus' power over water and his ability to use it for deliverance even when its destructive power is at its greatest. The disciples can be brought through the water and across the sea which separates the wilderness and the crowd from the village and synagogue, the place of feeding with physical bread from the place of feeding with spiritual bread. If anyone eats the flesh of the Son of Man and drinks his blood, he or she will have life (6:53–56). Jesus himself is true food and true drink (6:55). Therefore, if any thirst, they should come to him (7:37), for by drinking from (i.e., believing in) him they will have eternal life. Rivers of living water will flow from his belly. The narrator provides a partial explanation which links the motif with the giving of the Spirit through Jesus' death (7:39). Living water therefore points to Jesus, the revelation, the new life, and the means by which one enters it, the Spirit.

Following the heated debate over birth and paternity in chapter 8, Jesus sends the man who represents the universal condition of blindness to wash in the pool of Siloam. Siloam, the narrator explains, means "[the one] sent" (9:7). The pool and the washing therefore point away from themselves to the power of Jesus to relieve the condition of blindness with all its symbolic significance. The next washing, the washing of the disciples' feet, again depicts the cleansing action of Jesus' death and his word (cf. 15:3).[121] His death is implicitly understood to be the act of drinking the cup the Father has given him (18:11). With profound irony, the giver of living water must himself thirst (19:28), and the giver of good wine must drink vinegar or common wine.[122] His "cup" is a hyssop, like that used to sprinkle the blood of the paschal lamb on doorposts prior to the exodus (Exod. 12:22). Only in death does he hand over the spirit (19:30), and the river of living water from his belly is released by a spear thrust. John's development of the symbolism of water, like that of light, moves from earlier contexts in which its meaning and associations are more clearly defined, even if they change from one passage to another, to the point where the author assumes that mere references to the symbol, or words or images connected with it, will evoke the rich constellation of earlier references and associations. The impact is profound and moving, for the symbols increasingly elude efforts to interpret them and thereby invite further contemplation.

Bread. In contrast to the scattered and varied use of water, the intensive and more uniform development of bread as a symbol is localized almost exclusively in chapter 6. The setting is Passover, but Jesus is in Galilee rather than Jerusalem. Hence, it is in some sense an alternative celebration. Earlier, Jesus had responded to the disciples who had gone to buy bread for him by saying that he had food they did not know of (4:8, 32). Now he tests Philip: "How are we to buy bread, so that these people may eat?" (6:5). Even Philip recognizes the impossibility of buying sufficient bread. At the next Passover the disciples will mistakenly think that Judas was going out to buy something for the feast (13:29). The symbol should not be mistaken for the reality to which it points. In the economy of the Fourth Gospel true bread cannot be bought, it can only be given and received. After the feeding, the fragments are collected in twelve baskets, perhaps indicating that unlike the manna, which was perishable, the bread which Jesus gives does not perish. Accordingly, he admonishes the

---

[121] See above, p. 118 and Stemberger, *La symbolique du bien et du mal selon saint Jean*, pp. 152–70.

[122] See esp. Brown, *John*, vol. 2, pp. 927–30.

crowd not to work for food which perishes, but for food which abides to eternal life (6:27). This food is the counterpart of the living water which becomes "a spring of water welling up to eternal life" (4:14).[123] Bread is therefore a symbol which evokes the concept of "the true bread" (6:32).

Peder Borgen has shown that the discourse follows the form of a midrashic homily on the text quoted in 6:31.[124] In response to the crowd's call for a sign like Moses did, the giving of bread from heaven, Jesus corrects them on two points. The bread did not come from Moses but from the Father, and Jesus himself, not manna, is the "true" bread from heaven (cf. 3:13). The core symbol has therefore been expanded in various directions and will be expanded further as the discourse progresses. Materialistic eschatological concepts involving the renewal of the gift of manna (as in II Baruch 29:8) are rejected, and their fulfillment in another key is claimed for the descent of Jesus from heaven. The theme of bread from heaven is used to affirm Jesus' origin from above and the superiority of the bread Jesus offers (grace and truth) over the bread Moses gave (Law). The earlier statement that Jesus' food is the doing of the will of the one who sent him (4:32) is developed further in 6:38–40. The twin features of "the bread of God" are that it comes from heaven and gives life to the world (6:33). The nourishment of life, which is the primary function of bread, is then elaborated in terms of the role of the bread from heaven. John Dominic Crossan observes that the discourse on the true bread develops the relationship between feeding and teaching, bread and revelation. He schematizes the correspondence in parallel lists: "1) Source of Food, 2) Feeder, 3) Feeding, 4) Food, 5) Consumption of Food, 6) Consumer, 7) Bodily Life" and "(1') Source of Revelation, (2') Revealer, (3') Revealing, (4') Revelation, (5') Belief, (6') Believer, (7') Eternal Life."[125] In the terminology of the discourse the feeder then becomes the food. Twice Jesus says, "I am the bread of life" (6:35, 48) and twice "I am the (living) bread which has come down from heaven" (6:41, 51). Water, which is more closely tied to the Spirit, purification, and entrance into eternal life, is never used in an "I am" pronouncement and never identified with Jesus beyond the affirmations that he is its source and giver. Bread, on the other hand, whether because it was already identified with the Passover, wisdom, and the Torah in Jewish thought, or because it had eucharistic overtones, or because its function is the sustenance of life, has a greater attributive and interpretive role in symbolically defining Jesus' identity.

---

[123] Dodd, *The Interpretation of the Fourth Gospel,* p. 325.
[124] *Bread from Heaven.*
[125] "A Structuralist Analysis of John 6," p. 245.

The eucharistic overtones of 6:51–58 are universally recognized.[126] Just as the bread is not physical bread, and the life it sustains is eternal life, so the possibility must be considered that the eating of bread in a sacramental observance points to a profound appropriation of Jesus, the doing of the will of the one who sent him, and his death. Earlier it was said that coming to Jesus satisfies hunger and believing in him quenches thirst (6:35). The offensive starkness of the language of 6:51–58 causes many of the disciples to turn away, but crass cannibalistic and magical interpretations of the Lord's supper are rejected. It is the Spirit, not the flesh, which gives life (6:63). After all, Judas eats the bread ($\psi\omega\mu\iota\omega\nu$ not $\mathring{\alpha}\rho\tau o\varsigma$) which Jesus gives him at the last supper, and immediately Satan enters him. This event is connected with chapter 6 by the verbal parallel between the Old Testament quotation used to interpret it in 13:18, "he who ate [$\tau\rho\acute{\omega}\gamma\omega\nu$] my bread has lifted his heel against me" (Ps. 41:10). The same unusual verb for eating is used four times in 6:54–58: "He who eats my flesh and drinks my blood has eternal life" (6:54), "He who eats my flesh and drinks my blood abides in me, and I in him" (6:56), "He who eats me will live because of me" (6:57), and "He who eats this bread will live for ever" (6:58). Judas refused to eat the true bread; the bread he ate had no power to give life. No magical view of the eucharist can survive this narrative interpretation. Nevertheless, the sacrament is indirectly infused with profound meaning as the bread and wine are identified with the body and blood separated at Jesus' death,[127] while the eating is so interpreted that the sacrament must be understood as a symbol pointing to the true act of "eating" the bread from heaven.[128] In this case, the expansion of the core symbol explodes not the symbol but the sacrament—or at least inadequate interpretations of the sacrament—with which it was associated. Thereafter, the meal in John 21 glows with symbolic overtones. Jesus asks the disciples, who have caught nothing from fishing at night, "Do you have anything to eat?" They have not. The catch is linked with the coming of morning and the recognition of Jesus. Jesus himself, however, supplies the bread (21:9, 13) which he gives to them along with the fish.

---

[126] Although John 6:51c–59 has often been identified as a redactional interpolation, it is treated here as an integral part of the gospel. As stated in the Introduction, our concern is with the present form of the gospel, not any earlier stage of its composition. Moreover, these verses fit into the progressive development of various associations of bread in chapter 6, their idiom is thoroughly Johannine, and their harsh language helps to account for the defection of followers a few verses later.

[127] Crossan, "A Structuralist Analysis of John 6," p. 247.

[128] See also Painter, "Johannine Symbols," pp. 31–33.

Other symbols. Countless rich and significant symbolic references populate the text, but none of the other symbols appears with the frequency of the three core symbols. We have already seen that Jesus and the other characters have symbolic or at least representative functions, the geography, chronology, settings, and "signs" of the gospel are also inadequately understood until they are seen to point beyond themselves or their surface meaning. The settings, whether a wedding or the temple, the Jewish festivals or the cross, or even a breakfast by the lake, can be understood as metonymic or metaphoric expressions of the character of Jesus.[129] Each says something about him. Most of the other images, concepts, and material objects mentioned in the gospel also function symbolically. The Spirit descends as a dove (1:32; cf. 2:14, 16). Jesus is the lamb of God (1:29, 36), and his death coincides with the slaughter of the Passover lambs. Jesus drives out of the temple those who are selling sheep, sacrificial oxen, and pigeons (or doves) and replaces the temple with his body (2:14–22; cf. 14:2). In chapter 10 the image of his people as sheep receives extensive parabolic interpretation. The statement that the good shepherd lays down his life for his sheep provides a fresh perspective on Jesus' death and then reverberates when Peter is told to feed his sheep and warned about his impending death (21:15–19). Lazarus' tomb and grave wrappings (cf. 11:44; 20:7) and the anointing of Jesus, point ahead to Jesus' death, royal burial, and resurrection. Jesus' garments are mentioned in significant contexts (13:4, 12; 19:2, 5; 19:23–24). The thong of his sandals (1:27) and the towel he takes (13:4, 5) naturally serve as catalysts for meditation. Various parts of the body also have peculiar roles: feet (11:2, 32; 12:3; 13:5–14; 20:12), hands (3:35; 7:30, 44; 10:28–29, 39; 11:44; 13:3, 9; 20:20, 25, 27; 21:18), the finger (20:25, 27), arm (12:38), heel (13:18), legs (19:31–33), chest (13:25; 21:20), bosom (1:18; 13:23), side (19:34; 20:20, 25, 27), head (13:9; 19:2, 30; 20:7, 12), and heart (12:49; 13:2; 14:1, 27; 16:6, 22). Although it draws heavily from the associations found in the Old Testament and antiquity generally, a suggestive "anatomy" of the Messiah, his followers and his enemies could be constructed from these references. Jesus is also likened to a seed (12:24) and the true vine (15:1ff.), and the way in which each bears fruit is described. His robe is seamless (19:23), and the net remains untorn (21:6, 8, 11); these images remind the reader of the emphasis on the unity of Jesus with his Father and his followers (17:11, 21–23). Always the imagery is fluid and subservient to the evangelist's exploration of Jesus' identity and the responses to him.

---

[129] W. J. Harvey, *Character and the Novel*, p. 35.

Conclusion

Our analysis of the misunderstandings, ironies, and symbolism of the Fourth Gospel highlights its "deformation of language."[130] Images, concepts, and symbols common in its milieu are de-familiarized, given new meaning, and used idiosyncratically. In succession, various characters miss their meaning. The misunderstandings warn the reader not to mistake superficial for real meanings. By repeatedly exposing irony in the dialogue, the author calls the reader to share his elevated point of view on the story. Through the symbolism also the author tells the reader that things are more than they seem to be. He invites the reader to focus the portrait of Jesus, understand the non-answers he gives to his dialogue partners, and grasp and be grasped by the revelation embodied in Jesus. The dialogues, particularly those which employ misunderstandings and obvious irony, teach the reader how to read the gospel and detect its higher and subtler meanings. Everything is considered "from above." Concrete objects and symbolic metaphors point to abstract realities or concepts. As the core symbols expand and by repetition become pervasive motifs, mere allusions to them cast their light on new scenes and amplify their echoes in the reader's memory.

The themes of the misunderstandings, ironies, and symbols are often interwoven, as can be seen in the major discourses in John 4 (the Samaritan woman) and 9 (the blind man), and at the arrest and trial of Jesus. The metaphors and symbols are misunderstood by the dialogue partner, creating a setting for irony and underlining the importance of perceiving the symbolic meaning of Jesus, his words, and his works. This interweaving of themes through misunderstanding, irony, and symbolism, is the signature of the evangelist's insight and art. Words and scenes have a "surplus of meaning" which is not fully exhausted.[131] Jesus' words often have an oracular quality which means that they stand out individually from their context and must be absorbed one at a time. The text is therefore made discontinuous. More time and space is left between sentences, time for the reader to ascend again and again to the higher plateau of meaning.[132] The combination of symbols with a surplus of meanings which have been expanded to the point of explosion with a discontinuous,

---

[130] William A. Beardslee, *Literary Criticism of the New Testament*, p. 11. See also Ian T. Ramsey, *Religious Language*, pp. 123–24.

[131] Cf. Brown, *Rhythm in the Novel*, pp. 45–46, 85.

[132] Northrop Frye, "The Critical Path," pp. 117–18.

oracular text conveys to the reader the impression that there is always yet more there than he or she has grasped. Every re-reading provides additional insights into how various features of the text fit together and affords new glimpses of the mystery to which it points.

Rhythmic repetition of themes and symbols creates a sense of order. E. K. Brown's observations are also appropriate for the interpretation of John:

> To express what is both an order and a mystery rhythmic processes, repetitions with intricate variations, are the most appropriate idioms. Repetition is the strongest assurance an author can give of order; the extraordinary complexity of the variations is the reminder that the order is so involute that it must remain a mystery.[133]

John points to the mystery made present in Jesus, but what is seen in him is glory (1:14), the glory of the Father, and an order of life which must remain a mystery. The author can point and affirm but he cannot describe; his insight is "inexpressible in less than strictly symbolic terms."[134] Those terms, therefore, may be regarded as the signature of his insight.

The misunderstandings, ironies, and symbols also point to the central conflict in the gospel,[135] the conflict between that which is from above and that which is from below. Primarily the conflict is between Jesus, who is "from above," and those who cannot and will not recognize his identity. Some of the characters gradually recognize and move from the lower plateau of understanding to the higher. The symbols are predominantly dualistic: light and darkness, ordinary water and living water, plain bread and true bread ("which has come down from heaven"). These symbols are woven into the more extensive dualism of the gospel. As Jesus' followers move from one plateau to the other, they adhere to the symbols of the world above. Understanding of the symbols is therefore an index to the position and movement of the characters. By the end of the gospel, those who have accepted Jesus have been drawn into his conflict with those who have rejected him: the disciples meet behind locked doors, "for fear of the Jews" (20:19).

Paradoxically, however, the symbols drawn from "this world" (below) show that it is not inherently evil or opposed to the realm above. There is a profound relationship between the symbolism in John and its affirmation that Jesus is the *logos,* the creative agency. The creation is inherently good, and the created order eminently suitable for revealing the nature of

---

[133] *Rhythm in the Novel,* p. 115.

[134] P. J. Cahill, "The Johannine *Logos* as Center," p. 69.

[135] Cf. Friedman, *Form and Meaning in Fiction,* p. 299.

the creator. As Erich Auerbach observed in another context, ". . . the two realms of the sublime and the everyday are not only actually unseparated but basically inseparable."[136] This affirmation, as it is reflected in John, is the gospel's most profound sacramentalism. Everything in the world is capable of "re-presenting" the realm and reality of its creator. The sacraments serve this function but have no exclusive claim to the capacity to do so. The core symbols, and many of the others as well, have an attributive and interpretive role. They are one of the primary means by which the evangelist presents and interprets Jesus to the reader. Each of these symbols is an essential part of the context of life itself. Without light, water, and food there could be no life. And it is precisely these elements which are the core symbols for Jesus and the realm and life he represents. Through him, the evangelist affirms, the believer can, even through the experience of reading rightly, begin to share in his eternal life: "These [things] are written that you may believe . . . and that believing you may have life in his name" (20:31). The core symbols are therefore integrally related both to the purpose of the gospel and the affirmation of its prologue: "in him was life" (1:4), and he enabled those who accepted him to share in this life as "children of God" (1:12).

Finally, John's symbolism has a powerful and multi-faceted unitive effect.[137] True to their etymology, John's symbols "put together" the various elements and appendages of the literary work. Various parts of the gospel are interrelated by the recurrence of core symbols. The themes to which they are related are repeated and interrelated with challenging and enriching variations which cause various passages and contexts to resonate simultaneously, thereby allowing the sensitive reader to grasp the whole with increasing appreciation.[138] The Johannine symbols unite the concrete with the abstract, everyday life with John's distinctive theology. The world the reader knows points symbolically, at least when viewed from John's point of view, to the realm which neither author nor reader can fully comprehend. The symbols are in this regard bridges by which the reader may cross in some elusive sense into the reality and mystery, the life, which they represent. The symbols "sing of the existence" of that which they symbolize, but more, they move us to sing their song as well. They give it immediacy, approachability, and even perceptibility, while never robbing it of mystery or relieving the judgment upon those who fail to understand it or its symbols.

---

[136] *Mimesis*, p. 22.

[137] Tindall, "Excellent Dumb Discourse," pp. 345–46.

[138] Kim Dewey, *"Paroimiai* in the Gospel of John," p. 90, is undoubtedly right when he observes: "Overriding themes may be a more predominant unifying factor than structure, plot, or logical consistency."

The symbols, like the misunderstandings and irony which help the reader to understand them, are also a form of "silent" communication between the author and reader. Through these, author and reader are drawn together in a shared perception of meaning and reverence before mystery. Together, if the gospel is read in the way in which it calls for itself to be experienced, author and reader are united in the transformation effected by an experience of encounter with transcendent mystery. By proper reading of John as symbolic narrative, the reader is called to no less than the conviction that man and God can be united and that from this union new life is born in man, and specifically in the reader.

Chapter Seven

THE IMPLIED READER

No author, who understands the just boundaries of decorum and good-breeding, would presume to think all: The truest respect which you can pay to the reader's understanding is to halve this matter amicably, and leave him something to imagine, in his turn, as well as yourself.

For my own part, I am eternally paying him compliments of this kind, and do all that lies in my power to keep his imagination as busy as my own.

Laurence Sterne
Tristram Shandy

The author makes his readers. If he makes them badly—that is, if he simply waits in all purity, for the occasional reader whose perceptions and norms match his own, then his conception must be lofty indeed if we are to forgive him for his bad craftsmanship. But if he makes them well, that is, makes them see what they have never seen before, moves them into a new order of perception and experience altogether—he finds his reward in the peers he has created.

Wayne C. Booth
The Rhetoric of Fiction

The study of the reader of a narrative is one of the most important of recent developments in literary criticism. So sweeping is the change brought about by this development that M. H. Abrams summarizes the current scene as follows:

> The Age of Criticism, which reached its zenith in the mid-decades of this century, has given way to the Age of Reading, and whereas the American new critics and European formalists of the Age of Criticism discovered the work-as-such, current literary theorists have discovered the reader as such.[1]

Already the population of readers is growing at an alarming rate. There are intended readers, implied readers, historical readers, model readers, mock readers, ideal readers, and an equal number of narratees. Definition is essential. The key to such study is that narrative texts create their own readers. Just as the implied author is distinguishable from the real author, the narratee or implied reader is internal, created by the text, and not to be confused with actual, historical or contemporary readers.[2]

Within the growing literature on readers one discerns the pursuit of answers to two fundamental questions: Who is the reader? And, what must the reader do to read a text? A great deal of what has been put in earlier chapters of this book is related to what the reader of the Fourth Gospel must do to read it successfully. A full answer to that question would probably require another book of equal size. The first question—who is the reader?—is the easier of the two, and I shall be satisfied if some progress toward its answer can be made in the following pages.

READERS AND NARRATEES

Every narrative exerts some control over its readers. It sets up the mental moves required to experience and understand the text. Specifically, it hides and reveals in a sequence, it moves the reader about, it controls the

---

[1] "How to do Things with Texts," p. 566.
[2] See the diagram above, p. 6.

reader's clarity and confusion and his or her interest and emotional responses.[3]

Texts evoke the reader even if they do not repeatedly speak directly to the "dear" or "gentle" reader. Walter J. Ong cites the opening chapter of *A Farewell to Arms* as an example.[4] Hemingway draws the reader into the role of a bosom friend by referring to "the river" in such a way that the reader is aware that he or she is supposed to know which river from having been there before. Similarly, to read Camus or Conrad is to be drawn into a role as auditor in specific situations implied by the speech of the narrator. Even in texts which do not craft the role of the reader so deliberately that role is necessarily defined by the narrator or implied author.

The narrator's commentary is a major source of definition for the reader's identity. Actually, the narrator's commentary defines the role of the narratee, the one who hears the narrator, and in some texts the narratee is clearly distinguishable from the implied reader, who is defined by the implied author. In John, however, the narratee cannot be meaningfully distinguished from the implied reader. It does not have a fictional narratee or force the reader into a separate role.[5]

Peter J. Rabinowitz argues that there are at least four audiences in any narrative text: (1) the actual audience, (2) the authorial audience, (3) the narrative audience, and (4) the ideal narrative audience. The actual audience is the "real," flesh and blood reader. For our purposes, the actual audience may be either the historical (first-century) readers or contemporary readers. The historical readers can be described on the basis of other first-century documents, constructed from social and historical knowledge and literary conventions of the time, or extrapolated from the reader's role as laid down in the text.[6] The authorial audience is the audience for whom the "real" author thinks he is writing.[7] In the course of writing the author cannot avoid making certain assumptions about what readers will and will not know, understand, believe, or expect. Most writers, including the fourth evangelist, I think, attempt to minimize the distance between the

---

[3] See Wayne C. Booth, *The Rhetoric of Fiction*, pp. 122, 123, 274, 284, 302–4.

[4] "The Writer's Audience is Always a Fiction," pp. 62–69.

[5] The term "narratee" was coined by Gerald Prince: "Notes Toward a Categorization of Fictional 'Narratees,'" pp. 100–05; "On Readers and Listeners in Narrative," pp. 117–22; "Introduction à l'étude du narrataire," pp. 178–96. See further: Mary Ann Piwowarczyk, "The Narratee and the Situation of Enunciation," pp. 161–77; Peter J. Rabinowitz, "Truth in Fiction," pp. 121–41; Seymour Chatman, *Story and Discourse*, pp. 149–51, 253–62; and Ross Chambers, "Commentary in Literary Texts," pp. 323–37.

[6] Wolfgang Iser, *The Act of Reading*, pp. 27–28.

[7] See also Erwin Wolff, "Der intendierte Leser," pp. 141–66.

actual and authorial audiences. The greater the distance between them the more difficult it is for the actual reader to appreciate the book: "If historically or culturally distant texts are hard to understand, it is often precisely because we do not possess the knowledge required to join the authorial audience."[8] It is in this gap that exegesis and the study of Koine Greek, Judaism, and first-century Greco-Roman culture have played a vital role in the interpretation of John. The possibility remains, however, that by studying the authorial audience implied in the gospel a clearer picture may emerge of the audience for which the evangelist intended to write.

At least in fictional literature a third audience, the narrative audience, is present. In fiction the reader is asked to pretend that imaginary characters are "real," that certain situations "exist," and that various events are or are not possible. The narrative audience accepts the story on its own terms. Both the actual and the authorial audiences know better but willingly suspend their disbelief in order to enter into the story. In John the narrative audience accepts that all of the events took place as the narrator says: water turned to wine, men were healed, a multitude was fed, and Lazarus was raised from the dead. It may not have required any willing suspension of disbelief for the author's intended audience to become the narrative audience and accept the gospel as a realistic historical account. Later we will want to consider the task of the contemporary reader in joining the authorial reader when his or her assumptions and beliefs differ radically from those of the evangelist's intended audience. For the contemporary reader, reading the gospel may become an exercise in pretense, pretending to know and think what the evangelist assumed his first-century readers knew and thought and pretending to believe that water could be changed to wine and a man born blind could be given sight by obeying the command to wash clay and spittle from his eyes. Obviously there are different kinds of pretense or willing suspension of disbelief that are required of the gospel's actual, contemporary readers.

The fourth audience is one Rabinowitz calls the "ideal narrative audience." It is ideal in the sense that it believes the narrator, accepts his judgments, and appreciates his irony. Rabinowitz explains the relationships among the audiences as follows:

> As a general rule, the distance between authorial audience and narrative audience tends to be along an axis of "fact," either "historical" or "scientific." That is, the narrative audience believes that certain events could or did take place. The distance between the narrative audience

---

[8] Rabinowitz, "Truth in Fiction," p. 127.

and the ideal narrative audience tends to lie along an axis of ethics or interpretation. The ideal narrative audience agrees with the narrator that certain events are good or that a particular analysis is correct, while the narrative audience is called upon to judge him. Much of the problem—and most of the joy—of reading irony comes from sorting out these three levels, and feeling the tensions among them. But just as there are extremely realistic novels where the narrative and the authorial audiences are indistinguishable, so there are non-ironic works where the ideal narrative audience is virtually identical with the narrative audience.[9]

In John the ideal narrative audience adopts the narrator's ideological point of view, penetrates the misunderstandings, appreciates the irony, and is moved to fresh appreciations of transcendent mystery through the gospel's symbolism. The gospel is, ostensibly at least, entirely realistic. The narrative audience merges with the authorial audience, but the authorial audience is culturally, historically, and philosophically distant from the contemporary actual audience. We can concentrate, therefore, on the gospel's definition of its authorial audience and the work of the contemporary reader in adopting the perspective of that audience.

The narratee, discussed by Prince and Piwowarczyk, is closely related to the authorial audience and the narrative audience, but distinguishable from them. The narratee is defined as the hearer or reader of the narrator's voice. Prince defines a "degree zero" narratee, the minimally characterized narratee who knows only the language of the narrator and has no prior knowledge of the events, characters, locations, or narrator in the story. The status and spatial-temporal location of the degree zero narratee are also undefined. Deviations from this degree zero narratee can then be observed in various narratives. The narratee may be addressed or evoked more or less directly. Seven signs indicate the presence of a narratee: "direct references, inclusive and indefinite pronouns, questions and pseudoquestions, negatives, demonstratives, comparisons and analogies, and 'surjustifications'" (i.e., the narrator's explanations of the world of the characters, the motives for their acts, and the justification of their thoughts).[10] By these means the identity, spatial and temporal location, status, and roles of the narratee are defined.[11] The presence or absence of commentary invariably prints a portrait of the narratee.[12] If explanation

---

[9] "Truth in Fiction," p. 135.

[10] Piwowarczyk, "The Narratee and the Situation of Enunciation," p. 166; Prince, "Introduction à l'étude du narrataire," pp. 182–87.

[11] Piwowarczyk, "The Narratee and the Situation of Enunciation," pp. 167–77.

[12] Chambers, "Commentary in Literary Texts," pp. 327–28.

is provided, the narratee would not have understood otherwise; if explanation is absent, the narratee understands (or can figure it out). If a character is introduced, he or she would not otherwise have been known. Social customs may either be taken for granted or explained according to the narrator's assumptions about the narratee, or the author's assumptions about the reader. The question Howard Baker put so forcefully in the Watergate hearings can therefore be raised, in slightly modified form, concerning the narratee or authorial audience of the Fourth Gospel: What does it know, and when does it know it? The relations between the narrator, narratee, and characters may also be examined, for each may alternatively be placed near or far from each of the others.[13]

The work of Wolfgang Iser is seminal for the study of readers and reading. He is concerned not just with the identity the reader is required to assume in reading a narrative, but with the broader question of what a narrative text makes its actual reader do. The meaning of a text, he argues, is not inherent in it but must be produced or actualized by the reader. Iser's definitions of his "implied reader" are grounded in this thesis. The implied reader

> embodies all those predispositions necessary for a literary work to exercise its effect—predispositions laid down, not by an empirical outside reality, but by the text itself. . . . Thus the concept of the implied reader designates a network of response inviting structures, which impel the reader to grasp the text.[14]

Again,

> This term incorporates both the prestructuring of the potential meaning by the text, and the reader's actualization of this potential through the reading process. It refers to the active nature of this process—which will vary historically from one age to another—and not to a typology of possible readers.[15]

As the reader adopts the perspectives thrust on him or her by the text, experiences it sequentially, has expectations frustrated or modified, relates one part of the text to another, and imagines and works out all the text leaves for the reader to do, its meaning is gradually actualized. In a novel, or presumably any narrative text, prevailing social and philosophical norms are detached from their real context and embodied in a literary

---

[13] Chatman, *Story and Discourse*, p. 259.
[14] *The Act of Reading*, p. 34.
[15] *The Implied Reader*, p. xii.

one.[16] Here they can be examined and evaluated by the reader. The norms are contained in the narrative's "repertoire," which emerges from the perspectives of the narrator, the characters, the plot, and the reader.[17] The repertoire "reproduces the familiar, but strips it of its current validity."[18] In the narrative reproduction the familiar is put in a different context. Narrative texts may either set out to confirm existing values and thought systems which were being challenged or challenge the prevailing norms by exposing their weaknesses and deficiencies.[19] In either situation the same rule applies: ". . . literature counterbalances the deficiencies produced by prevailing philosophies."[20] Consequently, the literary historian should be able to reconstruct the prevailing thought system and its weaknesses. When prevailing norms are negated or their deficiencies exposed, the reader is compelled "to seek a positive counterbalance elsewhere than in the world immediately familiar to him."[21] The familiar thereby becomes obsolescent, "it belongs to the 'past,'" and the reader moves beyond it.[22] The reader's reflection on the thwarting of his or her expectations, the negations of familiar values, the causes of their failure, and whatever potential solutions the text offers require that the reader take an active part in formulating the meaning of the narrative. Literary texts, therefore, offer us—to paraphrase Iser—the opportunity to transcend the real world and become involved in the world of the narrative and so understand it and our own world more clearly.[23]

The question of the intended audience of the Fourth Gospel is certainly not new to Johannine studies, but it has hitherto been undertaken without an adequate understanding of the difference between the actual historical readers, the authorial or intended audience implied by the text, and the ideal narrative audience as these have been defined by Prince, Piwowarczyk, and Rabinowitz. The search for its readers has also been linked closely with the effort to define the purpose(s) of the gospel. Further progress may be possible if studies on the phenomenology of reading can be applied to the interpretation of John. It is hoped that this chapter and each of the previous ones will make some contribution to this task, but a fully developed application of the theories of reading proposed by Iser, Ingarden, Eco, Derrida, Fish, Bloom, Bleich, Culler, and others must be

---

[16] Iser, *The Implied Reader*, p. xii; *The Act of Reading*, p. 74.

[17] Iser, *The Act of Reading*, p. 96.

[18] Iser, *The Implied Reader*, pp. 34–35.

[19] Iser, *The Act of Reading*, p. 83.

[20] Iser, *The Implied Reader*, p. 28.

[21] Iser, *The Implied Reader*, p. xii.

[22] Iser, *The Act of Reading*, pp. 212–13.

[23] Iser, *The Implied Reader*, p. xi; *The Act of Reading*, p. 230.

put on a future agenda.[24] It will be enough if the outlines of the gospel's portrait of its reader can be traced from its surface and some factors which enter into the experience of reading the gospel can be considered.

JOHN'S READERS

The effort to define the setting, purpose, and audience of the Fourth Gospel has consumed a major share of the energies of Johannine scholars in the last two decades. Since the results are ably assessed by Robert Kysar, there is no need to do more than reiterate the basic positions. Kysar recognizes five solutions which were proposed between 1959 and 1971: (1) John was intended to serve as a missionary document for diaspora Jews (T. C. Smith, J. A. T. Robinson, and W. C. van Unnik—all published in 1959); (2) John was written in the context of sharp dialogue with the synagogue and was primarily intended to sustain and confirm believers and those on the fringe of the Christian community (J. L. Martyn, preceded by K. L. Carroll and E. Grässer, and supported by W. A. Meeks, R. Fortna, H. Leroy, J. Beutler, and M. de Jonge); (3) an antidocetic polemic (advocated by J. D. G. Dunn) was added as a secondary purpose late in the composition history of the gospel (R. E. Brown, B. Lindars, W. Wilkens, and G. Richter); (4) mission work among the Samaritans contributed significantly to the themes and theology of the gospel (J. Bowman, G. W. Buchanan, E. Freed, and in a more moderate form, W. A. Meeks); and (5) the purpose of the gospel was to transcend its immediate context and make a universal appeal to Christian believers from diverse cultural and intellectual milieux (C. K. Barrett, G. W. MacRae, P. Lamarche, and R. E. Brown).[25] Since the publication of Kysar's survey significant contributions to this discussion have been added by D. M. Smith, O. Cullmann, P. S. Minear, R. E. Brown, J. L. Martyn, M. E. Boismard, and W. Langbrandtner.[26] Each presents a view of the community, context, or audience of the Fourth Gospel. Although positions are refined in these publications, the major lines of debate over the context, purpose, and audience of the gospel are represented by the first,

---

[24] See esp. Roman Ingarden, *The Cognition of the Literary Work of Art;* Umberto Eco, *The Role of the Reader;* Jane P. Tompkins, ed., *Reader-Response Criticism;* and the following survey articles along with the bibliography they cite: Steven Mailloux, "Reader-Response Criticism?"; and Abrams, "How to do Things with Texts," pp. 566–88.

[25] Robert Kysar, *The Fourth Evangelist and His Gospel,* pp. 147–65.

[26] D. Moody Smith, "Johannine Christianity"; Oscar Cullmann, *The Johannine Circle;* Paul S. Minear, "The Audience of the Fourth Gospel"; Raymond E. Brown, *The Community of the Beloved Disciple;* J. Louis Martyn, *The Gospel of*

second, and fifth points above. Put most simply, the question is whether John was written as a missionary document for non-believers, a community document for believers, or a theological document for the church at large. Examination of the gospel's depiction of its authorial audience or intended reader may not lay the question to rest, but it may put the textual data in a fresh and fruitful perspective. Since the position, knowledge, and beliefs of the intended audience are at the center of the debate, we may return to the question raised earlier: What does the narratee know, and when does he or she know it? It should be noted, however, that a characterization of the narratee could be used in the debate over the actual, historical audience only on the assumptions that the narratee accurately represents the intended audience and that the author's judgments about his actual audience were also accurate. Historical questions aside, some understanding of the gospel's narratee is essential for a perceptive reading of the text.

We may begin by making the simple and perhaps overly wooden assumption that the character of the narratee can be drawn from the narration by observing what is explained and what is not. We will assume further that the narratee knows about things and characters that are alluded to without introduction or explanation but has no prior knowledge of things, persons, events, and locales which are introduced by the narrator. By the nature of the evidence we can say with more certainty what the narratee does not know than what he or she does know. By gleaning the relevant data from the voice of the narrator throughout the gospel, a portrait of the narratee can be drawn. We may characterize the narratee's knowledge or lack thereof in five areas: persons (or characters), places, languages, Judaism, and events. Some of the data are conflicting and some inferences can be drawn with more confidence than others, so the difficulties will have to be examined once we have attempted to trace the narratee's profile. The narratee is evoked explicitly in 19:35 and 20:31, both times with plural verbs and pronouns ("you," plural). A distinct group of readers is therefore in view, but it is not necessarily a homogeneous group. That determination can only be made after surveying all the data regarding the group to which the narrator speaks.

Persons. With which persons is the reader familiar, either from experience, from tradition, or from having heard the story or something like it before?

John in Christian History; Marie-Emile Boismard and A. Lamouille, *L'Evangile de Jean;* Wolfgang Langbrandtner, *Weltferner Gott oder Gott der Liebe.* See also R. Alan Culpepper, *The Johannine School.*

Do the readers (or narratee) know the narrator? Clearly it is assumed that they do, for the narrator uses "we" with no explanation in 1:14, 16 and 21:24. He also addresses the readers using the first person singular, "I," in 21:25. In 1:14, in the phrase "and dwelt among us," the word "us" may be a reference to mankind in general, a group of eye-witnesses, or a community within which there are some who saw "the Word." The "we" which follows is not necessarily co-terminus with the previous "us." Furthermore, it may or may not include the readers. The readers may or may not be a part of the group for which the narrator speaks, but they at least know the narrator (evangelist) and the group he represents.

Does the narratee have prior knowledge of Jesus, who is elaborately introduced by the combination of the prologue and John the Baptist's testimony? Together they establish his identity before he appears or speaks in the narrative (1:29). It is well known that *logos* has different meanings according to whether it is used in a Jewish or a Greek context. The evangelist does not define its meaning explicitly but assumes that the reader is familiar with the concept. The link between Jesus, the *logos,* and "he who comes after me," as the Baptist declares, is forged by John the Baptist's announcement: "This is he of whom I said . . ." (1:30). When this declaration is related to the Baptist's role as described in the prologue, the reader has no doubt who Jesus is. The point may be debated, but it looks as though the narratee has heard of Jesus before. Nevertheless, the author arranges the opening of the narrative so that he can present his interpretation of Jesus' role before Jesus is actually introduced. The name will be recognized, but the identity may be mistaken.

John the Baptist is given a scriptural sounding introduction in 1:6–8, and his role is carefully defined. Verse 6 implies that the reader has no prior knowledge of the Baptist, but the formal "there was a man . . ." may owe more to the evangelist's desire to imitate the style of the Old Testament than to the need to introduce John to readers who have never heard of him. The reason for the "special pleading" is that the tone of 1:6 conflicts with the polemical tone of verses 7–8, which can be more easily understood on the assumption that the reader has a mistaken regard for the Baptist. Moreover, John's activity is later explained with the comment, "for John had not yet been put into prison" (3:24). The implication is that the reader knows that John was imprisoned and may think he was imprisoned before Jesus began his ministry (cf. Mark 1:14–15). Should greater weight be given to 1:6 or 3:24? Is the narrator inconsistent? Is one of the references an editorial addition? Or, does the evangelist have in mind a group of intended readers some of whom will know John and some of whom will not? The latter thesis is certainly possible, but if 1:6 is explained as imitation of the style of Old Testament introductions, then a consistent picture emerges. The reader knows John the Baptist and knows of his arrest, but may have a mistaken notion of his role.

Does the reader also have some prior knowledge of the disciples? Individual disciples are introduced before the group is referred to. When the narrator does refer to "the twelve," and he does so very seldom (6:67, 70, 71; 20:24), he assumes the reader knows whom he means. Members of the group can be identified as "one of his disciples" (6:8; 12:4; 13:23; 18:25; cf. 18:15–16) or "one of the twelve" (6:71; 20:24). The individuals are treated with varying degrees of familiarity. Although Simon Peter has not yet been introduced, Andrew is said to be his brother and one of the disciples of John the Baptist (1:40). The identification is repeated in 6:8. There can be no question that the reader has heard of Peter before. An argument could be mounted either way concerning Andrew, however; he may be introduced repeatedly as Peter's brother simply because of Peter's fame, not because he is entirely unknown. No special effort is made to introduce Philip or Nathanael, though the circumstances of Nathanael's call are described in detail through the dialogue (1:43–51; cf. 21:2). Their names will presumably be recognized by the reader. In contrast to Andrew, Philip is not reintroduced when he appears later (6:5), so Philip seems to be better known. Andrew is reintroduced as "one of his disciples, the brother of Simon Peter" (6:8). Although he is regularly distinguished as "the twin" (11:16; 20:24; 21:2), Thomas too is probably expected to be recognized when he is introduced in 11:17. It is difficult to see how the designation "the twin" would have introduced him if he were unknown, but it gives him some individuality.

The comment in 6:64, that Jesus knew from the beginning who his betrayer was, implies that the reader knows about the betrayal of Jesus before the narrator tells about it.[27] In some tension with this aside, the narrator takes great pains a few verses later to explain who the betrayer was: "He spoke of Judas the son of Simon Iscariot, for he, one of the twelve, was to betray him" (6:71). Is the narrator providing a needed identification of the betrayer or is he using the comment to emphasize that Judas, the betrayer, was one of the twelve? Could the reader know of the betrayal (6:64) without knowing the identity of the betrayer (6:71), or are

---

[27] J. A. K. Thomson, *Irony*, pp. 36–38, contrasts the method of the modern dramatist in concealing *what* will happen with that of the Greeks, who concealed *when* it would happen: ". . . to see the things he has foreseen in the way he foresaw is actually more exciting than the unexpected events. . . . And to know that the inevitable feet of Death are thus visibly, thus measurably advancing on one whose history is known with a kind of passionate intimacy is to see a strange and awful light reflected forward upon all he will do and suffer."

these comments found in doublets of the same tradition, each intended for a different audience? Were they placed in the narrative by the same author or by different writers with different intended audiences in mind? Answers can only be suggested after all the pertinent references have been surveyed. Judas is repeatedly reintroduced (12:4; 18:2), often with his full name, but the repeated references to Judas' full name in 13:2 and 13:26 are partially explained by the introduction of Judas "not Iscariot" in 14:22. Judas (not Iscariot) and the sons of Zebedee are mentioned without introduction (14:22; 21:2), but the lack of an introduction may be due more to the fact that they have virtually no roles in the gospel than to the presumption that they would be known. One can argue, therefore, that all or most of the named disciples are known to the reader.

The Beloved Disciple, somewhat surprisingly, is introduced as a character unknown to the reader (13:23; 21:24). He is first referred to as "one of his disciples, whom Jesus loved" (13:23), not "*the* disciple whom Jesus loved" as he is in 19:26; 20:2; 21:7, 20. The difference is slight but shows that the reader is not expected to recognize the Beloved Disciple. At the end, the reader must also be told that it was the Beloved Disciple who bore witness to, and wrote, these things (21:24). So, the reader must be helped to recognize the Beloved Disciple. Is this because the Beloved Disciple has no "roots" in the tradition and his role is fictionalized to a greater degree than that of the other disciples? Probably. In the concluding verses of the gospel, "the brethren," who may be the intended readers, misunderstand about the Beloved Disciple's death. The readers know this disciple, therefore, but must be told of his role in the story, and the "Beloved Disciple" must be identified as the witness and author of the gospel. The "we" and the "I" of the final verses are also presumed to be known.

The Jewish groups are all recognized by the reader. No explanation is needed regarding the Jews, priests, or Levites. Similarly, the reader knows who the Pharisees, rulers of the Jews (3:1; 7:26), chief priests (7:32), and the high priest (11:49) are. The status of the βασιλικός (4:46) as an official or nobleman is known. Individuals such as Nicodemus (3:1), Caiaphas (11:49), Annas (18:13), and Joseph of Arimathea (19:38) must be introduced, but Pilate (18:29) and Caesar (19:12) are well known.

Lazarus must be introduced, but Martha and Mary are known (11:1). They were known outside Johannine Christianity (cf. Luke 10:38–42), but only in John are they said to have a brother named Lazarus (cf. Luke 16:19–31). Jesus' love for the three is emphasized (11:5). The reader's knowledge of the sisters is further indicated by the reference to Mary as the one who anointed Jesus, even though the anointing is not described until the following chapter (11:2; 12:3–8). Bethany, moreover, can be identified as the town of Mary and Martha (11:1). In John 12 the reader's

lack of familiarity with Lazarus is underscored by the seemingly gratu-
itous reminder, "Lazarus, whom he had raised from the dead" (12:9).

Jesus' brothers are referred to with no introduction (7:3), either because the reader has prior knowledge of them or would not be surprised
that Jesus had brothers. The servant whose ear is cut off at Jesus' arrest
must be identified as "Malchus" because he would otherwise not be
known. The identification adds credibility to the narrator's account, even
though Malchus' role is not developed further. Caiaphas is reintroduced
at 18:13–14 and 18:24. In sharp contrast, there is no need to introduce
Pilate or explain his position (18:28–29). More explanation is required
for the Jewish authorities than for Pilate or Caesar. Barabbas is also
unknown: "Now Barabbas was a robber" (18:40). It would be precarious
to infer any prior knowledge of the women at the cross on the basis of the
references to "Mary the wife of Clopas" and "Mary Magdalene" (19:25),
but the reader may have heard their names before. Joseph of Arimathea,
or at least his role as a secret disciple,must be introduced, and Nicodemus
is reintroduced (19:39; cf. 3:1; 7:50).

From this survey it appears that the reader is expected to recognize
most of the characters in the story. Those who need special introductions
are the Beloved Disciple, Lazarus, Nicodemus, Joseph of Arimathea,
Caiaphas, and Annas. Some question remains about John the Baptist and
Judas Iscariot. It is noteworthy that the Beloved Disciple, Lazarus, and
Nicodemus do not appear in the synoptic gospels, although a character in
a Lukan parable is named Lazarus. Caiaphas and Annas might not be
known to a non-Jewish audience or to Jewish readers late in the first
century. The roles of each of the others may be fictionalized to a greater
degree in John than in other traditions or accounts of Jesus' ministry. If
so, this may account in part for the fact that the narrator must introduce
them to the reader.

Places. The narrator assumes that the reader has a general knowledge
of the geography of the gospel story. The reader has at least heard of Jerusalem (1:19; 2:13), the region "beyond the Jordan" (1:28; 3:26; 10:40),
Galilee (1:44), Judea (3:22), and Samaria (4:4, 5, 7). For the name "Jerusalem" the narrator uses the Hellenized form Ἱεροσόλυμα exclusively
(twelve times) rather than the more Semitic Ἰερουσαλήμ, which is pre-
ferred by the author of Luke-Acts. The choice of the Hellenized form may
arise either from the idiom of the evangelist or that of his intended readers.

It is difficult to tell how much familiarity with Galilee is assumed.
Bethsaida is specified as the home town of Andrew and Peter (1:44;
12:21). There is no effort to locate Nazareth (1:45) or Capernaum (2:12;
4:46; 6:59), and Cana is simply "in Galilee" (2:1; 4:46). Their locations

are either assumed to be known or regarded as unimportant to the story. At the beginning of John 6 the narrator reports that Jesus crossed "the Sea of Galilee, which is the Sea of Tiberias." Some manuscripts, among them Codex Bezae, say that Jesus crossed "the Sea of Galilee to the region of Tiberias." The assumption is that the reader may be familiar with Tiberias either as the new city which had given its name to the lake or as a location which would identify where the feeding took place (cf. 6:23). The Greco-Roman name may therefore be of more help to the reader than the Jewish one, "Gennesaret," as an aid to identifying the Galilean location. In 21:1 the lake is called simply "the Sea of Tiberias." "The mountain" is never named or located (6:3, 15), but it is a typical setting in all the gospels. Although there is no effort to situate the Galilean towns in relation to each other or the Sea of Galilee, there is no evidence that the reader is familiar with their locations. What evidence there is, and it is not much, points in the other direction. The reader(s) do not seem to be familiar with Galilean locations, though they may have heard some of their names before.

Is the same true of the Judean sites? The towns outside Jerusalem are certainly not known to the reader. Ephraim is introduced as a little known village: "But [he] went from there to the country near the wilderness, to a town called Ephraim" (11:54). Bethany must also be described for the reader, first as "the village of Mary and her sister Martha" (11:1) and then as being located "fifteen stadia" (about two miles) from Jerusalem (11:18). In the next chapter it is reintroduced as the place where Lazarus was raised from the dead (12:1), implying that the reader would need such a reminder to remember where Bethany was. Aenon "near Salim" (3:23) may have been located in Judea, Samaria, or the Transjordan. It too was an unfamiliar site for the reader, who would not know there was water nearby (3:23), though the explanation "near Salim" may have located it.

The topography of Jerusalem is also generally unfamiliar to the reader. The narrator must say "now there is in Jerusalem . . ." when describing the Pool of Bethesda. It is located "by the Sheep Gate" (5:2). The Pool of Siloam is not located, but its name is translated (9:7). Locations in the temple are mentioned without explanation (the treasury, 8:20; and the Stoa of Solomon, 10:23) but it is impossible to say whether the reader would know precisely where these were or not. The Kidron valley seems to be a known landmark, but not the garden where Jesus was arrested: "When Jesus had spoken these words he went forth with his disciples across the Kidron valley [or 'winter-flowing Kedron'], where there was a garden" (18:1). The name Gethsemane does not appear in John. The site of "a place called The Pavement, and in Hebrew, Gabbatha" (19:13) and the place of the crucifixion, "the place called the place of a skull, which is called in Hebrew Golgotha" (19:17), and which is "near the city" (19:20), are both unknown to the reader. In the light of earlier translations of Hebrew words into Greek it seems likely that the Hebrew is provided here to authenticate the account rather than to identify the places for a reader who would know them by their Hebrew names. It is further possible that the reader would have heard the Hebrew names used but would not be expected to know where the places were located. The location of the tomb in the garden, near where Jesus was crucified, must also be described in detail (19:41). The resulting picture, which again must be very tentative due to the nature of the evidence, is that while the reader may have some idea of the topography of Jerusalem (the temple, the Pool of Siloam, the Kidron valley), most of the sites in the city are unfamiliar, and the reader knows little or nothing of Judea (Bethany and Ephraim).

The same can be said of the Samaritan and Transjordanian locations. Sychar, the only Samaritan city mentioned, is introduced as an unfamiliar one (4:4–5), and the reader must be told about the well and even that "Jews have no dealings with Samaritans" (4:9). We may infer that the reader has had little or no dealings with Jews, or Samaritans either. On the other hand, the reader presumably knows of "Bethany beyond the Jordan" (1:28; cf. 10:40).[28] The phrase "beyond the Jordan" may be added to distinguish this Bethany from the one in Judea, however. On the basis of this reference, the pattern of other geographical references, and the proximity of the Transjordan to the Galilean and Judean locations, it is difficult to conclude that the reader knows this area better than the others.

The nature of the evidence makes it easier to say what the readers do not know, and must be told, than what they do know. Our tentative conclusion is that the readers know the general regions but not specific locations. Where precise locations are significant (as with the Pool of Bethesda, the garden where Jesus was arrested, Bethany, Golgotha, and the tomb), these must be supplied by the narrator. The geography of the gospel is well known to the narrator but not to the reader.

Languages. It has been argued that a narratee knows the language of the narrative and only the language of the narrative unless there are indications to the contrary.[29] In John there are no clear indications to the contrary. The reader knows Greek and only Greek. Such common terms as "Rabbi" (1:38), "Messiah" (1:41), and "Rabboni" (20:16) must be translated. Names are also translated to convey their meaning (Cephas, 1:42;

---

[28] Cf. Cullmann, *The Johannine Circle,* pp. 59, 98.

[29] Piwowarczyk, "The Narratee and the Situation of Enunciation," p. 161.

Siloam, 9:7). Where Hebrew or Aramaic terms are introduced (Bethesda, Gabbatha, and Golgotha), they are referred to as foreign words ("in Hebrew," 5:2; 19:13, 17) rather than as the names by which the reader would know these locations. Their presence adds credibility to the account.

Related to the languages known to the reader is the issue of which system for reckoning the hours of the day is common to the narrator and reader. Recent commentators have held that John follows the Jewish system, but it is difficult to see how the narrator could assume the Jewish system, in which the day begins at six in the evening, when common Hebrew terms must be translated and Tiberias is more familiar than Gennesaret, or perhaps even "Sea of Galilee." Hours of the day are mentioned without explanation in 1:39 "the tenth hour," 4:6 "the sixth hour," 4:52 "the seventh hour," and 19:14 "the sixth hour." All of these work as well or better following the modern or Roman system, counting from midnight and noon, and there is some evidence that this system was used in Asia Minor.[30] The two disciples stayed with Jesus "that day" from ten in the morning rather than from four in the afternoon (1:39). The Samaritan woman came to the well in the evening, when Jesus was tired from a day's walking (4:6), rather than in the heat of the day. The fever left the official's son at seven in the evening and he started home the next day (4:52), and the crucifixion began at six in the morning rather than at noon. The noon hour coincides better with the time of the slaughter of the Passover lambs, but would be impossibly close to the beginning of the Jewish Passover that evening. The Roman system, therefore, fits both the chronological references and the data regarding locales and languages better than the Jewish system.

Judaism. For greater clarity we may distinguish three sub-points related to the issue of how much the reader knows about Judaism: the Old Testament, Jewish institutions and festivals, and Jewish beliefs and practices.

There are several indications that the implied reader has extensive knowledge of the Old Testament. In the latter half of the gospel the formula "that the scripture might be fulfilled" is repeated in 13:18; 17:12; 19:24, 36, with variations in 12:38 and 15:25. These references and the repeated quotations and allusions to the Old Testament scriptures imply

---

[30] For reckoning the hours from midnight and noon, see B. F. Westcott, *The Gospel According to St. John,* p. 282; Norman Walker, "The Reckoning of Hours in the Fourth Gospel," pp. 69–73; Jack Finegan, *Handbook of Biblical Chronology,* pp. 8, 12–13. The primary texts are Pliny, *Natural History,* II. 79. 188, and *Mart. Pol.* xxi.

that the fulfillment of scripture will confirm for the reader the truth of the evangelist's interpretation of the events. If it were simply that the fulfillment was important to the evangelist and he was attempting to persuade the reader of its importance also, he could not presuppose, as he apparently did, that the allusions to the Old Testament and its imagery and symbols would be understood by the intended reader. In the dialogue, for example, when the Jews ask John the Baptist whether he is Elijah or "the prophet" (1:21), no explanation is required. Knowledge of the story of Moses' lifting up the serpent in the wilderness can be assumed (3:14), and when the Jews claim "we are descendants of Abraham" (8:33) no explanation of Abraham's identity is required. The narrator himself speaks of Old Testament figures without explaining their importance. In contrast to the earlier introduction of John the Baptist, for example, the allusion to Moses and the Law in the prologue (1:17) can be made with the comfortable certainty that the reader understands. What must be emphasized to the reader is that "grace and truth came through Jesus Christ." The categorical assertion that "no one has ever seen God" (1:18) may imply that the reader could have mistakenly thought that Moses or some other figure could share with Jesus the claim to have seen God. The phrase "the prophet Isaiah" (1:23; 12:38) is probably a stock phrase in John, as it is in the other gospels, rather than an explanation based on the assumption that the reader would not know who Isaiah was.[31] The reader also knows the story of Jacob's giving land to Joseph (Gen. 48:22; Josh. 24:32), but is reminded that Joseph was Jacob's son. We may conclude from both the narrator's comments and the general use of scriptural material and images in the gospel that the intended reader had a rather extensive knowledge of the Old Testament.

Although Jesus' discourses at the Jewish festivals figure prominently in the organization and thematic development of the gospel, the narrator's references to the festivals can be dealt with briefly. In the first instance the reader is told that the festival was "the Passover of the Jews" (2:13). In John 6 the reader is reminded that "the Passover, the feast of the Jews, was at hand" (6:4), and the third time it is still "the Passover of the Jews" (11:55). These references leave the clear impression that the reader is not a Jew and that the narrator is placing some distance between himself and Judaism. A Jewish audience would not need such explanations. Like Passover, Tabernacles is also identified as "the Jews' feast" (7:2). Later the narrator notes that the festival of dedication, Hanukkah, took place in winter (10:22). A Jewish reader would hardly need to be told when the

---

[31] Cf. Matt. 3:3; 4:14; 8:17; 12:17; 13:35; Mark 1:2; Luke 3:4; 4:17; Acts 8:28, 30; 28:25.

festival was celebrated, since it occurs at the same time every year. Again, the reference to "the day of Preparation of the Passover" (19:14) does not require any special knowledge on the part of the reader. No explanations are offered regarding the synagogue or temple, but no great familiarity is presupposed either. The main problem posed by these texts is that the significance of the discourses which occur in the context of the festivals can only be grasped fully by readers who know something about the festivals themselves. The discourses therefore seem to presuppose more familiarity with the Jewish festivals than do the narrator's comments. Are the comments added for the sake of the non-Jewish readers while the heart of the narrative is intended for readers who would know a great deal about the festivals? Is the intended audience heterogeneous? Is the implied reader (projected throughout the narrative by the implied author) more familiar with Judaism than the narratee (who is shaped exclusively by the narrator's voice)? Or must one resort to a theory of redaction during stages of a long composition history in which the material was fashioned for different audiences?

Other comments which shed light on the reader's familiarity with Judaism deal with Jewish beliefs and practices. We may begin with the beliefs and practices which are mentioned but not explained. In view of the possible difference between the positions of the narratee and the implied reader, it may be significant to observe that some of these references occur in discourse rather than narration. Still, in view of the translations provided in the first chapter for "Rabbi" and "Messiah," it is somewhat surprising that no explanation of "the Son of man" (1:51) seems to be needed. The expectation of "the prophet" (1:21, 25) or "the prophet who is to come into the world" (6:14) seems to be sufficiently clear also; no explanation is given. The narrator refers to the devil (13:2) and Satan (13:27) and again assumes no explanation is needed. The reader has some understanding of the significance of the sabbath for the Jews (5:9), and when the disciples assume that the blind man's birth defect is related to sin the narrator assumes that the link between the two is sufficiently clear to the reader that again no comment is needed (9:2; cf. 9:34). When the chief priests and Pharisees collaborate in assembling a council (11:47), no explanation of their actions or the powers of such a council is offered. Caiaphas must be introduced as "high priest that year" (11:49), but the narrator does not anticipate any surprise on the reader's part when he says that the high priest prophesied (11:51).

Some Jewish beliefs and practices do require explanation, however. Matters pertaining to the practice of ritual purity are particularly obscure. The stone water containers are said to be "for [κατά] the Jewish rites of purification" (2:6), and, as we have already observed, the reader must be told that "Jews have no dealings with Samaritans" or, as Daube suggested, "Jews do not use vessels together with Samaritans" (4:9).[32] Similarly, the explanation for the Jews' refusal to enter the praetorium, that is, "so that they might not be defiled, but might eat the passover" (18:28), is based on the assumptions common to all explanations: it is needed, and it will be understood. The reader understands something about defilement, but the explanation is needed, perhaps both for clarity and for its irony. The materials used in the burial of Jesus, myrrh, aloes, and linen, are all known, but the reader is not familiar with the burial customs of the Jews (19:40).

The narrator's comments on the Old Testament and Jewish festivals, beliefs, and practices reveal that the reader is not Jewish but has extensive knowledge of the Old Testament and a general understanding of Jewish groups and beliefs. On the other hand, the reader (or at least the narratee) is not familiar with the Jewish festivals or practices related to ritual purity. The combination of knowledge of the Old Testament, especially regarding Moses, Elijah, and the expectations of a Messiah, the prophet like Moses, and the Son of Man, with indications that the reader is not Jewish and has little understanding of Jewish festivals and practices suggests that the reader is either a Christian or one familiar with Christianity.

Events. The final group of comments which add to the profile of the reader has to do with events in the story which have not yet been narrated. Does the reader know the story of Jesus, or parts of it, before it is told? The gospel suggests an affirmative answer. The meaning of baptism, whether John's or Jesus', does not need to be explained. Jesus' "hour" is not explained (2:4), either because the reader knows its meaning or because it is something the reader must infer from successive references later in the gospel. The reference to Jesus' resurrection in 2:22 is a crucial one. Not only is there no effort to conceal the outcome of the events which are occurring, but the reader—in a radical departure from Prince's "degree zero" narratee—is assumed to know about Jesus' resurrection already. In other words, the reader has some knowledge of the story before it is told. Nothing in the account to this point (2:22) has prepared the reader for this aside. The author presumes that the reader knows that Jesus was raised from the dead.[33]

The definiteness of the phrase "for [the] fear of the Jews" (7:13) may imply that the reader is acquainted with such fear. The basis for this fear is not explained until 9:22. Likewise, the comments in 7:30 and 8:20 that

---

[32] Daube, "Jesus and the Samaritan Woman," pp. 137-47.
[33] See above, pp. 173–74.

the Jews could not seize Jesus because his hour had not yet come are an explanation for the reader only if he or she knows what is meant by Jesus' hour. If its meaning is unknown, the comment provides a clue to its meaning while heightening the reader's awareness of its importance. The comment on Jesus' enigmatic statement in 7:38 conveys that the reader would not have understood the statement unaided and would be unaware, or might forget, that "for as yet the Spirit had not been given, because Jesus was not yet glorified" (7:39). The reader therefore assumes the presence of the Spirit and knows what is meant by Jesus' "glorification" (cf. 12:16). The danger is that the reader may be unaware that the Spirit had not yet been given at the time of Jesus' ministry. Admittedly, the Spirit is identified as "the Spirit which those who believed in him were to receive," but this identification again points to the difference between the reader's time and that of Jesus' ministry and ties the narrator's comment more closely to Jesus' metaphor in the previous verse. The explanation of the reason for the parents' fear of the Jews is that the Jews had already agreed to expel from the synagogue any who confessed that Jesus was the Christ (9:22). Are the readers unfamiliar with this decision or does the explanation provide the basis for them to see the similarity between their situation and that of the parents? From this comment alone it would be hard to tell, but the prominence of the word "already" suggests that the reader knows of the action but would not know that (in the narrative world at least) it has already been implemented during the ministry of Jesus. The narrator's reference to the anointing of Jesus before the event (11:2; 12:3–8) again shows that the reader knows this part of the story before it is told. Knowledge of John's imprisonment (3:24) and the identity of "the brethren" who misunderstand about the Beloved Disciple's death is also assumed.

In summary, the reader has prior knowledge of many of the key elements of the gospel story: Jesus' death and resurrection, John the Baptist's imprisonment, the presence of the Spirit, the synagogue ban, the fear of the Jews, the anointing of Jesus by Mary, and probably the betrayal of Jesus (6:64; cf. 6:70–71). The meaning of Jesus' "glorification" and perhaps Jesus' "hour" can also be assumed, and as we noted in the discussion of the evangelist's ironizing treatment of Jesus' origin, the evangelist and his intended audience share more understanding of Jesus' birth than is ever made explicit in the gospel.[34] If the intended audience is not Christian, it is certainly familiar with Christian beliefs and the Christian story.

---

[34] See above, pp. 170–71.

Synthesis of the Portrait

Doubtless other inferences could be made from a close reading of the gospel, but these are enough to suggest the possibility and difficulties of identifying the reader on the basis of the narrator's introductions, explanations, and comments. Our survey shows that the intended reader is expected to know most of the characters in the story. The exceptions are the Beloved Disciple, Lazarus, Nicodemus, Caiaphas, and Annas; and there is some ambiguity about the reader's knowledge of Judas Iscariot and John the Baptist. On the other hand, while the readers know the general regions in which the story takes place, they are unfamiliar with most of the specific locations. The readers, in other words, do not live in any of the areas mentioned in the gospel. Correspondingly, the readers know Greek but not Hebrew (or Aramaic), and the evangelist assumes they use the Roman rather than the Jewish system for reckoning the hours of the day. Knowledge of the Old Testament, and especially expectations of messianic figures, can be presupposed, but the readers seem to have little knowledge of the practice of ritual purity. Their knowledge of the Jewish festivals is uncertain because of the tension between the narrator's comments about the festivals, which imply that the reader knows little or nothing about them, and the content of discourses at the festivals, which require considerable knowledge on the reader's part if their full significance is to be grasped. In sum, it appears that the intended readers are not Jewish, but their prior knowledge of many parts of the gospel story shows that the intended audience is either Christian or at least is familiar with the gospel story.

On the whole, a remarkably coherent and consistent picture of the intended reader emerges from the narrator's comments. A different construction could be put on the results of this study, however, by assuming one or more of the following possibilities: (1) that the evangelist was careless or inconsistent in his comments and explanations, (2) that the explanatory comments from which we have inferred ignorance on the part of the intended reader have a different purpose (e.g., to emphasize the meaning or importance of a term or the role of a person, or to coordinate the narrative with oral tradition or the synoptic tradition), (3) that many of the comments and explanations are late additions to the narrative and reflect a change in the intended audience, or (4) that different writers working on this gospel made different assumptions about the audience. The consistency of the portrait we have traced means that none of these factors exerted a great influence on the gospel's projection of its intended audience. Carelessness can be ruled out, and the very nature of the comments suggests that they were intended as explanations rather than for emphasis or for harmonizing the Johannine account with synoptic tradition. The third and fourth alternatives do provide attractive explanations by which minor tensions and inconsistencies can be dealt with, however. The difficulty posed by the tension between presumption of familiarity with the Jewish festivals, especially in the discourses, and explanatory comments which make the gospel intelligible to readers unfamiliar with Judaism probably indicates that by the time the composition of the Fourth Gospel was completed a broader readership was envisioned than was originally intended. The later readership included gentile Christians who knew little about Judaism.[35]

This readership, however, still shares a common idiom and the ability to appreciate the gospel's use of particular images, ironies, and symbols. Readers familiar with this peculiar idiom can read the gospel with greater appreciation than others, but the narrator's comments and the object lessons furnished by the misunderstandings allow access to the narrative even for those who begin as outsiders to its idiom.[36] On the other hand, John is not a missionary tract for Jewish readers, as Robinson, Wind, and van Unnik have argued.[37] Further examination of the sequence in which disclosures are made to the reader may bear out Dodd's suggestion that John is written on two levels so that insiders (members of the Johannine community) can grasp the whole significance of the gospel from each episode, while outsiders find it built up step by step.[38] Analysis of the gospel's indications of its intended audience confirms, or at least complements, much of the recent research which has concluded that John was written for a particular community of believers. We still do not know, however, how different the language of the Johannine community was from that of others outside the community, or how insular or rigidly defined its membership was.

If the gospel was written for a Christian audience, what were its main purposes? As we have already noted, the gospel's statement of its purpose, its plot, characterization, comments, misunderstandings, irony, and symbolism all work together in leading the reader to accept the evangelist's understanding of Jesus as the divine revealer and to share in the evangelist's concept of authentic faith, faith which certifies the believer as one of

---

[35] Heinrich Lausberg, *Jesaja 55,10–11 im Evangelium nach Johannes,* pp. 141–44 [pp. 13–16], similarly distinguishes between a Semitic primary audience and a later Hellenistic audience.

[36] See the discussion of Meeks and Leroy in Chapter 6, pp. 153–54, 186–87.

[37] See above, p. 211.

[38] C. H. Dodd, *The Interpretation of the Fourth Gospel,* pp. 316–17.

the "children of God." Such faith must, in the eyes of the evangelist, be distinguished from the inauthentic faith of those who marvel at signs but do not grasp their significance or follow the one to whom they point. It must be distinguished from the faith of those who seek to remain within the synagogue, and it must be distinguished from that of those who eventually turn away (6:66). More will be said in the Conclusion about how the gospel moves readers to its vision of authentic faith.

One aspect of that faith must be noted here, however. The gospel, and the narrator's ideological point of view in particular, call for the reader to regard Jesus as the pre-existent *logos* and to see his crucifixion and resurrection as his exaltation. The intended readers are probably assumed to share in the misperceptions of one or more of the characters in the gospel. Some may not understand the relationship between Jesus and the creative *logos,* others may not accept the affirmation that the incarnate *logos* actually became human and died a real death. Speculation about the relationship between Jesus and the divine *logos* seems, therefore, to have been a significant issue for the Gospel's audience. John's contribution is that it insists on incarnation as well as pre-existence and affirms Jesus' death as a part of his work, even if it is to be interpreted as a manifestation of his glory, his enthronement as king, and his exaltation to the Father. The author therefore calls his readers to affirm the fulfillment of the Jewish heritage in Jesus and the divinity of the one "from above," who is not from "this world." At the same time, he proposes a narrative interpretation of Jesus which sets limits on Christian *logos* speculation. Jesus is the *logos,* and he was so before his birth. Nevertheless, he died a human death. This interpretation sets the gospel in contrast both to other early Christian interpretations and to the growing impetus to separate the humanity of Jesus from the divinity of the *logos,* deny the incarnation, and deny either the reality or the significance of Jesus' death.[39]

In contrast to the other disciples, as we have seen, the Beloved Disciple represents the paradigm of authentic faith. He does not resist Jesus' humility or his acceptance of his death. Neither does he dispute Jesus' resurrection and exaltation. Instead, he follows Jesus to the cross, is united with his mother, and witnesses the blood and water which flow from his side at his death. To such true disciples Jesus hands over the Spirit (19:30). This scandalous story of the creative *logos* which became flesh and died on a cross formed the core of the identity of this early Christian community. Readers found their identity in the gospel story and through it they could rise from their present struggles to hear their values and views reaffirmed, to hear again reassuring words from Jesus, to

---

[39] Cf. Brown, *The Community of the Beloved Disciple,* pp. 110–20.

glimpse the mystery of the world above, and find themselves, or at least their ideal, in the figure of the Beloved Disciple, whose witness was true and whose "place" was the bosom of the Lord.

Chapter Eight

CONCLUSION

Sartre is perhaps as good as any novelist can be without achieving real greatness; when we read his novels we say, "Yes, this is the Sartrean world"; but when we read one of the great masters we say, simply, "Yes, this is the world." The difference in our response may perhaps seem slight; in fact, it is crucial.

W. J. Harvey
Character and the Novel

In deciding whether a work *does* something well that is worth doing, or *is* something good that is worth being, the critic has only four or five general directions to look. We can admire a work because it is constructed unusually well (objective or formal criticism); because it expresses its author or his situation effectively (expressive); or because it does something to us with unusual force (rhetorical); or because it contains or conveys a true or desirable doctrine (didactic, or ideological); or because it culminates or illustrates a tradition or initiates a fashion (historical).

Since every work *is* all of these—a construction, an expression, an action on its audience, an embodiment of beliefs, and a moment in history—a critic stressing any one interest will find all works amenable to his judgments.

Wayne C. Booth
A Rhetoric of Irony

The diagram in the introductory chapter graphically depicts the model of literary analysis we have followed. It highlights various elements which are important in the communication between author and reader when one reads a narrative. As each of these has been examined, we have explored the "anatomy" of the Fourth Gospel, tracing its rhetorical form and studying the function of each of its organs. The study has set in sharp relief the uniqueness of this gospel and has, I hope, contributed to our understanding of what the gospel is and what gives it its power as a narrative.

The epigraph by Wayne Booth is quoted because it seems particularly well suited to the evaluation of the Fourth Gospel, not because it leads us to the banal conclusion that the gospel deserves to be regarded as an exceptional work, a great piece of literature, but because it helps us see the measure of the evangelist's achievement. As a construction, the gospel is magnificent but flawed. Magnificent in its complexity, subtlety, and profundity, but oddly flawed in some of its transitions, sequences, and movements. Recent criticism has repeatedly yielded fascinating views of how the gospel reflects the author's situation, and we have seen how artfully it expresses his view of the world. Its place in the canon of scripture testifies to its rhetorical power and the desirability of its doctrine. Finally, the Fourth Gospel is the magnificent culmination of the Johannine tradition and has been a vital force in shaping both Christian doctrine and "the representation of reality in western literature."[1] My aim has been to expose the Fourth Gospel's rhetorical power to analysis by studying the literary elements of its "anatomy."

In reading the gospel, one is drawn into a literary world created by the author from materials drawn from life and history as well as imagination and reflection. The narrator speaks retrospectively, telling a story that is a sublime blend of historical tradition and faith. Robert Browning described the gospel's retrospective point of view in a dramatic monologue:

But patient stated much of the Lord's life
Forgotten or misdelivered, and let it work:

---

[1] Erich Auerbach, *Mimesis,* argues that the gospels exerted a profound influence on subsequent literature. See esp. pp. 40–49, 555.

Since much of that at the first, in deed and word
Lay simply and sufficiently exposed,
Had grown (or else my soul was grown to match,
Fed through such years, familiar with such light,
Guarded and guided still to see and speak)
Of new significance and fresh result;
What first were guessed as points, I now knew stars,
and named them in the gospel I have writ.

. . . .

My book speaks on, because it cannot pass;
One listens quietly, nor scoffs but pleads,
"Here is a tale of things done ages since;
What truth was ever told the second day?"[2]

In this story of history interpreted by faith, the narrator leads the reader to view each character and event from his point of view. Although the implied author and the real author may be distinguished from the narrator in theory, in John the narrator is the voice of the author and the vocal expression of the choices and perspective of the implied author. One of the ways the gospel achieves its powerful effects is through the role of this narrator, who is omniscient, winsomely intrusive, and entirely reliable. By sharing with the reader his insights into points now known to be stars, he wins our trust from the outset and shapes our grasp of the whole.

The narrator's assistance is necessary because the story can only be understood when one sees its place in history between "the beginning" and "the last day." Only when the reader sees Jesus as the incarnation of the divine *logos,* which was active in creation and the history of Israel, and as the exalted Son of Man can the meaning of his ministry be understood. Moreover, although only a fraction of that ministry is narrated, the gospel conveys strong impressions by the way it conceals the gaps and uses repetition, summary, and allusion.

Within the gospel, one sees a world in which characters are sharply defined by their response to Jesus, by the measure of their ability to believe, and by their progress toward or away from the perspective of the narrator. The plot of the gospel is so crafted, however, that the narrator's view of Jesus is conclusively established before the reader is exposed to any challenge to it. Then, by the end of the gospel, the misperceptions of unbelief and the misunderstandings of those who do not see Jesus as the narrator sees him are completely exposed. On the other hand, the narrator's view of Jesus is confirmed throughout the gospel.

---

[2] "A Death in the Desert," lines 166–75, 368–71.

The characters one meets span the spectrum of responses to Jesus. The Pharisees and Jews reject him. Others, like Nicodemus and Joseph of Arimathea, refuse to confess their faith openly. Several of the characters are caught between Jesus and his opponents and must choose what their response will be. Pilate is the example of one who attempts to avoid the demand for a decision. The disciples, on the other hand, behold Jesus' glory and respond with belief, but each of them typifies a particular misperception or misunderstanding which must be overcome. The Beloved Disciple, whose perception and response to Jesus is clarified by belief and love, is the true witness and the paradigm of authentic faith. Together, the characters comprise the peculiar population of John's narrative world, and each is part of a unified continuum of responses to Jesus. The characters also typify reactions and problems the reader may share. By entering this narrative world through the experience of reading the gospel, readers may see more clearly what is lacking in their own response to Jesus. They may also be moved to embrace the response articulated by the narrator and dramatized by the Beloved Disciple and those who overcome their lack of understanding.

The gospel achieves its most subtle effects, however, through its implicit commentary, that is, the devices and passages in which the author communicates with the reader by implication and indirection. Here the gospel says more than it ever makes explicit. The extensive use of misunderstanding in the narrative teaches the reader how to interpret what Jesus says and warns the reader always to listen for overtones and double meanings. Through its irony, the gospel lifts the reader to the vantage point of the narrator so that we know what others in the story have not yet discovered and can feel the humor and bite of meanings they miss. A great deal of the agenda of Jesus' disputes with the Jews is interpreted for the reader by the gospel's irony. The folly of disbelief and misperception is thereby repeatedly exposed. The overtones of ironic words shade easily over into the effects of John's use of symbols. Core symbols, like light, water, and bread are used repeatedly and developed to the point where even allusions to them carry rich overtones. Through these symbols the gospel draws together the reader and the author, readers and Jesus, this world and the world above. Invitations to shared perceptions and shared judgments are accepted when readers sense meanings which are never stated. But the invitations, once sensed, cannot easily be declined. Readers dance with the author whether they want to or not, and in the process they adopt his perspective on the story.

Finally, the gospel derives much of its power from the way it depicts its implied reader. The original readers no doubt felt that the narrator was speaking to them and taking into account the limitations of their understanding and the predispositions they brought to the narrative. At the same time, beliefs they held dear were reaffirmed and clarified so that they were drawn deeper into the faith to which they had committed themselves. They were reassured by the community of faith they found in the company of the narrator, the Beloved Disciple, and the "we" who had beheld Jesus' glory.

The cumulative effect of all these elements of the gospel's narrative anatomy is exceedingly rich and powerful. While the plot focuses attention on the alternatives of belief or unbelief, the sequence of characters who encounter Jesus vividly depicts the common dilemmas, struggles, and misperceptions of those who must work out their response to the revealer. As we read, watching the encounters and forming judgments on each character, the narrator shapes the response we think we are making on our own and wins our confidence by elevating us above the characters to his position. From this vantage point the subtleties of the story, especially its irony and symbolism, are exposed and draw us further into the perspective of the author. The Gospel of John is therefore more unified and coherent than has often been thought because its unity is not found primarily in plot development, which as we have seen is rather episodic, or in the progression of action from scene to scene. It consists instead in the effect it achieves through thematic development, the spectrum of characters, and the implicit commentary conveyed through irony and symbolism. In other words, the unity of this "spiritual gospel" is more evident in the subtle elements of its narrative structure than in the obvious ones. The eagle soars when it reaches for the sublime and the subtle, but it is clumsy when it has to walk through some of the ordinary elements of a narrative. The rhetorical structures of the gospel nevertheless cohere and focus the affective power of its conflicts, characters, and comments. The effect is a profound challenge to accept the literary world as representative of reality, to see Jesus as the narrator sees him, and to see the world in which we live as a mere appearance concealing and revealing the reality of a higher plane of life which can only be experienced by accepting the perspectives affirmed by the gospel.

Our reading experience, however, must inevitably be different from that of the gospel's intended readers, for both their world and their assumptions about their world were much closer to the implied author's than ours are. Possessed of historical tradition, knowledge of his culture, and a resolute faith in Jesus as the creating and redeeming *logos,* the evangelist was able to construct a narrative with a literary world which shared enough with his intended readers' concepts of the real world for him to invite his readers to accept his vision of the world as the true, authentic (ἀληθινός) one. As Erich Auerbach wrote, "The world of the

Scripture stories is not satisfied with claiming to be a historically true reality—it insists that it is the only real world," so "we are to fit our own life into its world, feel ourselves to be elements in its structure of universal history."[3] But, as he and others have observed, this has become increasingly difficult as our world and our understanding of it have become different from the gospel's. What follows may therefore be regarded as a churchman's postscript.

First we notice that the past recorded in the gospel seems strangely different from our own time. We miss what Lionel Trilling has called "a culture's hum and buzz of implication."[4] The world that once surrounded the text is no longer there, and the text lives on in a new and different world with different activities, different understandings of life and history, and different "half-uttered or unuttered or unutterable expressions of value."[5] Not only may we mistake what was commonplace for what is distinctive in the narrative, but we also find it far more difficult to see our world mirrored there.

The incentive the narrative offers for accepting its world as the true understanding of the "real" world is enormous. It places the reader's world under the providence of God, gives the reader an identity with a past and a secure future,[6] and promises the presence of God's Spirit with the believer, forgiveness for sin, and an experience of salvation which includes assurances of life beyond the grave. The gospel offers contemporary readers a refuge from all the unreliable narrators of modern life and literature. It is not surprising then that it has survived through the centuries with a secure and much loved place in the canon of scripture.

Hans Frei, however, has insightfully chronicled what he called "the eclipse of biblical narrative," the historical and cultural changes which mean that biblical narratives can no longer be read as realistic narratives, as they once were: "In its own right and by itself the biblical story began to fade as the inclusive world whose depiction allowed the reader at the same time to locate himself and his era in the real world rendered by the depiction."[7] One part of this process has been the evolution of a profound distinction between empirical and fictional narratives.[8] History belongs to the former, imaginative literature to the latter. In order to retain their claim to truth and their role as revealed scriptures, biblical narratives came increasingly to be read as "literally" true by the standards of a

---

[3] *Mimesis,* pp. 14-15.
[4] "Manners, Morals, and the Novel," p. 232.
[5] Trilling, "Manners, Morals, and the Novel," p. 232.
[6] Cf. William A. Beardslee, *Literary Criticism of the New Testament,* pp. 19, 81.
[7] *The Eclipse of Biblical Narrative,* p. 50.
[8] Robert Scholes and Robert Kellogg, *The Nature of Narrative,* pp. 12–13.

positivistic historiography. Either the world and indeed the details of the events in the gospel narratives correspond precisely to those of Jesus' life, or else their claim to truth was felt to be denied or at least seriously compromised. Under such an alternative, the gospels have been read as "literally" true by most Christians. The choice has been either that the world of Jesus is accurately depicted by the narratives, in which case the narratives also tell us that our world is not at all as it is commonly understood today; or else, since the world must be as we know it, Jesus' world could not have been like that depicted by the narrative, in which case the gospel is not "true."

The struggle over this dilemma is most intense at precisely the gospel's central affirmation—the character of Jesus. For many modern readers the question is how they can accept the gospel's artful invitation to believe that God was in Christ revealing himself to the world when they cannot accept as historically plausible its characterization of Jesus as a miracle worker with full recollection of his pre-existence and knowledge of his life after death. Acceptance of this characterization after the modern divorce of truth from fiction and fiction from truth requires such a docetic reading of the gospel that its claim that Jesus was a man is contradicted. Refusal to accept the gospel's characterization, however, can only mean that it is fictional and therefore not true. This impasse has blocked meaningful dialogue between Christians and non-christians and has led Christian denominations to bitter controversies over the truth of the Bible, even though the controversies have generally dealt with statements regarding the "inspiration and authority" of scripture. The real issue is whether "his story" can be true if it is not "history."[9]

There is no way to return to the period before the Enlightenment, of course, and no way to treat the gospel as though the issue were not there. The future role of the gospel in the life of the church will depend on the church's ability to relate both story and history to truth in such a way that neither has an exclusive claim to truth and one is not incompatible with the other. Only then will the distorting blinkers of the contemporary world be set aside so that the gospel can be read as the evangelist assumed it would be. As long as readers require the gospel to be a window on the ministry of Jesus before they will see truth in it, accepting the gospel will mean believing that the story it tells corresponds exactly to what actually happened during Jesus' ministry. When the gospel is viewed as a mirror, though of course not a mirror in which we see only ourselves,[10] its mean-

---

[9] Cf. Raymond E. Brown, *The Birth of the Messiah,* p. 34: ". . . for a divinely inspired story is not necessarily history."

[10] See the discussion of the text as a window or as a mirror in Chapter 1.

ing can be found on this side of it, that is, between text and reader, in the experience of reading the text, and belief in the gospel can mean openness to the ways it calls readers to interact with it, with life, and with their own world. It can mean believing that the narrator is not only reliable but right and that Jesus' life and our response mean for us what the story has led us to believe they mean. Cultivation of a capacity to appreciate the Bible as literature can therefore contribute to the solution of the church's problem with how to read the Bible.[11]

When art and history, fiction and truth, are again reconciled we will again be able to read the gospel as the author's original audience read it. Original readers are now more vital to the accuracy of the text than original manuscripts. When once again we learn to read the gospel, we will be able to deal with the relationship between our world and its world "above" rather than the relationship between the evangelist's world and Jesus' world, or their world and our world. Then, when the horizons of our world and the world of the narrative merge,[12] we will have heard the gospel, the story will have fulfilled its purpose, and the truth to which it points can once again abide in its readers.

---

[11] As Brian Wicker so perceptively observes: "Perhaps it is only now, as a result of our long experience of reading *novels*, that is, narratives that once again combine the empirical and the fictional in a mode of narration more complex than either of these can be by itself, are we able to recover the true nature of narratives that were written before that split occurred" (*The Story-Shaped World,* p. 105.)

[12] Cf. David J. A. Clines, "Story and Poem," p. 127.

Bibliography

Abrams, M. H. *A Glossary of Literary Terms.* 3d ed. New York: Holt, Reinhart and Winston, Inc., 1971.
_____. "How to do Things with Texts." *Partisan Review* 46 (1979): 566–88.
Agourides, S. "The Purpose of John 21." Pp. 127–32 in *Studies in the History and Text of the New Testament—in Honor of K. W. Clark,* edited by B. L. Daniels and M. J. Suggs. Salt Lake City: University of Utah Press, 1967.
Aland, Kurt, Matthew Black, Carlo Martini, Bruce Metzger, and Alan Wikgren, eds. *Novum Testamentum Graece.* 26th ed. Stuttgart: Deutsche Bibelstiftung, 1979.
Alter, Robert. *The Art of Biblical Narrative.* New York: Basic Books, Inc., 1981.
Appold, Mark L. *The Oneness Motif in the Fourth Gospel: Motif Analysis and Exegetical Probe into the Theology of John.* Wissenschaftliche Untersuchungen zum Neuen Testament, Reihe 2, vol. 1. Tübingen: J. C. B. Mohr, 1976.
Auerbach, Erich. *Mimesis: The Representation of Reality in Western Literature.* Eng. trans. W. R. Trask. Princeton, NJ: Princeton University Press, 1953.
Barrett, C. K. "Christocentric or Theocentric? Observations on the Theological Method of the Fourth Gospel." Pp. 361–76 in *La Notion biblique de Dieu: Le Dieu de la Bible et le Dieu des philosophes,* edited by J. Coppens. Bibliotheca ephemeridum theologicarum lovaniensium 41. Louvain: Louvain University Press; Gembloux, Belgium: J. Duculot, 1976.
_____. "'The Father is Greater than I' (Jo 14, 28): Subordinationist Christology in the New Testament." Pp. 144–59 in *Neues Testament und Kirche: Für Rudolf Schnackenburg,* edited by J. Gnilka. Freiburg: Herder, 1974.
_____. *The Gospel According to St. John: An Introduction with Commentary and Notes on the Greek Text.* 2d ed. Philadelphia: Westminster Press; London: SPCK, 1978.
Bassler, Jouette M. "The Galileans: A Neglected Factor in Johannine Community Research." *Catholic Biblical Quarterly* 43 (1981): 243–57.
Baum, Gregory. *The Jews and the Gospel: A Re-examination of the New Testament.* London: Bloomsbury Publishing Co., 1961.
Beardslee, William A. *Literary Criticism of the New Testament.* Guides to Biblical Scholarship. Philadelphia: Fortress Press, 1970.
Becker, Jürgen. "Die Abschiedsreden Jesu im Johannesevangelium." *Zeitschrift für die neutestamentliche Wissenschaft* 61 (1970): 215–46.
Billings, J. S. "Judas Iscariot in the Fourth Gospel." *Expository Times* 51 (1939–40): 156–57.
Boismard, Marie-Emile, and A. Lamouille. *L'Evangile de Jean.* Synopse des Quatres Evangiles en Français, III. Paris: Cerf, 1977.
Booth, Wayne C. "Distance and Point of View: An Essay in Classification." *Essays in Criticism* 11 (1961): 60–79.
_____. *The Rhetoric of Fiction.* Chicago: University of Chicago Press, 1961.
_____. *A Rhetoric of Irony.* Chicago: University of Chicago Press, 1974.
Borgen, Peder. *Bread from Heaven: An Exegetical Study of the Concept of Manna in the Gospel of John and the Writings of Philo.* Novum Testamentum, Supplements 10. Leiden: E. J. Brill, 1965.
Bratcher, R. J. "'The Jews' in the Gospel of John." *The Bible Translator* 26 (1975): 401–9.

Brewer, Derek. "The Gospels and the Laws of Folktale: A Centenary Lecture, 14 June 1978." *Folklore* 90 (1979): 37–52.

Brooks, Cleanth, and Robert Penn Warren. *Understanding Fiction*. New York: F. S. Crofts & Co., 1943.

Brown, Edward K. *Rhythm in the Novel*. The Alexander Lectures, 1949–50. Toronto: University of Toronto Press, 1950.

Brown, Raymond E. *The Birth of the Messiah: A Commentary on the Infancy Narratives in Matthew and Luke*. Garden City, NY: Doubleday & Co.; London: Geoffrey Chapman, 1977.

_____. *The Community of the Beloved Disciple*. New York: Paulist Press, 1979.

_____. *The Gospel According to John*. Anchor Bible. 2 vols. Garden City, NY: Doubleday & Co., 1966 and 1970.

_____. Review of *Rätsel und Missverständnis* by Herbert Leroy. *Biblica* 51 (1970): 152–54.

_____, K. P. Donfried, and J. Reumann, eds. *Peter in the New Testament*. New York: Paulist Press; Minneapolis: Augsburg Publishing House; London: Geoffrey Chapman, 1973.

_____, K. P. Donfried, J. A. Fitzmyer, and J. Reumann, eds. *Mary in the New Testament*. New York: Paulist Press; Philadelphia: Fortress Press; London: Geoffrey Chapman, 1979.

Buchler, Justus, ed. *The Philosophy of Peirce: Selected Writings*. London: Routledge & Kegan Paul Ltd., 1940.

Bultmann, Rudolf. *The Gospel of John: A Commentary*. Eng. trans. G. R. Beasley Murray, et al. Philadelphia: Westminster Press; Oxford: Basil Blackwell, 1971.

_____. *Theology of the New Testament*. 2 vols. Eng. trans. K. Grobel. New York: Charles Scribner's Sons; London: SCM Press, 1955.

Cahill, P. J. "The Johannine *Logos* as Center." *Catholic Biblical Quarterly* 38 (1976): 54–72.

Caird, G. B. "The Glory of God in the Fourth Gospel." *New Testament Studies* 15 (1968–69): 265–77.

_____. *The Language and Imagery of the Bible*. Philadelphia: Westminster Press; London: Duckworth, 1980.

Carson, D. A. "Understanding Misunderstandings in the Fourth Gospel." *Tyndale Bulletin* 33 (1982): 59–91.

Casparis, Christian P. *Tense without Time: The Present Tense in Narration*. Swiss Studies in English, vol. 84. Bern: Francke Verlag, 1975.

Chambers, Ross. "Commentary in Literary Texts." *Critical Inquiry* 5 (1978): 323–37.

Chatman, Seymour. *Story and Discourse: Narrative Structure in Fiction and Film*. Ithaca, NY: Cornell University Press, 1978.

Chevalier, Haakon M. *The Ironic Temper: Anatole France and His Time*. New York and London: Oxford University Press, 1932.

Clavier, Henri. "L'ironie dans le quatrième évangile." Pp. 261–76 in *Studia Evangelica* I, Texte und Untersuchungen 73. Berlin: Academie-Verlag, 1959.

Clines, David J. A. "Story and Poem: The Old Testament as Literature and as Scripture." *Interpretation* 34 (1980): 115–27.

Cohen, Ted. "Metaphor and the Cultivation of Intimacy." *Critical Inquiry* 5 (1978): 3–12.

Collins, Raymond F. "Jesus' Conversation with Nicodemus." *The Bible Today* 93 (1977): 1409–19.

_____. "Mary in the Fourth Gospel. A Decade of Johannine Studies." *Louvain Studies* 3 (1970): 99–142.

_____. "The Representative Figures of the Fourth Gospel." *Downside Review* 94 (1976): 26–46; 95 (1976): 118–32.

Crane, R. S. "The Concept of Plot." Pp. 233–43 in *Approaches to the Novel*, edited by

Robert Scholes. Rev. ed. San Francisco: Chandler Publishing Co., 1966.

Crossan, John Dominic. "A Structuralist Analysis of John 6." Pp. 235–49 in *Orientation by Disorientation: Studies in Literary Criticism*. Presented in Honor of William A. Beardslee, edited by Richard A. Spencer. Pittsburgh Theological Monograph Series 35. Pittsburgh: Pickwick Press, 1980.

Cullmann, Oscar. *Early Christian Worship*. Eng. trans. A. S. Todd and J. B. Torrance. Philadelphia: Westminster Press, 1978; London: SCM Press, 1953.

———. "Der johanneische Gebrauch doppeldeutiger Ausdrücke als Schlüssel zum Verständnis des vierten Evangeliums." *Theologische Zeitschrift* 4 (1948): 360–72.

———. *The Johannine Circle*. Eng. trans. J. Bowden. Philadelphia: Westminster Press; London: SCM Press, 1976.

Culpepper, R. Alan. *The Johannine School: An Evaluation of the Johannine-School Hypothesis Based on an Investigation of the Nature of Ancient Schools*. Society of Biblical Literature Dissertation Series 26. Missoula, MT: Scholars Press, 1975.

———. "The Pivot of John's Prologue." *New Testament Studies* 27 (1980): 1–31.

Dahl, Nils. "The Neglected Factor in New Testament Theology." *Reflection* 73 (1975): 5–8.

Daube, David. "Jesus and the Samaritan Woman: The Meaning of *sygchraomai*." *Journal of Biblical Literature* 69 (1950): 137–47.

Davey, J. Ernest. *The Jesus of St. John: Historical and Christological Studies in the Fourth Gospel*. London: Lutterworth Press, 1958.

Dewey, Kim. "*Paroimiai* in the Gospel of John." *Semeia* 17 (1980): 81–100.

Dodd, C. H. *Historical Tradition in the Fourth Gospel*. New York and Cambridge: Cambridge University Press, 1963.

———. *The Interpretation of the Fourth Gospel*. New York and Cambridge: Cambridge University Press, 1953.

———. "Note on John 21, 24." *Journal of Theological Studies* 4 (1953): 212–13.

Donahue, John R. "A Neglected Factor in the Theology of Mark." *Journal of Biblical Literature* 101 (1983): 563–94.

Duke, Paul D. "Irony in the Fourth Gospel: The Shape and Function of a Literary Device." Ph.D. diss., Southern Baptist Theological Seminary, 1982.

Dunn, James D. G. "The Washing of the Disciples' Feet in John 13:1–20." *Zeitschrift für die neutestamentliche Wissenschaft* 61 (1970): 247–52.

Eco, Umberto. *The Role of the Reader. Explorations in the Semiotics of Texts*. Bloomington: Indiana University Press, 1979.

Egan, Kieran. "What is a Plot?" *New Literary History* 9 (1978): 455–73.

Fawcett, Thomas. *The Symbolic Language of Religion: An Introductory Study*. London: SCM Press, 1970.

Fennema, David A. "Jesus and God According to John: An Analysis of the Fourth Gospel's Father/Son Christology." Ph.D. diss., Duke University, 1979.

Feuillet, André. *Johannine Studies*. Eng. trans. Thomas E. Crane. Staten Island, NY: Alba House, 1964.

Fielding, Henry. *The History of Tom Jones*. Edited by F. Bowers. Oxford: Clarendon Press, 1974.

Finegan, Jack. *Handbook of Biblical Chronology: Principles of Time Reckoning in the Ancient World and Problems of Chronology in the Bible*. Princeton, NJ: Princeton University Press, 1964.

Forster, E. M. *Aspects of the Novel*. New York: Penguin Books, 1962.

Fortna, Robert T. "Theological Use of Locale in the Fourth Gospel." Pp. 58–95 in *Gospel Studies in Honor of Sherman E. Johnson*, edited by M. H. Shepherd, Jr. and E. C. Hobbs. Anglican Theological Review Supplementary Series 3 (1974).

France, Anatole. "The Procurator of Judea." Pp. 3–26 in *The Works of Anatole France*, vol. 2: *Mother of Pearl*, edited by F. Chapman. London: John Lane, The Bodley Head, Ltd., 1923.

Freedman, William. "The Literary Motif: A Definition and Evaluation." *Novel* 4 (1971): 123–31.

Frei, Hans W. *The Eclipse of Biblical Narrative: A Study in Eighteenth and Nineteenth Century Hermeneutics*. New Haven, CT, and London: Yale University Press, 1974.

Friedman, Norman. *Form and Meaning in Fiction*. Athens: The University of Georgia Press, 1975.

——. "Forms of the Plot." Pp. 145–66 in *The Theory of the Novel*, edited by Philip Stevick. New York: The Free Press, 1967.

Frye, Northrop. *Anatomy of Criticism: Four Essays*. Princeton, NJ: Princeton University Press, 1957.

——. "The Critical Path: An Essay on the Social Context of Literary Criticism." Pp. 91–194 in *In Search of Literary Theory*, edited by M. W. Bloomfield. Ithaca, NY: Cornell University Press, 1972.

——. *The Great Code: The Bible and Literature*. New York and London: Harcourt Brace Jovanovich, 1982.

Fuller, Reginald. "'The Jews' in the Fourth Gospel." *Dialog* 16 (1977): 31–37.

Gärtner, Bertil E. "The Pauline and Johannine Idea of 'To Know God' Against the Hellenistic Background." *New Testament Studies* 14 (1967–68): 209–31.

Genette, Gérard. *Narrative Discourse: An Essay in Method*. Eng. trans. Jane E. Lewin. Ithaca, NY: Cornell University Press, 1980.

Grässer, Erich. "Die antijüdische Polemik im Johannesevangelium." *New Testament Studies* 11 (1964–65): 74–90.

Gunn, Giles. *The Interpretation of Otherness: Literature, Religion, and the American Imagination*. New York and London: Oxford University Press, 1979.

Hahn, Ferdinand. "Die Jüngerberufung Joh. 1, 35–51." Pp. 172–90 in *Neues Testament und Kirche: Für Rudolf Schnackenburg*. Edited by J. Gnilka. Freiburg: Herder, 1974.

Hanson, Anthony T. *The New Testament Interpretation of Scripture*. London: SPCK, 1980.

Harris, Wendell V. "Mapping Fiction's 'Forest of Symbols.'" Pp. 133–46 in *University of Colorado Studies*. Series in Language and Literature 9. Boulder: University of Colorado Press, 1963.

Harsh, Philip W. *A Handbook of Classical Drama*. Stanford, CA: Stanford University Press, 1944.

Hartingsveld, Lodewijk van. *Die Eschatologie des Johannesevangeliums: Eine Auseinandersetzung mit R. Bultmann*. Van Gorcum's theologische bibliotheek, vol. 36. Assen, Netherlands: Van Gorcum & Co., 1962.

Harvey, A. E. *Jesus on Trial: A Study in the Fourth Gospel*. Atlanta: John Knox Press; London: SPCK, 1976.

Harvey, W. J. *Character and the Novel*. Ithaca, NY: Cornell University Press, 1966; London: Chatto & Windus, 1965.

Hawkin, David J. "The Function of the Beloved Disciple Motif in the Johannine Redaction." *Laval theologique et philosophique* 33 (1977): 135–50.

Hinderer, Walter. "Theory, Conception, and Interpretation of the Symbol." Pp. 83–127 in *Perspectives in Literary Symbolism*, edited by J. Strelka. Yearbook of Comparative Criticism, I. University Park: Pennsylvania State University Press, 1968.

Hirsch, E. D., Jr. *Validity in Interpretation*. New Haven, CT: Yale University Press, 1967.

Hodges, Zane C. "Problem Passages in the Gospel of John. Part 2: Untrustworthy Believers—John 2:23–25." *Bibliotheca Sacra* 135 (1978): 139–52.

Hoskyns, Edwyn C. *The Fourth Gospel*. Edited by F. N. Davey. London: Faber and Faber, Ltd., 1940.

Ingarden, Roman. *The Cognition of the Literary Work of Art*. Eng. trans. R. A. Crowley and K. R. Olson. Evanston, IL: Northwestern University Press, 1973.

_____. *Das literarische Kunstwerk.* Tübingen: Max Niemeyer, 1960.

Iser, Wolfgang. *The Act of Reading: A Theory of Aesthetic Response.* Baltimore: Johns Hopkins University Press, 1978.

_____. *The Implied Reader: Patterns of Communication in Prose Fiction from Bunyan to Beckett.* Baltimore: Johns Hopkins University Press, 1974.

James, Henry. "The Art of Fiction." Pp. 585–609 in *Henry James: Selected Fiction,* edited by Leon Edel. Everyman's Library. New York: E. P. Dutton & Co., 1953.

Jiménez, R. Moreno. "El discípulo de Jesucristo, según el evangelio de S. Juan." *Estudios bíblicos* 30 (1971): 269–311.

Jonge, Marinus de. *Jesus: Stranger from Heaven and Son of God,* edited and Eng. trans. by John E. Steely. Society of Biblical Literature Sources for Biblical Study 11. Missoula, MT: Scholars Press, 1977.

Jónsson, Jakob. *Humor and Irony in the New Testament.* Reykjavik: Bokautgáfa Menningarsjóts, 1965.

Käsemann, Ernst. *The Testament of Jesus According to John 17.* Eng. trans. G. Krodel. Philadelphia: Fortress Press, 1968.

Kelber, Werner H. *Mark's Story of Jesus.* Philadelphia: Fortress Press, 1979.

Kennedy, George A. *Classical Rhetoric and Its Christian and Secular Tradition from Ancient to Modern Times.* Chapel Hill: University of North Carolina Press, 1980.

Kermode, Frank. "Figures in the Carpet: On Recent Theories of Narrative Discourse." Pp. 291–301 in *Comparative Criticism, A Yearbook: 2,* edited by Elinor S. Shaffer. Cambridge and New York: Cambridge University Press, 1980.

_____. *The Genesis of Secrecy: On the Interpretation of Narrative.* The Charles Eliot Norton Lectures, 1977–78. Cambridge, MA: Harvard University Press, 1979.

_____. *The Sense of an Ending: Studies in the Theory of Fiction.* New York and London: Oxford University Press, 1967.

Koch, Klaus. *The Growth of the Biblical Tradition: The Form-Critical Method.* Eng. trans. S. M. Cupitt. New York: Charles Scribner's Sons; London: A. & C. Black, 1969.

Kossen, H. B. "Who Were the Greeks of John XII 20?" *Studies in John: Presented to Dr. J. N. Sevenster.* Novum Testamentum, Supplements 24. Leiden: E. J. Brill, 1970.

Krafft, Eva. "Die Personen des Johannesevangeliums." *Evangelische Theologie* 16 (1956): 18–32.

Krieger, Murray. *A Window to Criticism: Shakespeare's Sonnets and Modern Poetics.* Princeton, NJ: Princeton University Press, 1964.

Kysar, Robert. *The Fourth Evangelist and His Gospel: An Examination of Contemporary Scholarship.* Minneapolis: Augsburg Publishing House, 1975.

Lakoff, George, and Mark Johnson. *Metaphors We Live By.* Chicago and London: University of Chicago Press, 1980.

Langbrandtner, Wolfgang. *Weltferner Gott oder Gott der Liebe: Die Ketzerstreit in der johanneischen Kirche.* Beiträge zur biblischen Exegese und Theologie 6. Frankfort: Lang, 1977.

Langer, Susanne K. *Philosophy in a New Key: A Study in the Symbolism of Reason, Rite, and Art.* 4th ed. Cambridge, MA: Harvard University Press, 1960.

Lausberg, Heinrich. *Jesaja 55, 10–11 im Evangelium nach Johannes.* Minuscula philologica (V). Nachrichten der Akademie der Wissenschaften in Göttingen, I. Philologisch-historische Klasse, 1979, No. 7. Göttingen: Vandenhoeck & Ruprecht, 1979.

Leal, Juan. "El simbolismo histórico del iv evangelio." *Estudios bíblicos* 19 (1960): 329–48.

Lee, Edwin K. *The Religious Thought of St. John.* London: SPCK, 1950.

Léon-Dufour, Xavier. "Towards a Symbolic Reading of the Fourth Gospel." *New Testament Studies* 27 (1981): 439–56.

Leroy, Herbert. *Rätsel und Missverständnis: Ein Beitrag zur Formgeschichte des Johannesevangeliums.* Bonner biblische Beiträge 30. Bonn: Peter Hanstein, 1968.

Levin, Harry. *Contexts of Criticism.* Harvard Studies in Comparative Literature 22. Cambridge, MA: Harvard University Press, 1957.

Lewis, C. S. "Modern Theology and Biblical Criticism." Pp. 152–66 in *Christian Reflections,* edited by Walter Hooper. Grand Rapids: Wm. B. Eerdmans, 1967.

Lindars, Barnabas. *The Gospel of John.* New Century Bible. Grand Rapids: Wm. B. Eerdmans, 1981; London: Marshall, Morgan & Scott, 1972.

Lotman, J. M. "Point of View in a Text." *New Literary History* 6 (1975): 339–52.

Lubbock, Percy. *The Craft of Fiction.* The Travellers' Library. London: Jonathan Cape, 1921.

Lucas, Frank L. *Tragedy in Relation to Aristotle's Poetics.* Hogarth Lectures on Literature 2. London: Hogarth Press, 1930.

Macgregor, G. H. C. *The Gospel of John.* Moffatt New Testament Commentary. London: Hodder and Stoughton, 1928.

McHugh, John. *The Mother of Jesus in the New Testament.* London: Darton, Longman & Todd, 1975.

MacRae, George W. "Theology and Irony in the Fourth Gospel." Pp. 83–96 in *The Word in the World: Essays in Honor of Frederick L. Moriarity, S. J.,* edited by R. J. Clifford, S. J. and G. W. MacRae, S. J. Cambridge, MA: Weston College Press, 1973.

Mailloux, Steven. "Reader-Response Criticism?" *Genre* 10 (1977): 413–31.

Malatesta, Edward. "Blood and Water from the Pierced Side of Christ (Jn 19, 34)." Pp. 165–81 in *Segni e Sacramenti nel Vangelo di Giovanni,* edited by Pius-Ramon Tragan. Studia Anselmiana 66. Rome: Editrice Anselmiana, 1977.

Martyn, J. Louis. *The Gospel of John in Christian History: Essays For Interpreters.* New York: Paulist Press, 1978.

_____. *History and Theology in the Fourth Gospel.* Rev. ed. Nashville: Abingdon Press, 1979.

Meeks, Wayne A. "'Am I a Jew?'—Johannine Christianity and Judaism." Pp. 163–86 in *Christianity, Judaism, and Other Greco-Roman Cults: Studies for Morton Smith. Part One: New Testament,* edited by J. Neusner. Leiden: E. J. Brill, 1975.

_____. "The Divine Agent and His Counterfeit in Philo and the Fourth Gospel." Pp. 43–67 in *Aspects of Religious Propaganda in Judaism and Early Christianity,* edited by E. S. Fiorenza. Notre Dame, IN: University of Notre Dame Press, 1976.

_____. "Galilee and Judea in the Fourth Gospel." *Journal of Biblical Literature* 85 (1966): 159–69.

_____. "The Man From Heaven in Johannine Sectarianism." *Journal of Biblical Literature* 91 (1972): 44–72.

Michaels, J. R. "Nathanael Under the Fig Tree." *Expository Times* 78 (1967): 182–83.

Minear, Paul S. "The Audience of the Fourth Evangelist." *Interpretation* 31 (1977): 339–54.

_____. "'We Don't Know Where . . .' John 20:2." *Interpretation* 30 (1976): 125–39.

Miranda, Juan P. *Der Vater, der mich gesandt hat: Religionsgeschichtliche Untersuchungen zu den johanneischen Sendungsformeln.* Europaische Hochschulschriften, Reihe 23: Theologie, vol. 7. Bern: Herbert Lang, 1972.

Moloney, F. J. "From Cana to Cana (Jn. 2:1–4:54) and the Fourth Evangelist's Concept of Correct (and Incorrect) Faith." *Salesianum* 40 (1978): 817–43.

Moule, C. F. D. "The Meaning of 'Life' in the Gospel and Epistles of St. John. A Study in the Story of Lazarus, John 11:1–44." *Theology* 78 (1975): 114–25.

_____. "A Note on 'Under the Fig Tree' in John 1.48, 50." *Journal of Theological Studies* 5 (1954): 210–11.

Muecke, D. C. *The Compass of Irony.* London: Methuen & Co., 1969.

_____. *Irony.* The Critical Idiom 13. London: Methuen & Co., 1970.

Neyrey, J. H. "Jacob Traditions and the Interpretation of John 4:10–26." *Catholic Biblical Quarterly* 41 (1979): 419–37.

Nuttall, A. D. *Overheard by God: Fiction and Prayer in Herbert, Milton, Dante and St. John.* New York and London: Methuen, 1980.

Nuttall, Geoffrey. *The Moment of Recognition: Luke as Story-Teller.* Ethel M. Wood Lecture, 1978. London: University of London, Athlone Press, 1978.

Olsson, Birger. *Structure and Meaning in the Fourth Gospel: A Text-Linguistic Analysis of John 2:1-11 and 4:1-42.* Eng. trans. J. Gray. Coniectanea biblica, New Testament 6. Lund: C. W. K. Gleerup, 1974.

Ong, Walter J. *Interfaces of the Word: Studies in the Evolution of Consciousness and Culture.* Ithaca, NY: Cornell University Press, 1977.

O'Rourke, John J. "Asides in the Gospel of John." *Novum Testamentum* 21 (1979): 210-19.

_____. "The Historic Present in the Gospel of John." *Journal of Biblical Literature* 93 (1974): 585-90.

Painter, John. "Johannine Symbols: A Case Study in Epistemology." *Journal of Theology for Southern Africa* 27 (1979): 26-41.

_____. *John: Witness and Theologian.* 2d ed. London: SPCK, 1979.

Pancaro, Severino. *The Law in the Fourth Gospel. The Torah and the Gospel, Moses and Jesus, Judaism and Christianity according to John.* Novum Testamentum, Supplements 42. Leiden: E. J. Brill, 1975.

_____. "'People of God' in St. John's Gospel." *New Testament Studies* 16 (1969-70): 114-29.

Paschal, R. Wade, Jr. "Sacramental Symbolism and Physical Imagery in the Gospel of John." *Tyndale Bulletin* 32 (1981): 151-76.

Petersen, Norman R. *Literary Criticism for New Testament Critics.* Guides to Biblical Scholarship. Philadelphia: Fortress Press, 1978.

_____. "When is the End not the End? Literary Reflections on the Ending of Mark's Narrative." *Interpretation* 34 (1980): 151-66.

Peterson, Peter M. *Andrew, Brother of Simon Peter: His History and His Legends.* Novum Testamentum, Supplements 1. Leiden: E. J. Brill, 1958.

Piwowarczyk, Mary Ann. "The Narratee and the Situation of Enunciation: A Reconsideration of Prince's Theory." *Genre* 9 (1976): 161-77.

Pollard, T. E. "The Raising of Lazarus (John xi)," in *Studia Evangelica* VI, Texte und Untersuchungen 112. Berlin: Academie-Verlag, 1973.

Potterie, I. de la. "Das Wort Jesu, 'Siehe, deine Mutter' und die Annahme der Mutter durch den Jünger (Joh. 19, 27b)." Pp. 191-219 in *Neues Testament und Kirche: Für Rudolf Schnackenburg,* edited by J. Gnilka. Freiburg: Herder, 1974.

Prince, Gerald. "Introduction à l'étude du narrataire." *Poetique* 14 (1973): 178-96.

_____. "Notes Toward a Categorization of Fictional 'Narratees.'" *Genre* 4 (1971): 100-05.

_____. "On Readers and Listeners in Narrative." *Neophilologus* 55 (1971): 117-22.

Rabinowitz, Peter J. "Truth in Fiction: A Reexamination of Audiences." *Critical Inquiry* 4 (1977): 121-41.

Ramsey, Ian T. *Religious Language: An Empirical Placing of Theological Phrases.* New York: Macmillan Co.; London: SCM Press, 1957.

Rhoads, David. "Narrative Criticism and the Gospel of Mark." *Journal of the American Academy of Religion* 50 (1982): 411-34.

_____, and Donald Michie. *Mark as Story: An Introduction to the Narrative of a Gospel.* Philadelphia: Fortress Press, 1982.

Richardson, Peter. *Israel in the Apostolic Church.* Society for New Testament Studies Monograph Series 10. New York and Cambridge: Cambridge University Press, 1969.

Ricoeur, Paul. *Interpretation Theory: Discourse and the Surplus of Meaning.* Fort Worth: Texas Christian University Press, 1976.

_____. "Narrative Time." *Critical Inquiry* 7 (1980): 169-90.

Robinson, J. A. T. "The Destination and Purpose of St. John's Gospel." *New Testament Studies* 6 (1959–60): 117–31.

_____. *The Roots of a Radical.* London: SCM Press, 1980.

_____. "The Use of the Fourth Gospel for Christology Today." Pp. 61–78 in *Christ and Spirit in the New Testament: Studies in Honor of C. F. D. Moule,* edited by B. Lindars and S. S. Smalley. New York and Cambridge: Cambridge University Press, 1973.

Russell, D. A., and M. Winterbottom, eds. *Ancient Literary Criticism: The Principal Texts in New Translations.* Oxford: Clarendon Press, 1972.

Ryken, Leland. "Literary Criticism and the Bible: Some Fallacies." Pp. 24–40 in *Literary Interpretations of Biblical Narratives,* edited by K. R. R. Gros Louis, J. S. Ackerman, and T. S. Warshaw. Nashville: Abingdon Press, 1974.

Sacks, Sheldon. *Fiction and the Shape of Belief: A Study of Henry Fielding, With Glances at Swift, Johnson, and Richardson.* Berkeley and Los Angeles: University of California Press, 1964.

Schnackenburg, Rudolf. "Das vierte Evangelium und die Johannesjünger." *Historisches Jahrbuch* 77 (1958): 21–38.

_____. *The Gospel According to St. John.* Vol. 1, Eng. trans. K. Smyth; Vol. 2, Eng. trans. G. Hastings, et al. Herder's Theological Commentary on the New Testament. New York: Herder and Herder, 1968 and 1979.

Schneiders, Sandra M. "History and Symbolism in the Fourth Gospel." Pp. 371–76 in *L'Evangile de Jean: Sources, Redaction, Théologie,* edited by M. de Jonge. Bibliotheca ephemeridum theologicarum lovaniensium 44. Gembloux: Duculot; Louvain: Louvain University Press, 1977.

_____. "Symbolism and the Sacramental Principle in the Fourth Gospel." Pp. 221–35 in *Segni e sacramenti nel Vangelo di Giovanni,* edited by Pius-Ramon Tragan. Studia Anselmiana 66. Rome: Editrice Anselmiana, 1977.

Scholes, Robert, and Robert Kellogg. *The Nature of Narrative.* New York and London: Oxford University Press, 1966.

Schrenk, G. "*Graphō.*" Pp. 742–73 in G. Kittel and G. Friedrich (eds.), *Theological Dictionary of the New Testament* 1. Eng. trans. G. Bromiley. Grand Rapids: Wm. B. Eerdmans, 1964.

_____. "*Patēr.*" Pp. 945–58, 974–1022 in G. Kittel and G. Friedrich (eds.), *Theological Dictionary of the New Testament* 5. Eng. trans. G. Bromiley. Grand Rapids: Wm. B. Eerdmans, 1967.

Schulz, Anselm. *Nachfolgen und Nachahmen: Studien über das Verhältnis der neutestamentlichen Jüngerschaft zur urchristlichen Vorbildethik.* Studien zum Alten und Neuen Testament 6. Munich: Kösel-Verlag, 1962.

Schweizer, Eduard. *Lordship and Discipleship.* Studies in Biblical Theology 28. London: SCM Press, 1960.

Scott, Ernest F. *The Fourth Gospel: Its Purpose and Theology.* The Literature of the New Testament. Edinburgh: T. & T. Clark, 1908.

Smalley, Stephen S. *John: Evangelist and Interpreter.* Exeter: The Paternoster Press, 1978.

Smith, D. Moody. *The Composition and Order of the Fourth Gospel: Bultmann's Literary Theory.* New Haven, CT: Yale University Press, 1965.

_____. "Johannine Christianity: Some Reflections on its Character and Delineation." *New Testament Studies* 21 (1975): 222–48.

_____. "The Presentation of Jesus in the Fourth Gospel." *Interpretation* 31 (1977): 367–78.

Smith, Jonathan Z. "The Influence of Symbols Upon Social Change: A Place on Which to Stand." *Worship* 44 (1970): 457–74.

Snyder, G. F. "John 13:16 and the Anti-Petrinism of the Johannine Tradition." *Biblical Research* 16 (1971): 5–15.

Sontag, Susan. *Against Interpretation and Other Essays.* New York: The Noonday Press, 1966.

Stagg, Frank. *The Book of Acts; The Early Struggle for an Unhindered Gospel.* Nashville: Broadman Press, 1955.

Stemberger, Günter. *La symbolique du bien et du mal selon saint Jean.* Parole de Dieu. Paris: Editions du Seuil, 1970.

Sternberg, Meir. *Expositional Modes and Temporal Ordering in Fiction.* Baltimore and London: Johns Hopkins University Press, 1978.

Sterne, Laurence. *Tristram Shandy.* Intro. by G. Saintsbury. Everyman's Library. London: J. M. Dent & Sons Ltd.; New York: E. P. Dutton & Co., 1912.

Stevick, Philip, ed. *The Theory of the Novel.* New York: The Free Press, 1967.

Strachan, R. H. *The Fourth Gospel: Its Significance and Environment.* 3d ed. London: SCM Press, 1941.

Summers, Ray. *Behold the Lamb: An Exposition of the Theological Themes in the Gospel of John.* Nashville: Broadman Press, 1979.

Talbert, Charles H. *What is a Gospel? The Genre of the Canonical Gospels.* Philadelphia: Fortress Press, 1977.

Tannehill, Robert C. "Tension in Synoptic Sayings and Stories." *Interpretation* 34 (1980): 138–50.

Tenney, M. C. "The Footnotes of John's Gospel." *Bibliotheca Sacra* 117 (1960): 350–64.

_____. "Topics from the Gospel of John. Part I: The Person of the Father." *Bibliotheca Sacra* 132 (1975): 37–46.

Thompson, A. R. *The Dry Mock: A Study of Irony in Drama.* Berkeley: University of California Press, 1948.

Thomson, J. A. K. *Irony: An Historical Introduction.* London: George Allen & Unwin, Ltd., 1926; Cambridge, MA: Harvard University Press, 1927.

Thurian, Max. *Mary: Mother of the Lord, Figure of the Church.* Eng. trans. N. B. Cryer. London: The Faith House, 1963.

Tindall, William York. "Excellent Dumb Discourse." Pp. 335–54 in *The Theory of the Novel,* edited by Philip Stevick. New York: The Free Press, 1967.

Tomashevsky, Boris. "Thematics." Pp. 61–95 in *Russian Formalist Criticism,* edited and Eng. trans. by Lee T. Lemon and Marion J. Reis. Lincoln: University of Nebraska Press, 1965.

Tompkins, Jane P., ed. *Reader-Response Criticism: From Formalism to Post-Structuralism.* Baltimore: Johns Hopkins University Press, 1980.

Trilling, Lionel. "Manners, Morals, and the Novel." Pp. 121–36 in *Approaches to the Novel: Materials for a Poetics,* edited by Robert Scholes. San Francisco: Chandler Publishing Co., 1961.

Trollope, Anthony. *The Warden, and Barchester Towers.* New York: The Modern Library, 1936.

Trudinger, L. Paul. "The Meaning of 'Life' in St. John. Some Further Reflections." *Biblical Theology Bulletin* 6 (1976): 258–63.

Unnik, W. C. van. "The Purpose of St. John's Gospel." Pp. 382–411 in *Studia Evangelica* I, Texte und Untersuchungen 73. Edited by K. Aland, et al. Berlin: Akademie-Verlag, 1959.

Uspensky, Boris. *A Poetics of Composition. The Structure of the Artistic Text and Typology of a Compositional Form.* Eng. trans. V. Zavarin and S. Wittig. Berkeley and Los Angeles: University of California Press, 1973.

Vouga, François. *Le cadre historique et l'intention théologique de Jean.* Paris: Beauchesne, 1977.

Wahlde, Urban C. von. "The Johannine 'Jews': A Critical Survey." *New Testament Studies* 28 (1982): 33–60.

_____. "The Terms for Religious Authorities in the Fourth Gospel: A Key to Literary Strata?" *Journal of Biblical Literature* 98 (1979): 231–53.

_____. "The Witnesses to Jesus in John 5:31–40 and Belief in the Fourth Gospel." *Catholic Biblical Quarterly* 3 (1981): 385–404.

Walker, Norman. "The Reckoning of Hours in the Fourth Gospel." *Novum Testamentum* 4 (1960): 69–73.

Watt, Ian. "Realism and the Novel Form." Pp. 73–99 in *Approaches to the Novel: Materials for a Poetics,* edited by Robert Scholes. Rev. ed. San Francisco: Chandler Publishing Co., 1966.

Wead, David W. "The Johannine Double Meaning." *Restoration Quarterly* 13 (1970): 106–20.

_____. "Johannine Irony as a Key to the Author-Audience Relationship in John's Gospel." Pp. 33–50 in *AAR Biblical Literature: 1974,* compiled by Fred O. Francis. Missoula, MT: Scholars Press, 1974.

_____. *The Literary Devices in John's Gospel.* Theologischen Dissertationen, vol. 4. Basel: Friedrich Reinhart Kommissionsverlag, 1970.

Weimann, Robert. *Structure and Society in Literary History: Studies in the History and Theory of Historical Criticism.* Charlottesville: University Press of Virginia, 1976.

Weiss, Herold. "Foot Washing in the Johannine Community." *Novum Testamentum* 21 (1979): 298–325.

Wellhausen, Julius. *Das Evangelium Johannis.* Berlin: G. Reimer, 1908.

Westcott, B. F. *The Gospel According to St. John.* London: John Murray, 1892.

Wheelwright, Philip E. *Metaphor and Reality.* Bloomington and London: Indiana University Press, 1962.

White, Hayden. "The Value of Narrativity in the Representation of Reality." *Critical Inquiry* 7 (1980): 5–27.

Wicker, Brian. *The Story-Shaped World: Fiction and Metaphysics, Some Variations on a Theme.* Notre Dame, IN: University of Notre Dame Press; London: University of London, Athlone Press, 1975.

Wilder, Amos N. *Early Christian Rhetoric: The Language of the Gospel.* Cambridge, MA: Harvard University Press, 1971.

Wilson, Rawdon. "The Bright Chimera: Character as a Literary Term." *Critical Inquiry* 5 (1979): 725–49.

Wind, A. "Destination and Purpose of the Gospel of John." *Novum Testamentum* 14 (1972): 26–69.

Wolff, Erwin. "Der intendierte Leser." *Poetica* 4 (1971): 141–66.

Woll, D. Bruce. *Johannine Christianity in Conflict: Authority, Rank, and Succession in the First Farewell Discourse.* Society of Biblical Literature Dissertation Series 60. Chico, CA: Scholars Press, 1981.

Wuellner, Wilhelm. "Narrative Criticism and the Lazarus Story." Unpublished Society for New Testament Studies Seminar Paper, 1981.

Index

Authors

Abrams, M. H.   17, 80, 102, 106, 205, 211
Agourides, Savvas   121
Aland, Kurt   5
Alter, Robert   106, 136
Appold, Mark L.   66
Auerbach, Erich   8, 10, 86, 201, 231, 234

Baker, Howard   209
Balzac, Honoré de   102
Barlach, Ernst   189
Barrett, C. K.   24, 45, 65, 66, 108, 112, 154, 158, 161, 165, 169, 170, 171, 211
Bassler, Jouette M.   131
Baum, Gregory   125
Beardslee, William A.   4, 8, 52, 84, 87, 199, 235
Becker, Jürgen   64, 141
Beutler, Johannes   211
Billings, J. S.   124
Bleich, David   210
Bloom, Harold   210
Boeckh, August   10
Boismard, Marie-Emile   211, 212
Booth, Wayne C.   15, 16, 17, 21, 22, 32, 34, 47, 104, 150, 166, 167, 168, 172, 178, 179, 204, 206, 230, 231
Borgen, Peder   196
Boswell, James   8
Bowman, John   211
Bratcher, Robert J.   125
Braun, F.-M   134
Brewer, Derek   79, 85
Brooks, Cleanth   20
Brown, Edward K.   189–90, 199, 200
Brown, Raymond E.   5, 24, 41, 45, 46, 64, 65, 66, 109, 112, 121, 123, 124, 133, 134, 136, 137, 139, 140, 143, 154, 158, 161, 165, 171, 172, 195, 211, 226, 236
Browning, Robert   231
Buchanan, G. W.   211
Buchler, Justus   182
Bultmann, Rudolf   24, 45, 53, 130, 133, 152, 153, 155, 156, 158, 160, 171
Byatt, A. S.   100

Cahill, P. J.   200
Caird, G. B.   112, 166
Camus, Albert   206
Carlyle, Thomas   150, 183
Carroll, K. L.   211
Carson, D. A.   154
Casparis, Christian P.   31
Chambers, Ross   206, 208
Charles, R. H.   69
Chatman, Seymour   6, 16, 17, 26, 32, 42, 53, 81, 102, 109, 206, 209
Chevalier, Haakon M.   168
Clavier, Henri   166
Clines, David J. A.   237
Cohen, Ted   181
Collins, Raymond F.   104, 123, 134, 136, 140
Connolly, Cyril   178
Conrad, Joseph   206
Crane, R. S.   79, 81, 82
Crossan, John Dominic   197
Culler, Jonathan   53, 210
Cullmann, Oscar   165, 187, 211, 218
Culpepper, R. Alan   15, 43, 66, 88, 112, 118, 123, 212

Dahl, Nils   112
Daube, David   222
Davey, J. Ernest   108
Derrida, Jacques   210
Dewey, Kim   201
Dodd, C. H.   39, 42, 45, 65, 73, 133, 141, 152, 165, 166, 171, 173, 185, 191, 196, 225
Donahue, John R.   112
Douglas, Norman   100
Duke, Paul D.   150, 166, 170, 176, 180
Dunn, James D. G.   95, 118, 211

Eckhardt, K. A.   141
Eco, Umberto   210, 211
Egan, Kieran   78, 80
Eisler, R.   141

Fawcett, Thomas   182, 184
Fennema, David A.   112

PRIMARY TEXTS

Subjects